RELIGION
AND
PERSONALITY
IN THE SPIRAL
OF LIFE

David Belgum, Rudolph 1922-

School of Religion
The University of Iowa

UNIVERSITY
PRESS OF
AMERICA

LANHAM • NEW YORK • LONDON

All University Press of America books are produced on acid-free
paper which exceeds the minimum standards set by the National
Historical Publications and Records Commission.

58,027

Dedicated to Colleen Lewis

with appreciation for valuable help

in preparation of this and other manuscripts

ACKNOWLEDGMENTS

Appreciation is hereby expressed for permission to use previously published material.

Augsburg Publishing House, Minneapolis, Minnesota

Benuska, Daniel Alan, El Paso, Texas

Iowa State University Press, Ames, Iowa

Macmillan Publishing Company, Inc., New York City
The Individual and His Religion, Copyright by
Macmillan, 1950; renewed 1978 by Robert B. Allport.

Pantheon Books, a Division of Random House, Inc.,
New York City. Material from Memories, Dreams
and Reflections, by C. G. Jung, edited by Aniela
Jaffe, translated by Richard and Clara Winston.
Copyright © 1962, 1963 by Random House, Inc.
Reprinted by permission of Pantheon Books, a
Division of Random House, Inc.

Scripture quotations unless otherwise noted are from
the Revised Standard Version of the Bible, copyright
1946, 1952, and 1971 by the Division of Christian
Education of the National Council of Churches.

PREFACE AND PERSPECTIVE

Two scholars in a great university were intent on investigating a rose from the perspective of their divergent disciplines. The one was a biochemist, the other a professor of art. Now admittedly, each has a legitimate approach depending upon the desired outcome. The art professor set the rose in a vase and placed it against a draped background that suited his purpose. He then asked the students in the art class to paint what they saw, paying special attention to line, form, shadings of color, texture, etc. Across the river the chemistry professor lectured on the organic composition of the rose and asked her students to take it to the laboratory, grind it up and test it for pigments, proteins, vitamins, etc. The one study resulted in a beautiful painting for which one student received a grade of "A"; the other resulted in a contribution to medical research with a yet unknown application for therapy.

Would it be possible, as with the rose, to crush or distort personality or religious experience by studying it too closely or heavy-handedly? Some fear so. A famous self-help group turned a cold shoulder to my interest in investigating their therapeutic approach to see what factors contributed to successful outcome. Their reply was, "We're too busy helping people to get involved in that kind of research." I got the impression that it would be like grinding up that beautiful rose in the chemistry lab, and they wanted no part of it. Perhaps studying faith or prayer scientifically, even if that were possible, would distort the experience beyond recognition. Patients at our university hospital who are asked to participate in an interview or questionnaire study have to sign consent forms for human experimentation just as if they were being subjected to a potent, experimental drug on the assumption that it can be as dangerous to tamper with the mind as with the body.

From the vantage point of which school of psychology should we view the terrain of religion and the dynamics of personality? Obviously, some theories, such as Skinnerian stimulus-response behaviorism, are too limited to suffice. This is not to say that such a method would not be useful to answer certain specific questions such as what kind of alarm system would most effectively and quickly alert a pilot to trouble, an audible or visual signal. Freudian psychoanalytic thinking in its classic form contains such heavy-handed determinism that it lacks the freedom we desire for the human spirit. Needless to say, depth psychology has enriched our understanding of the role of the unconscious in both abnormal and normal psychic life, as a component of motivation and as a valued insight in counseling. We shall rather draw upon many insights in an eclectic manner as we find any research or theory useful. Because of their humanistic approach, two psychologists have been helpful to me as I have tried to understand the significance of religion for personality development, namely, Gordon W. Allport and Erik H. Erikson.

Allport championed the idiographic method, the legitimacy of studying the uniqueness of the person. He called it the science of personology. The focus of attention is not on isolated parts of experience such as sensation, perception, memory, nor a study in which the individual may be ranked comparatively with others of the same age, sex, ethnic group or educational category. Rather, nothing more nor less than the whole person, the individual, is the focus of Allport's personology. This avoids the reductionism on the one hand and losing the individual in the mass on the other. This approach has also been referred to as the biographical, life history, or case study method. It is distinctly different from the mind set of the psychologist who replied, when asked how his wife was, "Compared to what?"

As an Episcopalian, Allport wrote a pamphlet for that denomination's Advent Papers series entitled "The Roots of Religion." He took a keen interest in the psychological study of religion as part of his concern for the development of a theory of personality. His investigations of prejudice and values were closely related to religion. His peers acknowledged his leadership by electing him president of the American Psychological Association (1939) and the Society for the Psychological Study of Social Issues (1944). He was editor of the Journal of Abnormal and Social Psychology. He died in October, 1967 after having served on the Harvard University faculty for about thirty-five years. His writings were translated into ten languages. Some of his books are:

Personality: A Psychological Interpretation.
New York: Henry Holt and Company, 1937.

The Individual and His Religion.
New York: Macmillan Company, 1950.

The Nature of Prejudice.
Cambridge, Mass.: Addison-Wesley Pub. Co., 1954.

Becoming: Basic Considerations for a Psychology of
Personality.
New Haven, Conn.: Yale University Press, 1955.

Personality and Social Encounter.
Boston: Beacon Press, 1960.

Pattern and Growth in Personality.
New York: Holt, Rinehart and Winston, 1961.

Letters from Jenny (edited).
New York: Harper and Row, 1965.

The Person in Psychology.
Boston: Beacon Press, 1968.

Erikson has pioneered along the same line with a method
called psychohistory, tracing the development and unfolding
of the person through his eight stages of the life cycle, calling it the "epi-genesis of identity."[1] The hurdles, crises,
stresses, and accommodations of the individual are the subject
of such research. To some it seems unscientific because it
lacks the statistics and "control groups" of experimental
psychology. Yet, it seems that the investigations of these
two ego psychologists have been fruitful and insightful.
Others of the so-called humanistic psychology movement could
be drawn upon, those who focus on the wholistic patterning or
"gestalt" of the individual personality.

Erikson was born of Danish parents in 1902, and the very
beginning of his life and early childhood may have prompted
his concern for the "identity crisis" concept which he made
famous. His father abandoned his mother before Erik was born.
She travelled to Germany where her son was born, and she married the pediatrician, Dr. Theodor Homburger. Erik's Jewish
step-father was seemingly good to him, but both parents kept
secret the facts of his origin and birth. When this tall,
blond, blue-eyed boy attended his step-father's temple, he was
called a "goy," whereas his schoolmates referred to him as a
"Jew." Even his last name is symbolic. It is neither the

name of his biological father nor his stepfather. He simply
chose it later in life in consultation with his family. His
first interest in children was in teaching them art, which he
did in Vienna. Anna Freud witnessed his work with children
and trained him in the psychoanalysis of children. Although
he shows a keen interest in the development of personality
through childhood and adolescence, he is also concerned about
later stages of life. When he came to America, he took extensive field trips among American Indians observing their child
rearing patterns.

Martin Luther and Ghandi became subjects for Erikson's
full-scale investigation using his psychohistory method. The
book which catapulted him to fame was Childhood and Society.
He is now retired from the faculty of Harvard University. Some
of his more significant books are listed in chronological
order. All were published by W. W. Norton & Company, Inc., of
New York.

Childhood and Society, 1950.

Young Man Luther, 1958.

Insight and Responsibility, 1964.

Identity: Youth and Crisis, 1968.

Ghandi's Truth, 1969.

Life History and the Historical Moment, 1975.

Toys and Reasons, 1977.

DEFINITIONS

It is only fair to provide two definitions for you to
think about if we are going to talk about religion and personality. Without definitions we may not be talking about the
same thing. You are certainly free to write your own. This
is mine:

Religion is the faith, values, and actions whereby a person is bound in a comprehensive and
integrating way to Whom or what one considers
fundamental in the universe, which includes
relationship to nature, to society in historical perspective, to one's own psycho-physical
experiences, and to one's destiny.

Such a definition includes belief system, morality, and ritual, which are usually present in dominant or implicit form in any religion. The integrating function provides for meaning concerning one's external environment of other persons and things as well as a mode of perceiving of one's selfhood. It also attributes significance to one's origins as well as destiny. The alternative of personal and impersonal description of the object of one's highest loyalty is provided to accommodate any system which does not refer to a personal deity. This is offered as a functional definition and does not pretend to deal with the content or faith commitments of any particular religion.

Personality is also difficult to define considering the numerous activities and experiences involved in human existence.[2] See if the following definition is comprehensive enough:

> Personality is the capacity of an individual to co-ordinate the actions of anatomical and physiological parts toward meaningful goals within a social context while experiencing that the feelings and meaning of the activity are one's own.

Our definition includes thought, emotion, and behavior together with the self-awareness and self-direction needed for motivation. It further implies the inter-personal relationship necessary for the growth and development of the person. The capacity for organizational structure, commonly referred to as the self or soul, provides the integrating factor which lifts the person above mere random and unconnected behavior patterns. Yet personality is not defined as an ethereal entity since attention is also given to the body with its organic parts.

DO YOU HAVE ANYONE IN MIND?

Neither personality nor religion exist in abstractions, but are embodied in concrete individuals. It will make your study more meaningful if you apply the principles, dynamics, and interpretations of this book to someone in particular. The case you have in mind may be the religious leader of a religious group or congregation to which you belong, the founder of a denomination like Martin Luther or John Wesley, a favorite heroine or saint like Joan of Arc or Saint Teresa of Avila, a reformer like Harriet Beecher Stowe or Norman Thomas, a grandparent or even yourself. The following are just a few of the questions you might find provocative in searching for leads, clues, traits, and characterizations:

Was religion a positive factor (peace of mind, purpose, sense of identity and worth, reconciliation, etc.), or was it a negative element (fear, bigotry, isolation, unresolved guilt, self-depreciation)?

What hurdles did the subject have to jump or overcome (handicap, poverty, illness, social prejudice)?

What was the person's mission in life? Was there a red thread or continuity which ran through the warp and woof of the personality fabric, perhaps such a trait as self-doubt, self-sacrifice, concern about status, search for peace with God, etc.?

Was there a particular aspect that "marked" the person such as being born out of wedlock, a dramatic conversion experience in adolescence, a series of utopian dreams, each leading to failure and defeat, a burning calling or vocation in life like being a missionary like Judson, a central commitment like Schweitzer's "reverence for life," or Harriet Beecher Stowe's abolition of slavery concern?

Did the subject have to wrestle with a persistent temptation like despair, pride, procrastination, alcoholism, etc.?

What special strength or resource did the subject find in interpersonal relationships and significant others such as family, congregation, spouse, meditation and prayer, the consensual validation from others, and proven success and approval in a given venture?

Naturally, all the above questions would not be equally relevant to every subject for a case history. Allport stresses the need to consider the unique nature of each individual personality. Yet there are certain basic facts which are always helpful: family setting and constellation, socioeconomic class membership, educational background, religious affiliation, physical characteristics and health as well as mental health and stability. What part did the person play in larger social contexts (Martin Luther King, Jr., within the civil rights movement or Mahatma Ghandi in the larger setting of British India on the eve of emancipation, or Martin Luther

at the end of one era and the beginning of another)? Finally,
do you have enough empathy to feel into the other person's
life, as an Indian saying goes, "Walk in another person's moc-
casins"?

Our Preface grows too long, and now that you know the plot,
I hope that you are becoming impatient to turn to the story of
the person, the writing about the life of the self, maybe even
the auto-bio-graphy that is you.

NOTES

1. Chapter III, "The Life Cycle: Epigenisis of Identity,"
   Identity, Youth and Crisis, New York: W. W. Norton, 1968.

2. Gordon W. Allport, Pattern and Growth in Personality,
   New York: Holt, Rinehart and Winston, page 28 ff.

   Allport's classic treatment of the problem of definition
   of personality may be found in Chapter II of his Personality: A Psychological Interpretation, New York: Henry
   Holt and Company, 1937, pp. 24-54. When he revised this
   book nearly twenty-five years later, he gave the following
   definition: "Personality is the dynamic organization
   within the individual of those psychophysical systems that
   determine his characteristic behavior and thought."
   Pattern and Growth in Personality, New York: Holt, Rinehart and Winston, 1961, p. 28.

TABLE OF CONTENTS

(See the next four pages for a more detailed outline
of the contents of the book.)

PART I

YOU IN THE SPIRAL OF LIFE

From the moment you became alive, about nine months before you were born, until now, you have been caught up in the spiral of life. You first spun around in a little space, indeed, and could hardly move off dead center in your crib. The only way your radius could be extended was for a big, strong parent to pick you up and carry you about the room. You operated at a low and elemental level of slight awareness and little thought; and only later would you come to know in any ordered way that you were thinking.

Through a remarkable combination of nature and nurture you began to reach out, to walk, to talk, and to relate in increasingly complex patterns of behavior. Later you not only walked, but ran around the school yard playing games of many kinds. You not only reached out but could replace the spark plugs in your Dad's car and play a recognizable piece on the piano. Your talking took on many forms of conversation with friends and strangers, responding in a classroom, each sample of talking revealing your feelings and temperament as well as ideas. In the spiral of life you were not only enlarging your circle of living space but ascending to an ever higher level of complex organization as far as your personality was concerned.

All this growing and developing took place in a social and cultural environment with significant others ordering, asking, persuading, and pleading with you to shape your life according to some desired plan, to measure up to their standard of righteousness, an ideal. For countless people this whole project of moulding character and pointing individuals in the right direction is motivated by religious faith commitments and belief systems, is guided by values and ethics derived from religious sources, and is supported by group consensus, shared worship,

1

and social reinforcement. This is true in synagogues, mosques, churches, and prayer breakfasts around the world. We see signs of this involvement of religion in personality development in shrines, symbols, sacraments, and religious art.

Unless you are acutely and terminally ill or are planning your suicide, you have no idea how long your own personal spiral will continue to evolve and spin. Many believe it will continue dynamically beyond their death in an eternal life. As you read these words you are in the present tense, but as you reflect back upon the early beginnings of your life spiral, you are oriented to the past. When I ask you where you plan to live five years from now and what kind of person you are striving to become ten years from now, you shift your perspective into the future tense. Thus, if the horizontal radius of your spiral represents space, the vertical dimension indicates time. Could you place an "X" on the spiral indicating where you are today? See Figure 1.

Note how the repetitious theme of "religion in personality in religion in personality in religion" continues throughout life. There is an interaction, and knowing where to begin is as impossible as finding the answer to the question, "Which came first, the chicken or the egg?" Even before your own birth, your parents had been influenced concerning their own sense of worth as persons by their religious perspective and the "value" and meaning they attributed to your being born into their young family. Secondly, the spiral has some advantage over the image of "life cycle." To "come full circle" means to come back to one's beginning, the familiar image of "second childhood" notwithstanding.

Religion is not content with objective measurement of time and space. Meaning of life, quality of relationship, values, intention, and motivation are only a few of the hard-to-measure aspects of the reality of human existence. Obviously, even if we were to use a three-dimensional cone instead of a spiral on a piece of paper, we could not begin to diagram the complexity which is inherent in the relationship between religion and personality as they interact upon each other.

Ask yourself throughout Part I, "How does religious orientation, belief, practice, ceremony, or membership assist the person in developing through one stage of life into the next? In what specific ways may religion be said to be a resource for the individual in surmounting this hurdle or that crisis on life's journey?" Let us not assume that every possible religious thought or deed fosters constructive growth and mature mental health. Some of the most destructive forces in society can

2

also be set in motion by religious zealots motivated by sadism or masochism, by self-righteous pride or a hunger for power over others.

One purpose of our present study is to trace out the many influences of religion on personality development and maintenance. The corollary of that goal is to note what influence personality type has on the way religion is perceived and experienced, for surely introverts and extroverts, to say nothing of pessimists and optimists, view life quite differently from each other. We are indebted to the many helpful insights of Erik Erikson and will not hesitate to draw upon his model of the "life cycle" in which he traces the various stages of personality development from birth to death. Part I of our study deals with religion in personality. If you let yourself get involved, it can become "the auto-biography that is you." I hope you will get to know yourself better as you are learning about personality in general. That is an invitation.

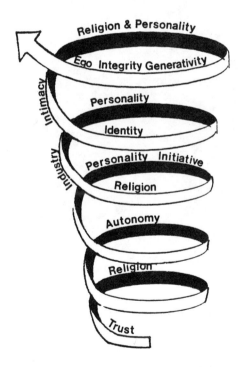

Fig. 1   You in the Spiral of Life

CHAPTER 1

IS IT OK TO BE BORN ?

Are you a blessed fulfillment of the Covenant, or are you just part of the population problem? Abraham heard as good news the Lord's promise, "I will indeed bless you, and I will multiply your descendents as the stars of heaven and as the sand which is on the seashore." (Genesis 22:17) Today we hear of young couples who have themselves sterilized even before marriage to make sure they do not bring any children into an already over-populated world. Is it still OK to be born?

Religions have always devoted much attention to childbirth. Granted, it has sometimes been negative as in cases of infanticide of unwanted girl babies or even sacrifice of children to idols. An Islamic friend tells that in his homeland, Egypt, it is common to have a festive party celebrating the first week of birth when the child is seven days old. Circumcision of baby boys has been practiced in the Jewish tradition for millenia.

Today Reformed Jews may call their relatives and friends together for a "naming ceremony" thirty days after the birth of either a boy or girl. The parents pray as follows:

> "Blessed is the Lord our God, Ruler of the universe, for giving us life, for sustaining us, and for enabling us to reach this happy day. O God, for the gift of this child we give thanks, praying that we will be worthy of the blessing and responsibility of parenthood."

The Rabbi prays for either the boy or girl as follows:

"May the One who blessed   (or)   "May the One who blessed
our fathers, Abraham,   our mothers, Sarah,

5

Isaac, and Jacob, bless this child with life and health. May he be a joy to his parents. May he live to bring honor to the House of Israel, blessing to humanity, and glory to the name of God."

Rebekah, Leah and Rachel, bless this child with life and health. May she be a joy to her parents, may she live to bring honor to the House of Israel, blessing to humanity, and glory to the name of God."

"Now, in the presence of loved ones, we give to this child the name . . . . Let it become a name honored and respected for wisdom and good deeds. May God's blessing rest upon this child now and always."[1]

Most Christians practice infant Baptism within a short time after the birth. A leaflet used by a Baptist church, which holds to "believer's Baptism," contains a brief ceremony entitled "Order of Service for the Parental Dedication of Little Children." The attitude of all such ceremonies and sacraments is summed up in this famous saying of Jesus:

"Let the children come to me, do not hinder them; for to such belongs the kingdom of God. Truly, I say to you, whoever does not receive the kingdom of God like a child shall not enter it."

(Mark 10:14b-15)

The Rites of the Catholic Church, in its 1976 version, stressed the responsibility of parenthood as well as the support offered by the community for their new role.

"You have asked to have your children baptized. In doing so you are accepting the responsibility of training them in the practice of the faith. It will be your duty to bring them up to keep God's commandments as Christ taught us, by loving God and our neighbor. Do you clearly understand what you are undertaking?"

Then the priest addresses the godparents asking them if they are ready to help the parents in their duty as mother and father. Announcing the name of any to be baptized, he states that "the Christian community welcomes you with great joy.....I now trace the cross on your foreheads, and invite your parents (and godparents) to do the same."[2]

Anthropologists refer to rites of passage as those which

6

support a person passing from one stage of life to the next. Surely the passage from pre-natal existence within the womb into the external world of hubbub and self-breathing is a dramatic transition and worth celebrating. To begin life with a positive welcome, social acceptance, and assured worth as a Child of God tends toward an affirmative answer to the question, "Is it OK to be born?"

BEGINNING LIFE WITH TRUST OR TRAUMA

A person begins life with a basic trust if he/she is wanted and welcomed into the world. A child does not have to understand the words of adults to discover whether or not it was OK to be born. Cuddling security, the desire of the parent to hold the child closely and lovingly, the dependable feeding and bathing, the gentle rocking, and the soothing tune hummed softly; all of these constitute a clear message which the pre-verbal child picks up through the five senses. All the religious ceremonies and sacraments mentioned above foster such concern and focus of attention on the welfare of the child; and they give strong social support to the worthy vocation of parenting.

Contrast with the preceding positive introduction into the world the sad and traumatic beginning of an infant who suffers child abuse almost from day one. Milder forms of rejection are the brusque manner in which the mother changes the dirty diaper and plunks the puzzled baby down into the crib as if to communicate, "Well, that chore is over for a while;" the stiff plastic tray some infants are laid upon for feeding so their sticky little bodies will not mess up the mother's dress; and many other ways of distancing oneself from the baby. Such a child gets the message that it might be better if he/she had not intruded into the scene like a personna non grata or an uninvited guest.

Erik Erikson inter-relates trust and hope with faith in his discussion of this first stage of life. The baby has a distinctive need such as hunger, which reaches out for or hopes for satisfaction. Trust is built up because again and again the other is faithful and can be relied upon to satisfy the needy, hungry child. It is not difficult to see the implications of such early confidence for adult religious faith. The foundations for later faith are laid exceedingly early in life. It is easier for an adult to pray, "Our Father who art in heaven" if the earliest experiences with the father image are reminiscent of security, love, and acceptance.

WHEN CONDITIONS AREN'T QUITE RIGHT

Conditions more personal than the problem of global over-population contribute to the hazards of rejected, or semi-rejected childbirth. The following statements have been heard in maternity wards:

> "We were not planning on having a child until Jack finished his education and we were settled. I had been working...and now this added expense."

> "My husband's mother is upset that we didn't wait longer for the second baby."

> "I am kind of embarrassed having this little one since our youngest just began junior high. We get a lot of kidding. But he's cute anyway. My husband doesn't talk much about the baby."

> "I won't be having a husband. We were engaged, but not quite ready to get married. When I became pregnant, my fiance wanted me to have an abortion; and when I couldn't go along with that, it turned out to be a choice between my boy friend and my baby. He took off for California. Now I want my little baby boy baptized here in the hospital because I don't dare take him the 350 miles home without taking care of that. What if something should happen to him?"

Note the apprehension in this last statement, almost as if to say that if something bad did happen it would not be an unexpected punishment. The hospital chaplain had several sessions with the mother before performing the baptism in order to give her ample opportunity to deal with her sorrow and loneliness and guilt. Although every effort was made to indicate full acceptance of her and the little, healthy child, the young mother cried steadily throughout the ceremony. Her brother and another patient were the only witnesses to this heroic attempt to give the baby a positive start in life. One could only hope that her parents to whom she was returning and the religious community to which she belonged would be supportive, and that somehow the child would come to believe that it was OK to be born.

THE CASE OF THE SHRIVELLED ARM

Lest we become too deterministic in our conviction that the switches set so early in life inevitably send a person down an irreversible track, the following case is in order.

8

A woman in her early thirties gave birth to her eagerly
awaited son. The couple's new house was ready to receive this
pride and joy. There could not have been a more welcoming attitude. Then the shock came. The nurse held up the new-born
baby boy for the mother to see. The horrified mother screamed
at the nurse to take that baby away and not bring him back
until she was told to. The right arm was half as long as it
should have been, and what vestigial fingers were visible pro-
truded slightly from the forearm. Clearly that boy would never
shake hands properly with his right hand, nor catch a ball, or
hold a bat. It was tragic. The mother began to knit furiously
a small stocking-like garment to slip over the grotesque stub
of an arm. Only after that had been tied in place to cover up
the deformity could the disappointed mother bear to hold and
look at her baby boy.

Before you jump to the conclusion that this initial bad
start in life would permanently damage the boy's personality,
let me quickly jump ahead to the happy ending. The mother,
father, and son became a close knit and secure family. The members of the congregation showed acceptance and support. The
boy became a well adjusted young man, graduated from a prestigious engineering school, is the happily married father of normal
children, and is doing very well as a mature and balanced adult.
Sometimes children seem exceedingly fragile and at other times
remarkably resilient. Parents likewise!

THE ONCE-BLESSED BABY

One Saturday afternoon a young pastor was casually raking
leaves in the yard when a phone message explained that the baby
born a month ago to a church couple was "critically ill, and
maybe wouldn't live long." As soon as he could whip on his
clerical collar and black suit, he drove out to the suburban
home where he expected to administer emergency infant baptism.
Imagine his surprise when he saw the parents and two sets of
grandparents standing calmly in the front hall of the home
greeting him. He asked, "Where is the baby?" The reply was
unexpected. "Oh, he is napping in his crib." Obviously the
baby was not bleeding to death right on the spot. Yet a crystal bowl of water was set upon a pedestal in the hall in preparation for the baptism.

As the mother and pastor stood beside the crib, she explained the state of affairs. She had returned that morning
from the doctor's office after the one-month check-up. It had
turned out not to be a routine once-over. The doctor told the
mother that his later tests had confirmed his earlier suspici-
ons: the child had the condition of mongolism, which he explained would result in mental retardation, and might mean that

the child would have a foreshortened life expectancy since some mongoloid persons do not live to maturity. (Actually the child died at age six.) Note how the mother had re-interpreted the statement to mean that the child was in imminent danger of death. An understandable case of wishful thinking. The second reason for wanting the baptism right now in the home was that it would be less embarrassing than to have the poor little child up in front of the church for all to see. Ironically, during the first month, many had commented on how cute the boy was and how he resembled the paternal grandfather. One final comment on the mother's acceptance of the child. There was great haste in placing the child in a foster home in another community as soon as arrangements could be made. The mother appeared to feel an unresolved guilt for what seemed later to be hurried abandonment and gave herself much psychic punishment for it in several hospitalizations in a mental hospital.

The potency of religious symbolism and sacrament can be illustrated by what took place during the baptism that day, but which the young pastor did not discover until three years later. The question for the young cleric was whether to go ahead with the so-called emergency baptism when it was not an emergency. Would it be better for the couple to have the support of their friends in the church? (The boy with the shrivelled arm was baptized in the church and the result was seemingly positive.) Yet, reluctantly, he went ahead with it, thinking that if the child did die unexpectedly, he would feel awful about having denied their request in this special case.

Different liturgical practices have developed in this denomination. The young minister was accustomed to making the Sign of the Cross once over the child when the blessing was spoken. Previous pastors in that church had used the formula, "in token whereof I make the Sign of the Cross upon thy brow and upon thy breast (making the sign twice)." Some years later the still troubled and depressed mother said, "Pastor, I knew of course that you could not bless his head because he wasn't right mentally." Such is the power of religious symbolism, both to comfort and to disturb.

Some children begin their life in an atmosphere of trust and security, acceptance and love. Others begin with trauma, rejection, and mistrust. We now turn to the implications of this difference for the possibility and nature of faith later in life.

EARLY BEGINNINGS ON THE JOURNEY OF FAITH

In spite of what has been said about the spirituality of the child-like state of mind, that is the beginning and not the

desired end of the journey. Saint Paul said, "When I was a
child, I spoke like a child, I thought like a child, I reasoned
like a child; when I became a man, I gave up childish ways."
(I Corinthians 13:11)

TWO ROUTES AND A DANGEROUS TURN

The little child takes things at face value without considering all the complicating conditions beyond immediate sense
perception. "Daddy can lift me, my tricycle, a grocery bag. I
even saw him lift Mommy off the ground once when he kissed her.
My Daddy can lift anything." Ergo, Daddy is OMNIPOTENT. The
child lives in a simple universe. But, of course, someday con-
flicting evidence brings disillusionment. There is that time
that Daddy's car slid off the icy road into a snow bank, and he
could not lift the car back on the road. Another man came with
a wrecker and pulled the car out of the ditch. What a let down!
The child now doubts the primary belief.

Unanswered prayer can be the beginning of doubt. The
little child asks God (or Santa Claus) for a little red wagon
for her birthday. Sure enough, the birthday cake with five
candles is on the dining table; and underneath is the little red
wagon. A farmer prays for rain on his corn field and hopes for
a good crop. His neighbor prays for sunny weather because he
is making hay which he hopes will not rot in the field. If they
both have a child-like belief, one of them is going to be disillusioned. This painful realization comes to different persons
at different times in their development and in unique experiences. Figure 2 illustrates two routes on the journey of faith.
The upper line assumes a simple and gradual progression upward
from point A to point B. The lower line shows the dip of doubt
which comes in later childhood or at least by adolescence, a
concept for which I am indebted to Gordon W. Allport.[3]

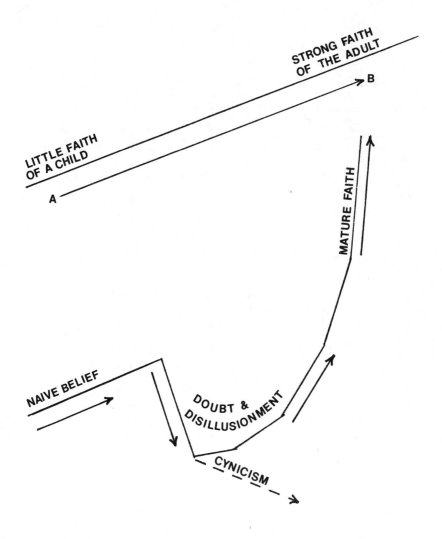

STRONG FAITH OF THE ADULT

B

LITTLE FAITH OF A CHILD

A

MATURE FAITH

NAIVE BELIEF

DOUBT & DISILLUSIONMENT

CYNICISM

Fig. 2.   Two Models of the Development of Faith

X The little child takes everything in an undiscriminating
way, at face value. There is an immediacy of simple knowledge,
a credulity which easily believes what seems so obvious. It is
left to the experienced adult to judge that things are not always what they seem, that "all that glitters is not gold." Most
of us cannot even remember what it was like when we believed
what we saw and said what we thought without filtering experience through social convention. By calling this earliest kind
of belief "naive" we simply mean it is natural and spontaneous,
uneducated.

The critical juncture of doubt is a crucial one because a
person can take two directions from there on: (1) upward toward what Teilhard de Chardin called the Omega Point, or what
Saint Paul called the Crown of Righteousness, a destiny in which
little red wagons and rain on corn fields are quite secondary,
or (2) downward toward a negative and bitter cynicism. The latter is more likely among those whose earliest childhood experiences were characterized by mistrust.

X A mature religious faith needs to be "heuristic," a Greek
term meaning open to new discovery. Allport wrote, "It is
characteristic of the mature mind that it can act whole-
heartedly even without absolute certainty."[4] It is the bigot
who has absolute certainty and won't even discuss it. That
person's very security depends upon not "rocking the boat" with
new evidence or the benefit of other perspectives. Such belief
is not to be shared but protected. That kind of "old time religion" may simply mean what was believed in very young childhood and never examined, never reflected upon.X

X We should distinguish between faith and knowledge. Knowledge is dependent upon facts, scientific investigation, observation and proofs. Faith is more intuitive, subjective in the
sense of involving a commitment, willing to risk. Belief may
be a strong statement, as in "I believe Acme Food Company is a
strong, honest company." Faith, on the other hand, is involved
in "I have just invested my last $50,000 in Acme Food Company."
It is one thing to believe so-and-so is a nice person, and
another to commit oneself to a lifetime of marriage; that takes
something like faith. Actually faith is not having to "know."X

It is a long step from the limited perspective of childlike and simple belief to the kind of broad faith required in
adulthood. A mature faith should be inclusive and comprehensive
enough to be able to encompass the laws of nature and the needs
of society, joy and sorrow, health and sickness, satisfaction
and frustration, righteousness and sinful failure, life and
death, yes, even getting a red wagon and not getting a red

13

wagon, rain and sunshine.

INTRINSIC AND EXTRINSIC RELIGION

Studies of religious participation comparing statistics of group membership and frequency of worship service attendance can be superficial and misleading, as Allport and Ross have pointed out.[5] Their research on prejudice revealed that the crucial difference was not so much in the quantity of religious participation as whether the individual's orientation toward religion was "extrinsic" or "intrinsic."

Extrinsic use of religion is self-serving. Consider the real estate salesman who moves into a city and is interested in making as many sales contacts as possible. He may join Rotary, a bowling league, the Chamber of Commerce, and for good measure the largest protestant church in town, which happens to be Methodist. After having gone through the Methodist prospects and "contacts," he transfers to the second largest church in town. Obviously, he is primarily interested in what he can get out of this religious "connection." It is mostly self-seeking and self-serving. He would pray, serve on committees, even tithe if he thought it would increase his sales, pretty much an adult version of the "little red wagon." This is not the exercise of faith, but rather manipulation and utilitarianism.

Regardless of how cute little babies and very young children may be, and completely apart from whether one believes in a doctrine of the Old Adam or original sin, it is quite obvious that the orientation of infants is self-gratification. The infant cries to be fed or changed quite oblivious to the disturbance this may cause for the mother who is trying to be a good hostess to her bridge club downstairs. The child spends very little time worrying about the economic and legal aspects of daily life and only gradually, and with considerable effort at social learning, is willing to take the needs of older brothers and sisters into account. Some persons remain fixated at this ego-centric orientation or may even regress back to it later in adult life in various forms such as self-pity, dependency, or illness.

The intrinsically oriented person appreciates worship for its own sake, seeks meaning and guidance for life from religious teaching and inspiration, is genuinely willing to be led into service of others and enlarging fellowship. A person thus motivated believes it is more blessed to give than to receive. There is a ring of authenticity in the person's voice and a stamp of integrity upon that person's behavior. One senses that this individual has grown into a mature, adult religious faith,

14

which permeates many aspects of personality and life.

THE ROLE OF FAITH IN PERSONALITY

How shall we avoid an implied utilitarianism in discussing
the function of faith? As soon as a person says to himself,
"If faith is so good for my mental health and personality adjustment, I guess I'll believe then, and get those good benefits," then the process becomes extrinsic, a means to an end.
Faith and worship are sufficient ends in themselves. Once we
have that straight, then we can back up and ask what function
this process seems to be fulfilling for the person. In short,
is there a basic "need" for faith which is natural and inherent
in human personality as we know it?

MEANING AND ORDER

Someone has said that the person needs a cognitive house to
live in as well as a physical dwelling. One needs cupboards,
shelves, and drawers in which to sort out ideas into helpful
categories. Some of these are answers to questions, such as:
my relationship to nature, time, space, other persons, society,
history, and destiny. In contrast to animals much lower on the
evolutionary scale, the human being is aware of his/her own
existence, and has the capacity to ask and wonder about the
meaning of the above list of concepts. It seems endemic to
tribes and peoples around the globe and throughout history that
every group has had some specified way to think and believe
about nature, the self, and society. In more sophisticated cultures this way of believing has usually been formulated into
creeds and elaborated with doctrines. Sometimes these beliefs
are considered so absolutely essential to the good order of the
group that deviant thinking has been labelled heresy and very
dangerous.

"As he thinketh in his heart, so is he..." (Proverbs 23:7a
King James Version) is still a valid saying. Consider how the
Nazi SS officer was shaped to conform to the ordered thinking
of Hitler's doctrine about the superiority of the Aryan race.
It seemed to create a "new order" within the Reich, but it created a cataclysmic disorder in world society. Perhaps one test
of heresy could be whether it works in the long run and whether
it is beneficial to others as well as myself. The ultimate of
private thinking with no felt need for the consensual validation of others is that of the psychotic patient in a private
world of delusional ideas and hallucinations. He is the only
one in the room who believes that the Russians are sending him
messages through the light bulb in the ceiling. His disordered
behavior is in keeping with this disordered thinking even to

15

the point of self-inflicted injury. What one thinks and what one believes to be important is an integral part of one's personality.

Logotherapy was developed by Viktor Frankl to explain the function of meaning in personality adjustment.[6] He was a Jewish, Viennese psychoanalyst who gained a new perspective from his concentration camp experience. He broke from psychoanalytic doctrine, which held that man had a primary "will to pleasure" (Freud) or "will to power" (Adler), by asserting man's unique "will to meaning" as of basic importance. He ascribed the fact that some inmates survived longer than others, even though on the same diet and work regimen, to their sense of purpose or meaning in life. Those who gave in to the sense of meaninglessness, which their captors tried to impose through various dehumanization processes such as serial numbering instead of naming, shaving the head, and indistinguishable clothing; those despairing and purposeless persons became hopeless and did not survive as long as the others. We speak of persons without an integrating purpose as "falling apart" or "lost souls." It was Frankl's contention that the middle of the twentieth century could be characterized by meaninglessness or a vague ennui.

Perhaps this explains the great popularity of certain cults, such as Hari Krishna, The Church of the New Song, Scientology, Numerology, Satan worship, "true believer" communes such as Jonestown in Guyana, etc. When a belief vacuum developed within persons, often disenchanted youth or disenfranchised poor, anyone with a strong voice of authority and a ready-made system of belief fulfilled a need for some system to make sense out of life. It is as though any belief were preferable to no belief even if it meant that the leader (e.g., The Rev. Jim Jones of the People's Temple) advocated suicide as some kind of highest good. It also made perfectly good sense for the Japanese Kamikaze (means "divine wind") pilots to fly off on suicide missions under the religio-political commitment to the Emperor.

A young couple who had dropped out of church was married not by the girl's clergyman father, but by a justice of the peace. When asked why they had chosen Thursday, November 14th, for their wedding day, since weekends are much more common, the bride said, "My man is into Numerology, and 14 has always been good to him." They could not believe in God or the Apostles' Creed, but they could believe in #14. Of course, some persons have several levels of belief operative concurrently: holding a given doctrine of religion intellectually, planning for the future as though they believed in fatalism, while intuitively committed to magic. Since the mind is a dynamic and complex process, it is doubtful that any of us are as logical and consistent as we may think.

It is outside the scope of this study to make pronounce-
ments on the truth or falsity of specific doctrines; that is
dealt with in the discipline of Systematic Theology. We can observe, however, that from the perspective of personality
function, some beliefs seem to have a destructive and other
beliefs seem to have a constructive consequence for the individual, to say nothing of the impact made upon society. Religion
has been used to intimidate, shame, manipulate, and attack with
consequences for the individual of loss of self regard, the
stultifying impotence of fear, and isolating withdrawal. Religion has also been supportive, accepting, promoting warm interpersonal relations and a sense of purpose. One criterion
used by religious thinkers is the concept of heresy. Since the
assumption is that heresy creates disorder and right belief is
helpful, we should consider the dynamics of heresy from a psychological (not theological) point of view.

Distortion is a useful touchstone or test for heresy for
our purpose. Weird beliefs are frequently perfectly good ideas
carried to an extreme. "Honor your father and your mother..."
is a commandment which is widely believed not only in the
Judaeo-Christian tradition but elsewhere. It can foster a
wholesome relationship between children and parents serving as
a model of how to relate to authority and power in many situations outside the family in the larger society. A parent needing to find a rationalization for child abuse and sadism finds
it useful to blow this commandment way out of proportion from
the authority side. All kinds of corporal punishment will be
justified by such a parent if he comes across the passage "Spare
the rod and spoil the child."

The civil rights of each citizen is a doctrine to which an
increasingly large majority have by now subscribed. It is helpful in bringing about social justice, moderating race prejudice,
etc. All one needs to do to make a distortion out of this useful teaching is to season it well with paranoia, a psychiatric
diagnostic term coming from two Greek words meaning "beside" and
"mind" as in "He's beside himself with jealousy." Such a person
searches with hyper-sensitivity for any possible slight or remark that can be remotely interpreted as an insult. A law professor remarked that every community has a "litigating nut," a
malcontent who is bent on taking the slightest issue to court
on the basis of "principle." A person insistent on that kind
of "justice" will always be disappointed. Even when invited to
sit at the head table at the banquet he will suspect that the
seating arrangement is a derogatory reflection on "his group,"
whether the group he is referring to is religious, racial, ethnic, socio-economic, geographic, or age oriented.

17

Even love can be misused if focused upon as the only virtue or value of any importance. So-called "smother love" can be damaging to a child. Useful discipline is a mixture of love and justice, teaching the child fairness while supporting him/her with loving acceptance. A love that sets no limits deprives the growing child from learning to assume larger and larger types of responsibility. Love needs to supply the child's needs but also deprive the child of harmful and damaging things.

Clearly what a person believes is not only important but formative as far as personality is concerned. It can provide meaning and order, a firm foundation upon which to build.

MEANING AND MOTIVATION

Excepting autistic and psychotic persons, who are supposedly "not in control of themselves," one's thinking and what one believes precede behavior. Jesus placed such a high value on thinking as to equate it with behavior. Hence the passage made famous by President Carter: "You have heard that it was said, 'You shall not commit adultery.' But I say to you that every one who looks at a woman lustfully has already committed adultery with her in his heart." (Matthew 5:27-28) It is clear here that the beginning of the trouble (adultery) lies in the person's thinking about it in such a way as to tend in that direction. Hence intention is the link between thought and deed. The thinking about it is not incidental; it is prerequisite to the act. Thus if one believes arrogantly in the superiority of one's own race, one is likely to act quite differently from the person who believes in civil rights. Thinking and believing are inextricably related to motivation, which lies behind the act itself and leads to the behavior.

Mao Tse Tung perceived of himself as a teacher. One of his most important doctrines was that exploitation was evil and the cause of many of the problems of the old China. Important among these was the exploitation of women by men. Phrases such as "Women hold up half the sky" became popular. Pornography, prostitution, and foot binding were shunned as evils unworthy of a good citizen of the new China. Through his charismatic capacity to persuade the masses to follow his teachings, a remarkable change took place in the status, rights, and self-regard of women. The assumption was that what persons believed about themselves and others was the starting point, the beginning of motivation. People were not merely following orders but understood the meaning behind the new motivation to regard women differently. To advocate prostitution under Mao would have been viewed as a heresy--strange, weird thinking. Brain washing would be in order for anyone with such dirty thoughts,

18

which needed to be replaced by Mao Tse-tung thought. The person intending to respect and not exploit women is not likely to think about opening up a house of prostitution, producing an X-rated film, nor publishing a pornographic magazine; nor would such a person desire to patronize any of the above three enterprises.

Allport devoted a section to intention in his chapter on "The Nature of Faith" referred to above. Thinking and believing can be referred to as acts, mental acts; just as walking and riding a bicycle are physical acts.

> "To act mentally is to intend an object that represents our goal. One can name no condition of mental life that is not one of stretching toward, aiming at, or otherwise intending a goal. Always the individual is trying to do something. One might say that the grammatical part of speech most typical of mental life is the active participle, for at every moment of time the individual is occupied in comprehending, comparing, judging, approving, disapproving, loving, hating, fearing, rejecting, yielding, adoring."

> (Catholic theologians writing about intention would say) "...that intention is never indifferent to the means employed. To desire an end is to desire appropriate means. If a person intends health for himself he is bound to intend the means to achieve health."

> "Faith is basically man's belief in the validity and attainability of some goal (value). The goal is set by desires. Desires, however, are not merely pushes from behind (drive ridden). They include such complex, future-oriented states as longing for a better world, for one's own perfection, for a completely satisfying relation to the universe. So important is this forward thrust in all desires emanating from mature sentiments that I propose 'intention' to depict the dynamic operation we are endeavoring to describe. Better than 'desire' this term designates the presence of the rational and ideational component in all productive striving. Some sort of idea of the end is always bound into the act itself. It is this inseparability of the idea of the end from the course of the striving that we call faith."[7]

We have come a long way from our discussion of infant trust at the beginning of this chapter. We have seen how various religious practices and teachings have the potential for affirming the young child's sense that it was OK to be born. There is the unfolding and development of childlike belief into mature faith as the person grows outward and upward in the spiral of life. That very faith serves parents in good stead when it is their turn to be role models and supportive guides to their own infants. Erikson sums up this aspect of personality development poignantly:

> "The parental faith which supports the trust
> emerging in the newborn, has throughout history
> sought its institutional safeguard (and, on
> occasion, found its greatest enemy) in organized
> religion. Trust born of care is, in fact, the
> touchstone of the actuality of a given religion...
> The clinician can only observe that many are
> proud to be without religion whose children can-
> not afford their being without it. On the other
> hand, there are many who seem to derive a vital
> faith from social action or scientific pursuit.
> And again, there are many who profess faith,
> yet in practice breathe mistrust both of life
> and man."[8]

EXAMPLES OF TRUST AND MISTRUST

Soren Kierkegaard was a complex person of mixed moods. He could enter into deep despair and yet experience ecstatic spiritual joy and peace. He disclosed so many fragments of his life that one is tempted to try to piece them together in a quilt. His writings are so numerous and symbolic that it would be the work of a lifetime to do justice to him in an Eriksonian psychohistory. This brief case illustration may serve not only to individualize the material of this chapter but to entice the reader to explore SK's life further through his journals and other writings.

Born in 1813, Soren compressed a prodigious amount of living into his short span before dying in 1855. What concerns us now is the tremendous role his father played in his formative years both positively and negatively. As the favorite child of his later middle age (57 years of age), Michael lavished an inordinate amount of attention upon Soren. He played with him as a companion or buddy rather than establishing a father-son relationship. Perhaps this was to compensate for Soren's physical defect: curvature of the spine and a hunching of the back which gave him an awkward gait and made him look somewhat odd.

The heavy doses of religion were along a pietistic and rigid line without much grace to soften the impact on the impressionable child. On the positive side, fostering trust, was this intimate and strong relationship with a wealthy father who provided security and close companionship. On the negative side was a vague, intangible gloom, which hung over his father and the household. Because of its indefiniteness it led to anxiety in the developing son.

It did not become clear to Soren until he was in his early twenties what caused the curse which hung over his melancholic father. This revelation, the secret which the father may have disclosed or the son may have discovered or pieced together from fragments of evidence, came to Soren as an EARTHQUAKE. He described it in an entry in his journal in 1835.

> "Then it was that the great earthquake
> occurred, the terrible revolution which suddenly
> forced upon me a new and infallible law of in-
> terpretation of all the facts. Then I suspected
> that my father's great age was not a divine
> blessing but rather a curse; that the outstanding
> intellectual gifts of our family were only given
> to us in order that we should rend each other
> to pieces: then I felt the stillness of death
> grow around me when I saw my father, an unhappy
> man who was to outlive us all, a cross on the
> tomb of all his hopes. There must be a guilt
> upon the whole family, the punishment of God
> must be on it; it was to disappear, wiped out
> by the powerful hand of God, obliterated like
> an unsuccessful attempt, and only at times did
> I find a little alleviation in the thought that
> my father had been allotted the heavy task of
> calming us with the consolation of religion,
> of ministering to us so that a better world should
> be open to us even though we lost everything
> in this world, even though we were overtaken by
> the punishment which the Jews always called down
> upon their enemies: that all recollection of
> us should be utterly wiped out, that we should
> no longer be found."[9]

The father felt perpetually guilty for two offences. First, as an eleven-year old shepherd boy, brought up in hardship and poverty, he had stood on a hill and cursed God for his unfortunate estate in life. Secondly, there was the adultery with a servant girl, the complex implications of which are clearly set forth in Alexander Dru's introduction to The

"Shortly after the death of his first wife,
who died childless, in April 1796, Michael Peder-
sen wound up his affairs and sold his business.
Within a year, in April 1797, he had married his
servant, and less than five months later their
first child was born. Behind that sequence of
events, the death of his first wife, to whom he
was devoted, his retirement, and his hurried
second marriage, lies the secret on which he
began to brood, and which his son was to discover with such tremendous consequences. He
had loved his first wife, and to the end of
his life continued to regard her as his real wife
and himself as responsible in some sense for
her death--perhaps she had learnt of his relations
with their servant. If Kierkegaard's expressions
are any guide, he accused himself of seducing,
if not raping, the girl who lived under his
roof and under his protection, and who became
the mother of his children. Outwardly fortunate,
eminently successful, a close friend of Mynster,
the future Primate of Denmark, and widely respected for his uprightness and his intelligence,
he was inwardly broken by remorse. His vigorous
mind was imprisoned in a narrow, disfiguring
Protestantism, an arid predestinarian theology
and a meagre pietism that accentuated the personal dependence of man on God at the price of
confining it in an almost mechanistic concep-
tion of Divine Providence. To him the chain
of cause and effect, of guilt and punishment
reached from his first rebellion against God,
down through his sensuality to the successive
deaths of his children. It was a religion
which neither education nor vision had touched;
it remained morose, intense, and sterile. In
a softened light it was the Christianity which
Kierkegaard himself was offered and against
which he reacted healthily, though to the end
his mind was coloured by it."10

Basic seeds of mistrust and despair can be sown in the
heart of a child without that little person knowing the source
thereof. Only in retrospect might the tortured patterns of
personality and character formation be seen and understood.
Such vague forebodings that all is not as it should be in the
household are more difficult to deal with than specific and

obvious problems. A tangible danger can be feared, avoided, combatted, dealt with; but in the case of anxiety the enemy is unknown, and there is no way to get a handle on the problem. This is why the secrets of hypocrisy are more damaging than the pain of revelation. So often, as in the case of Soren, the secret becomes known later on anyway, but only after years of befuddlement and confusion and often battling straw men.

The basic unworthiness, the haunting curse, what is so often referred to as "bad blood in the family," was to influence Soren in many ways in his later life. For example, at age 27 he was engaged to Regine Olsen, had finished his theological education, and could supposedly have settled down to enjoy some happiness in life. But NO! He was not able to proceed. He may have picked up some unworthiness on his own in his student days of revelry, but there seems always to have lurked in the background this basic and unsettling sense of divine wrath.

> "But there was a divine protest, that is how I understood it. The wedding. I had to hide such a tremendous amount from her, had to base the whole thing upon something untrue....."

> "It was a time of terrible suffering: to have to be so cruel and at the same time to love as I did. She fought like a tigress. If I had not believed that God had lodged a veto she would have been victorious....."

> "How great is womanly devotion.--But the curse which rests upon me is never to be allowed to let anyone deeply and inwardly join themselves to me....."11

The curse Soren seemed to bear in his nature from the beginning, the rumblings and reverberations of it, affected his later stages of personality development as these excerpts show. It affected his sense of autonomy, shaped the course of his industry, influenced his search for identity, and markedly limited his capacity for intimacy.

* * * * * * * * * * *

Contrast the gloomy household of Soren with the positive atmosphere and attitudes of the home of a Jewish girl in which religion was a supportive and natural part of life. This is an excerpt from a term paper drawn from real life, but in which all personal anonymity is preserved.

Sarah's family was a closely-knit and loving one. She was given the expected amount of love as an infant and, thus, began to trust those around her. This was very easy, for the Jews formed their own little community in the city of 250,000, and a good part of it was related to her mother and her family. Before she went to school her playmates were her own cousins or children whose parents belonged to the synagogue.

Raised in the tradition of "the people of the Book," there was a great emphasis put upon learning. When Sarah started public school she also started Sunday School, Hebrew School, and Talmud Torah. The importance of learning instilled in her by her family and peers, coupled with her own intelligence, made this course of study no hardship, but the natural thing to do. Even today her mother can read and write Hebrew.

Sarah went to school each week day except when there was a Jewish holiday. These were fairly numerous, and on these days there was no school for her and her friends. Instead they celebrated with their families. There was always a big meal including symbolic delicacies and attending the synagogue for prayer and worship. The security so basic to a human being, as pointed out by Allport, was obtained by her, to a large degree, in the rituals of the Jewish religion.

Every Friday night little Sarah and her sister came home to help their mother clean the house for the sabbath. They would put on their good clothes and await the return of their father. The father would close his kosher wholesale store early for the sabbath. When the sun went down the mother would light the sabbath candles. There were four candles because of the four members in the family. The blessing was very beautiful and traditional. The mother of the house put a scarf over her head and recited in Hebrew, "Blessed art thou O Lord our God, King of the universe, who has commanded us to kindle the sabbath lights."

Following the sabbath meal the family would all go to the synagogue and afterwards she attended Talmud Torah class with her friends where she received talmudic instruction.

This is an example of how Sarah successfully reached the third stage in life, according to Erikson. In this stage the child grows together. That is, initiative forms a basis and a reason. This young girl was able to take action and see reason in this action. Through the sabbath service I described above, I've tried to point out how repetition gave security to Sarah. Symbolism was illustrated in this example and it proved the assimilation of the tangible and the intangible. She got

24

stability through the closeness of her family and the families of all of her friends.

As to the question of intellectual motivation rather than emotional experience and symbolism, Sarah didn't necessarily rely on one or the other, but it was as if the two were joined. The traditions of her religion were emotional and symbolic and were taught to her with love. Thus, they were detached from intellectual motivation as such. She did not have to resolve the two in the usual way.

Sarah attended Hebrew school three nights a week after public school classes were over. Her social events were like those of her family and friends, centered around the synagogue. They always attended Bar Mitzvahs which were in celebration of a person's thirteenth birthday, thus acknowledging growing to adulthood. This was a social event as well as a religious cere-mony. There was always a dinner and party accompanying this event. Weddings, too, made social events, as well as public ac-knowledgement of the crises in one's life; so did happy holidays.

These things are perfect examples of how religion united physical, mental, and emotional needs in young Sarah into one being.

NOTES

1. _____ Gates of the House: The New Union Home Prayer-book.
   New York: Central Conference of American Rabbis, 1977, pp. 118, 119.

2. _____ The Rites of the Catholic Church.
   New York: Pueblo Publishing Co., 1976, pp. 198, 199.

3. Gordon W. Allport, The Individual and His Religion.
   New York: The Macmillan Company, 1950, ch. 5, "The Nature of Doubt" and ch. 6, "The Nature of Faith."

4. Ibid., ch. 3, "The Religion of Maturity." This is a good summary of the mature religious sentiment. Page 81.

5. Gordon W. Allport (with J. Michael Ross) Journal of Person-ality and Social Psychology, 1967, 5:432-43.

6. Viktor Frankl, Man's Search for Meaning.
   Boston: Beacon Press, 1963.

7. Gordon W. Allport, The Individual and His Religion.

25

pp. 143, 146, and 149.

8. Erik H. Erikson, Childhood and Society (revised). New York: W. W. Norton & Company, Inc., 1963, pp. 50, 51.

9. Alexander Dru (editor), The Journals of Kierkegaard. New York: Harper and Brothers, 1958, p. 39.

10. Ibid., pp. 12, 13.

11. Ibid., pp. 72, 73, and 76.

QUESTIONS AND ISSUES FOR DISCUSSION

1. Can you see the dynamics referred to in this chapter operative in your own life or in the life and experience of someone you know personally?

2. How would the points brought up in connection with trust and faith help to explain the significance of some personality adjustment problems in later life?

3. Have you witnessed or participated in a recent ceremony commemorating birth? What did the experience seem to mean to various people involved?

4. In what sense can we say that Erikson's "Trust vs. Mistrust" test is foundational for later life? In what way would it compare with preventive medicine?

5. Give several examples of attitudes toward childbirth or infant care as evidenced by magazine or TV advertisements. Would these have positive or negative impact upon the child? Explain.

6. How would the subject of abortion relate to this chapter?

7. At what age would a child become aware that discussions about population control and planned parenthood have implications for his/her own existence?

8. Is there any relationship between the material of this chapter and suicide?

9. Just because a switch is thrown as a train leaves Chicago does not mean we can be sure the train will end up in New Orleans, Omaha, or Minneapolis. There may be many switches

along the way. It may be that our discussion has been over-simplistic or has seemed deterministic to you. Please criticize the chapter (positively or negatively) from that angle.

10. What other impact or implications do you see concerning religion and this first stage of the development of an individual's personality?

CHAPTER 2

IS IT SAFE TO BE A CHILD ?

Developmental stages overlap with one another and cannot be confined to a specific time span in a rigid fashion. Just as the person continues, at periods other than infancy, to be confronted with the question of whether it was OK to be born, so the process of individuation does not wait to begin until the first stage is completed. During childhood there is the possibility of picking up two burdens, which for some become heavy, excess baggage on life's journey: shame and guilt. No wonder psychologists have viewed childhood as a crucial stage of personality formation.

BECOMING A SELF-CONSCIOUS SELF

Awareness of autonomy emerges sometime after the baby begins to realize that he/she and the mother are two separate entities. Some have speculated that hours and days after birth the infant still does not distinguish self from non-self. For all the baby knows, the mother's breast is as integral a part of his own self as his hand or nose. Later experience teaches him that whereas the mother goes away and comes back, there are other realities that are still with him, the parts of his body. This differentiation of the self from other selves, this individuation process, accelerates in a short time.

AUTONOMY: FREEDOM AND CHOICE

Toilet training has become recognized as a classic period of self-discovery. The young child realizes that instead of being a passive recipient of care, she is expected to co-operate with another person. Although she cannot conceptualize any doctrine of freedom of the will, something akin to "will" is being dramatically acted out. It dawns upon the child that the mother is asking her to exercise control over a part of herself. The mother is helpless without the child's participation. These sphincter muscles belong to the child and not to the mother. Any parent who has been stumped in this enterprise has been able to translate the thoughts of the cute but stubborn kid on the toilet training seat to read, "I'll do it in my own good time!" If the first stage posed the question of "To be or not to be?", this stage of development raises the possibility of "To do or not to do."

As the child progresses from crawling to toddling, the spiral of life covers a larger area. What were random movements become more purposeful. If one swings one's arm in the right direction, the red ball will go bouncing along the floor. If one pinches the rubber duck, it squeaks. The child becomes aware of his visibility. In the environment of a safe and loving home, it is not only OK for you to be who you are but to be where you are. Increasing amounts of autonomy are granted to the child as he or she is promoted from the crib to the play pen to the whole living room floor to the vast expanse of the outside play yard. The child now stands out on the landscape as a self-actualizing little person, has a privately owned name, high chair, and bed. Higher up on this spiral, one's place in the world becomes a little more complex. Not only is the red ball bouncing along the floor, but it is I, myself, who am making it bounce. This growing self-consciousness is pretty heady stuff.

A passage from Erikson indicates the significance of this stage of personality development as far as character formation and other larger issues are concerned.

> ".....As the infant's senses and his muscles grasp at opportunities for more active experience, he faces the double demand for self-control and for the acceptance of control from others. To will does not mean to be "willful," but rather to gain gradually the power of increased judgment and decision in the application of drives .....Here, no doubt, is the genetic origin of the elusive question of Free Will, which man, ever again, attempts to master logically and theologically.....A sense of defeat (from too little or too much training) can lead to deep shame and a compulsive doubt whether one ever really willed what one did, or really did what one willed."[1]

SHAME: "DON'T BE LIKE YOU ARE!"

Note that at this stage Erikson speaks of shame rather than guilt. This is a pre-moral stage in which the child is yet unable to use the adult categories of right and wrong, good and evil. A scolding at this age makes the child feel it is not all right to be who he is. In this case the sin and the sinner are one. Later this self-conscious child may have stage fright during a school skit and wish he could disappear through a hole in the floor. This feeling of not being willing to be seen can precede and be independent of any "mistake" or misbehavior during the performance. Shame is a natural successor to mistrust, rejection, and depreciation. A sense of legitimate and spontaneous autonomy would be more likely the experience of a child who had spent his first stage of life in an atmosphere of trust and accepting love.

Shame is the alternative to autonomy in the sense that a child thus stigmatized is not worthy to do anything. Obviously if you are a nobody, you should do nothing; at least you are not entitled to do anything on your own. Just as we predicted it would be difficult for a child surrounded by mistrust to have faith later in life, so it may be difficult for a person whose self-image is shrouded with a sense of shame to grasp the meaning of grace in adult life. Grace means that God loves and accepts you and looks upon you as worthy just because you are created in his image completely apart from what you do or accomplish. Instead of the castigating, "Don't be like you are!", the comforting words of Charlotte Elliott's hymn are heard, "Just as I am, thou wilt receive." We shall return to this dynamic again in discussing vocation.

REACHING OUT AND RISKING MISTAKES: GUILT AND MORALITY

As long as the child bounces the rubber ball along the floor, there is still no conflict with the values of the adult world. One adventuresome day the child swings his arm just as purposefully and knocks a colorful teacup from the table onto the floor. This is a delightful experience; the noise, the shiney pieces catching the sunlight, the mother running in excitedly from the other room. It could well be the first significant clash between the values of the mother (Take good care of the expensive tea set your parents-in-law gave you for Christmas) and the priorities of the child (Have fun with colorful objects and loud noises). This is but the first step on a long journey of discovering what is right and wrong, good and evil, acceptable and unacceptable in society. This encounter will be followed by the following:

31

"Leave your brother's things alone."

"Keep your hands out of the cookie jar."

"When you finish raking the leaves, you may go and play ball." (Work is good and is rewarded.)

"Practice your piano lessons because anything worth doing is worth doing well." (Righteousness is its own reward.)

"Thou shalt not steal." (...nor even cheat on thy income tax when IRS is not looking)

"Thou shalt not commit adultery." (...nor even look upon a woman to lust after her)

"Thou shalt have the right attitude toward management while working for this company."

Morality is a progressive discovery ranging from the judgment about very specific and isolated behaviors of childhood to the more pervasive values of adulthood such as patriotism, loyalty to one's colleagues, and even the attitudes and intentions which underlie behavior. What takes place in this complex transformation of values is that what began as "must" commands given by external authority figures, become assimilated and internalized into the "ought" of conscience. A child must not run the wrong way down a one-way street, and his Daddy will forcibly remove him from that danger if necessary and place him back on the path of righteousness, namely, the sidewalk. We hope that the mature adult will abide by traffic regulations out of a sense of social responsibility as well as for his own safety. He ought to be a good citizen. If he fails to act in an adult and socially responsible way, the Daddy (in the uniform of a police officer) tells him he must keep his hands out of the store's cash register, the bank's vault, or any other cookie jar which attracts him. But making this transition from must to ought takes many years, longer for some than others.

THE DILEMMA OF THE WILL

"I can will what is right, but I cannot do it. For I do not do the good I want, but the evil I do not want is what I do." (Romans 7:18b-19)

The child now has the ingredients for having reached the "age of discretion," the capacity to recognize the difference between good and evil and the capacity to make a responsible choice

32

between them. The Jewish boy who undergoes the Bar Mitzvah ceremony becomes a "son of the commandment," morally responsible for his acts. Catholics set a time when children go to confession and receive First Communion under the assumption that at this age the child is capable of sin and a repentant attitude toward that sin. Ancient Greeks used the term <u>akrasia</u>, meaning want of self-control, incontinence, intemperance. It was much like Saint Paul's dilemma: knowing the good but not doing it.

Belief and morality are closely linked, as in the remark, "I believe it is the right thing to do." The embezzler begins by having "good" reasons for acquiring the unearned $40,000 from the bank where he is teller.

1. My mother needs $10,000 worth of surgery and treatment.

2. My gifted son deserves to go to Harvard, which otherwise we could not afford.

3. My wife deserves a nice vacation in Hawaii for our 25th wedding anniversary, which I have long promised her.

4. My boss has grown too rich anyhow, and the other investors in the multi-million dollar bank won't miss these few thousands.

You may disagree with belief #4, but are not the first three all <u>good</u> and loving things to do? The embezzler believes in and concentrates on what he thinks is good in the long run. He does not intend nor think much about disaster. He does not say to himself, I shall embezzle $40,000 in order to:

1. Bring shame to my sick mother.

2. Destroy my marriage as I languish in the penitentiary.

3. Cause my son to disrespect me.

4. Lose my job and get my name in the headlines which read: "LOCAL CHURCH DEACON ARRESTED FOR STEALING MONEY FROM HIS NEIGHBORS."

Rationalization has this in common with heresy that it is a distortion. It begins with something that is basically true (A loving son should help his mother with her health problems + My mother needs the money more than my rich boss) and ends up

33

with something illegal (Therefore, I am justified in stealing $40,000 from this bank).

Alcoholics Anonymous members have used a phrase to describe the disordered thinking and beliefs of their addiction life style. They call it "stinkin thinkin." The alcoholic travel-ing salesman has had a bad week falling far below his quota even though he has made many calls on customers. Both his wife and his salesmanager will be disappointed. He reasons thus: "Anyone who has worked as hard as I have all week is entitled to a little happiness or reward. Several drinks will make me more happy; therefore, I should stop in at this bar and have several drinks." He does not say to himself, "I shall now pro-ceed to destroy my body and mind, my marriage and reputation. The most effective way to do this is to get drunk, end up in jail, lose my job, and come down with delirium tremens."

Some pathologically disordered minds seem to know evil and deliberately seek it. The first type, the sociopath, has never incorporated the rules and laws of society into his psyche, has never assimilated them in such a way as to bring them and his own personal conscience into some working agreement. He has never found the esteem of his parents or society significant; perhaps interpersonal relations have never been rewarding to him. The caution, "Wouldn't your parents be disappointed with you if you did that?", has no power to influence his decision. He says, "What's that to me? They don't care about me anyway. My father deserted seven years ago, and my mother is always down at the bar and wants only one thing from me--that I stay out of her way." Such a person is unsocialized, not integrated into society, not sensing any obligation to play the game ac-cording to the same rules that control the conduct of the vast majority. Such a person seems to have nothing to lose socially nor emotionally.

The second type of disorder is masochism. Although the behavior may be as destructive and negative as that of the socio-path, the motivating goal is different. What is unusual and seemingly perverse about it is that good and bad are reversed; pain is perceived as pleasure, and illness is perceived as de-sirable. Such persons may be accident prone and injure them-selves "deliberately," not consciously but through a disordered, unconscious motivation for self-retribution or to satisfy some other unmet need. That is why it is considered a pathological state and must be treated by psychotherapy rather than by a direct appeal to the will or reason.

For the purpose of our discussion of the dilemma of the will we should exclude these two disordered forms of thinking:

34

sociopathy and masochism. Supposedly persons with these afflictions do not have the capacity to make a responsible choice between good and evil, right and wrong. At the very least we would have to grant that their freedom has been greatly limited.

PARADIGM OF WILL

Having discussed various alternative approaches to decision-making, we see that Saint Paul is speaking of only some of the alternatives in his classic statement, "...I do not do the good I want." In Figure 3 the following formula is used: behavior is classified as active or passive and as positive (good) or negative (evil). From a strictly mathematical calculation there would be quite a few alternatives if one also added two other factors: what one wants and what one does.

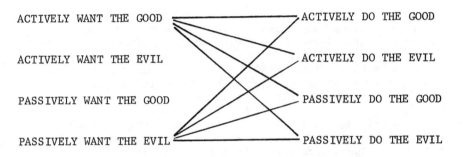

ACTIVELY WANT THE GOOD   ACTIVELY DO THE GOOD

ACTIVELY WANT THE EVIL   ACTIVELY DO THE EVIL

PASSIVELY WANT THE GOOD   PASSIVELY DO THE GOOD

PASSIVELY WANT THE EVIL   PASSIVELY DO THE EVIL

Fig. 3   Alternatives of Wanting and Doing

What the above diagram implies is that it is possible to have four types of behavior stemming from four types of motivation or "wanting." This is what moral theology means by sins of commission and sins of omission. In the parable of the Good Samaritan, the sin of the Priest and Levite was not that they actively added to the stricken man's injuries, but their sin lay in their passivity, their not helping him. Which of the above patterns in Figure 3 would describe them morally? Perhaps our efforts to classify the moral alternatives still fall short in spite of our complex patterns of alternatives. It may not be sufficient to say that they passively want the good and passively do the evil. The problem was that in their passivity they did not do the good.

TYPES OF MORAL RESPONSE

Rather than try to perfect our diagram to cover all possible alternatives, let us cite other examples of the moral dilemma of the will.

1. A son who appreciates and loves his mother decides to visit her on her birthday and bring a present.

2. A Nazi SS officer carefully carries out his assignment of executing Jews in a concentration camp after medical "experiments" have been carried out on temperature endurance and survival.

3. The alcoholic persuades himself he deserves some happiness and gets drunk as in the case of the salesman already referred to.

4. An obese person tries to stay on his diet but ends up eating half a chocolate cake between lunch and dinner.

5. A youth hates his school teacher and wants to hurt the old bastard by slashing all four of her tires in the parking lot beside her apartment building late at night.

6. A wife agrees adultery is wrong and wants to remain faithful to her husband but does not live up to this desirable standard and sleeps with her husband's best friend.

7. A person needs transportation to another city and "uses" another person's car without permission. When asked if he feels sorry for this crime of theft, his reply is, "So what's the big deal? I needed it so I took it."

8. A member of the Ku Klux Klan, in his role of real estate salesman, does not tell a prospective black customer about a house within his financial capacity to buy. It overlooks a quiet lake in Briarwood Hills suburb.

9. An obese person tries to stay on her diet, is offered a piece of chocolate cake after dinner, but politely refuses it.

10. A Japanese youth, under MacArthur's occupation regime, said he never wanted to be a Kamikaze pilot anyway.

11. "A man had two sons; and he went to the first and said, 'Son, go and work in the vineyard today.' And he answered, 'I will not'; but afterward he repented and went. And he went to the second and said the same; and he answered, 'I go, sir,' but

he did not go. Which of the two did the will of his father?"
(Matthew 21:28-31a)

How would you match the following descriptions with the
above eleven moral situations?

     a. Sociopath

     b. Sinner tempted by the Deceiver

     c. Masochist

     d. Conformist

     e. Saint Paul's dilemma

     f. Sinner (work of the "flesh")

     g. Not aware of unconscious motivation

     h. Sinner with "hardness of heart"

     i. Morally victorious ("fruit of the Spirit")

     j. Sadist

     k. Morally ambivalent

     l. Lacking in will power

     m. _____ (other)

You may wish to make your own chart or follow Fig. 4 for analyz-
ing this process including at least the following categories:

Moral Social Reality	Person's Private Belief	Person's Actual Attitude	Behavior Finally Performed	Descriptive Type
Act is Good	Act is Good	Really Wants the Evil	Does the Evil	Sinner ("Work of the flesh")
Act is Evil	Act is Evil	Wants the Evil	Does the Evil	Sinner ("hardness of heart")
Act is Good	Believes Act is Good	Wants the Good	Does the Good	Integrity
Act is Good	Act is Evil	Wants the Evil	Does the Good	Conformist
Act is Evil	Neutral	Expediency	Does the Evil	Sociopath
Act is Evil	Act is Good	Wants the Evil (thought to be good)	Does the Evil	Sinner (tempted by "Deceiver")
Act is Good	Act is Good	Really wants the Evil	Does the Evil	Now aware of unconscious motivation
Act is Evil	Act is Evil	Wants the Good	Does the Evil	Saint Paul's Dilemma
Act is Evil	Act is Good	Wants the Evil (misperceived as Good)	Does the Evil	Distortion of Masochism (re: self) or Sadism (re: others)
Act is Good	Act is Good	Wants the Evil but wants the Good more	Does the Good	Victorious ("Fruit of the Spirit")
Act is Good	Act is Evil	Does not want the True Good	Does the Evil	Racist (in #8 above)

Fig. 4   Reality, Belief, Attitude and Moral Behavior

Sometimes the religious person feels he/she is in a bind or even a double bind. For example, a person may interpret the total depravity of humanity view in such a way as to think, "If I do wrong I'm wrong, and if I do right I am wrong." That does not lead to constructive moral guidance. Others hold that each person is so complexly ambivalent that every act is a composite of positive and negative motivations. There is so much good in the worst of us and so much bad in the best of us that none of us should cast the stone of judgment. "Judge not, that you not be judged." That is all well and good as far as judgment is concerned, but it may confuse the child who is gradually learning how to develop an internalized and socially functional moral sense. With current moral thinking in our society ranging from arbitrary and bureaucratic rules and regulations at the one extreme to so-called situation ethics on the other, it is little wonder that many personalities are ill-equipped to cope with the dilemma of the will.

One way of understanding the quote from Saint Paul about not doing what one wants and doing what one does not want is to check the "want" against the behavior. Perhaps people do what they really want, not what they say they want nor even what they think they want. The way to find out whether the obese person "wanted" loss of weight more than the satisfaction of eating chocolate cake is to wait and find out what that person actually did. The person did what was wanted more intensely, more pervasively, or more insistently. The growing child wrestles with this when saying, "I didn't really mean to hit my sister; I just did it."

UNIQUENESS THROUGH SECRETS AND PLAY

Paul Tournier explains the child's use of secrets as an early experimentation with autonomy.[2] "I know something you don't know," is an oft heard taunt between siblings. A sense of power comes from the fact that the supposedly all-powerful and all-knowing parent does not know that the child has a forbidden firecracker or frog skeleton tucked into the back corner of the bottom dresser drawer. Being the only person privy to such wonderful information makes one a bit special, unique, even somewhat powerful.

Even later in life persons still use secret information as a commodity with which to barter for friendship or influence. In prison, where all other personal property is reduced to a minimum, there remains the special significance of rumor, which makes the owner thereof a valued and influential person. Membership in a fraternity, sorority, or the Masonic Order is made more special by secret passwords, handshakes, and clandestine initiation ceremonies unknown to the "outsider." Mystery cults from the ancient Gnostics to the People's Temple sect in Guyana have relied upon secrets to bolster members' sense of worth and uniqueness.

Tournier carefully distinguishes between childish secrets and adult lying. A little girl is told by her mother to stay on a certain side of the street on her way to school so as not to be endangered by the busy traffic. Nevertheless, one day she skips across the street to buy some penny candy and thus disobeys her mother. When she comes home that day, her mother inquires if she stayed only on the safe and prescribed side of the street; and the daughter says, "Yes." The point Tournier makes is that this is not so much a matter of formal lying (although technically it is that, too) as of autonomy, an experiment in claiming one's individuality. Incidentally, the girl also discovers that the mother cannot see around corners, and that it is possible to have a little secret all one's own.

Some children are not allowed to become autonomous persons because, when they have little secrets, they are cajoled by their parents and threatened not to have anything, even a thought, that is privately their own. Carried to its extreme, this is the totalitarian brainwashed state. But individuals, stunted in this period of development, can also create their own personal totalitarian state of mind and live furtively long into adulthood. One very successful middle-aged farmer felt so intimidated by his wife that as he and a neighbor farmer rode home from the village where he had delivered a load of grain, he remarked to his companion, "We'll eat these peaches and throw away the pits and the bag before we get home. Hannah doesn't have to know about this."

The person developing in a healthy manner toward maturity acquires enough sense of worth to be able to deal realistically with events and other persons and does not need to "play games" nor resort to secret manipulation to get along in the world. Such a person knows when to think out thoughts in private and when to present them in a motion at the committee meeting if such action seems constructive. This is quite different from worrying that others will find out what you are thinking or what you are doing. "Secret" behavior among children in the sense described by Tournier is developmentally normal; whereas the same childish behavior in an adult could be labelled "hypocrisy." The mature adult is willing to accept responsibility for his/her own thoughts and actions and take the consequences for the same. We will return to this issue in Chapter 7 in connection with morality and sin.

In Erikson's recent book, _Toys and Reasons_, he demonstrates that children use play and toys to create meaning out of their environment and to interpret their relationship to persons and objects as well as to significant events in their lives. In play therapy a child may be able to express fear, hostility, love, and loneliness through the handling and placement of dolls representing members of the immediate family. A three-year-old boy in my parish saw his father kill his mother with a hammer on the kitchen floor. He was so traumatized that he lost his capacity to speak and became totally mute. Only after a play therapist helped him work through this gruesome scene with dolls representing the family was he able to re-enter the real world and speak to it again. In short, what children do in their play is not nonsense but testing out life on a small scale.

An experience from John Woolman's childhood shows how the same moral issue which the adult Quaker would confront in objection to killing in war was for the playful boy also a moral problem.

> "On going to a neighbor's house, I saw on the
> way a robin sitting on her nest, and as I came
> near she went off; but having young ones she
> flew about, and with many cries expressed her
> concern for them. I stood and threw stones
> at her, and on striking her she fell down dead.
> At first I was pleased with the exploit, but
> after a few minutes was seized with horror,
> at having in a sportive way, killed an innocent
> creature while she was caring for her young."[3]

Likewise, children test out adult vocations by "playing" doctor, fireman, preacher, nurse, farmer, etc. The rules of their little games are not unlike the regulations of later life such as taking turns, being fair, not taking more than your share, keeping score, and the like.

The corollary of this process may be found among adults in whom it is just as easy to read their true values and self image in their play and recreation as in their supposedly serious statements in the business or professional world. Imagination and creativity require a certain amount of playfulness. Even religious liturgies and rituals are re-enactments of scenarios (the Mass in relation to the Crucifixion or the very descriptive term: The Lord's Supper, a re-enactment of The Last Supper). We also speak of the Army's practice exercises as "War Games." A person may not be promoted because he displays unsportsmanlike behavior and does not follow "the rules of the game" in the business world.

41

> "In sketching the ontogeny of playfulness,
> then, we are inclined to go beyond those theo-
> ries which assign legitimate play in adult life
> only to games or rituals taking place in 'tempo-
> rary worlds within the ordinary world dedicated
> to the performance of an act apart'--that is,
> on toy table, playgrounds, or theatrical stages,
> on game boards and sport fields, or, indeed, in
> high rituals reflecting a collective's mythology.
> No, the spirit of playfulness can pervade the
> visionary schemes which attach to human activi-
> ties of utter practicality and consequence,
> whether such schemes are altogether implicit, or
> are, in fact, expressed in terms of playful
> metaphors..."4

It seems that some adults develop excessive rigidity if they have never learned how to sit back and view their vocations or even society itself with a touch of playfulness and humor. Allport suggested that humor and religion have this in common: that they help to put issues of life into perspective.

> "For the religious person, as well as for the
> irreligious, the design of the universe is by
> no means apparent at all times, and its non-
> sequiturs, its 'mechanical inelasticities' are
> fair game for laughter.....Humor helps to inte-
> grate personality by disposing of all conflicts
> that do not really matter."5

Clearly there is a continuity between the child's searching for autonomy, discovering that he/she is a unique self, and a later sense of freedom to act "on one's own," a sense of respon-sibility for one's own behavior as belonging to oneself. Early secrets and play can be a useful way for the young child to test out the basic issue of autonomy.

KEEPING SCORE: SUCCESS AND/OR FAILURE

One aspect of gamesmanship of which our American society is painfully and compulsively aware is that of keeping score. Very early the child is led to believe that competence, accomplishment and excellence in performance are what guarantee the worth of an individual.

You may recall conversations at the family reunion about whether Alice was weaned as early as Jane and whether Bill learned to walk, talk, or whatever, as early as Jack. Then there are the Scout badges, trophies, school grades, aptitude tests, tests of basic skills, basketball tournaments, college entrance exams, job performance appraisals, promotions, demotions, honors, citations, etc., in a never-ending evaluative process. Currently there is a stress on even dying in the right way, namely with dignity, in contrast to other ways which are "wrong." Whence this fascination with keeping score, with needing to make a determination of success and/or failure at every turn?

Even when there has been a deliberate effort to down-play comparative evaluation and competition, the process re-asserts itself as if by necessity. Descriptive paragraphs were written in the student's record in place of letter grades; and categories were broadened to the simple distinction of "pass/fail." This was supposed to reduce pressure on students so they could be more themselves and not worry about grades. Graduate admissions committees were troubled by this lack of discrimination since they quite naturally wanted the cream of the crop, and now the cream was not even being separated from the milk; students had become homogenized. In my one-room country school house days, grades were given on a percentage basis. Later A, B, C, D, and F were used. One school that became disenchanted with pass/fail returned part way to a formula of H, AA, P, and F (Honors, Above Average, Pass, and Fail - obviously an ABC, omitting the D). One professional school rates students as Top 10%, Top 12.5%, and Top 37.5% of the class, which would be helpful for firms that wished to interview applicants only from a certain category. These scores, numbers, and percentages loom very large for a person who has set a goal which simply must be reached in order for that individual to be an acceptable or worthy person.

A CULTURAL NORM OF COMPETITION

In highly developed countries with great stress on upward social mobility such as West Germany, Japan, and the United States, some persons may enter into a full scale mental breakdown or even resort to suicide because they were ranked 101 or 103 when there were only 100 positions open in a given category. Unless they "succeed" their life is evidently not worth living. Not only each culture or country but each family and individual set a standard of accomplishment or success that implies personal worth. Erikson described the crucial issue at this stage of development as characterized by the alternatives of "industry vs. inferiority."

> "The child's danger, at this stage, lies
> in a sense of inadequacy and inferiority. If
> he despairs of his tools and skills or of his

43

status among his tool partners, he may be dis-
couraged from identification with them and with
a section of the tool world. To lose the hope
of such 'industrial' association may pull him
back to the more isolated, less tool-conscious
familial rivalry of the oedipal time. The child
despairs of his equipment in the tool world and
in anatomy, and considers himself doomed to
mediocrity or inadequacy.....

"On the other hand, this is socially a most
decisive stage: since industry involves doing
things beside and with others, a first sense of
division of labor and of differential opportunity,
that is, a sense of the <u>technological</u> <u>ethos</u> of
a culture, develops at this time."6

Erikson's use of the term "mediocrity" deserves a cultural
and etymological footnote. The term "mediocre" comes from two
old Latin parts: <u>medi</u> (middle) and <u>ocris</u> (rugged mountain);
literally a mountain of medium height or in the middle of a
range. How often have we heard a snide remark that someone is
"below average" or as the dictionary defines the term, mediocre,
"only ordinary." The fact of psychological testing is that indeed millions of people, in fact the vast majority, are average
or ordinary. The bell-shaped curve is true of IQ, height and
weight, as well as many other characteristics.

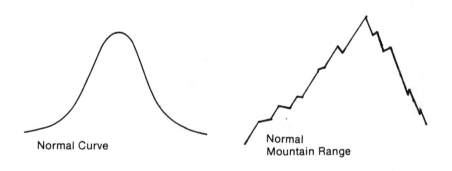

Normal Curve

Normal
Mountain Range

Fig. 5   Reality

According to many it would be ideal if no one were below average, at least not their children. We would then need to get used to a new curve of human capacity as well as new kinds of mountains which have no middle peaks, thus:

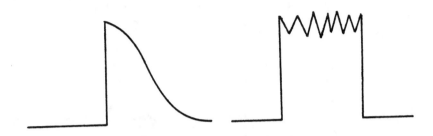

Fig. 6   Ideal

If mental health means accepting reality, it would be healthier not to juggle the facts nor even to idealize unreality. Both mountains and people come in all sizes and shapes, all sorts of textures and colors. Why is it necessary to place an odium on one and an accolade on another? Various efforts to take an egalitarian attitude have been attempted. Perhaps the most ambitious campaign was mounted by Mao Tse-tung whose goal was to minimize class and rank distinctions, stress the great worth of the peasants and workers, the masses, who had been looked down upon because they were so far below average. It is very hard to keep such a goal constantly in sight because someone will soon ask, "Who is the best, most faithful, hardest working comrade in our work brigade?" Comparative and superlative adjectives creep back into the vocabulary until such "right roaders" are purged and a better attitude is re-established.

In an elementary school in the People's Republic of China, I saw sixteen children playing tug-of-war, each side trying to

45

pull the red flag across their line. The teacher explained how this exercise was to foster co-operation, pulling together, in keeping with their motto "Friendship first, competition second." They were to try to win, but not with the philosophy of Coach Lombardi, who said, "Winning isn't everything; it's the only thing." After one side had won in the tug-of-war game, the children changed positions so that they worked together with another group.

12345678	ABCDEFGH		1234ABCD	5678EFGH
12AB56EF	34CD78GH			

Fig. 7

Rotating Teams to Teach "Friendship First, Competition Second"

Malcolm X College in Chicago has taken a leaf from the behavior modification therapists in developing a new grading system. Professors record achievements but not failures. Thus, if a student does not learn enough in a term to receive a passing grade, he/she simply gets no grade. If, the third time the course is taken, there is satisfactory completion of the course, the student receives, for example, a grade of C for three hours of American History. Since many of their students are disadvantaged persons from the lower socio-economic class, they do not have the burden of two grades of F to add to their low self-image. Meanwhile, it in no way lowers the academic standard because the student was not given the C until he/she had earned it. This method has the self-directing vocational guidance feature of dealing with reality rather than judgment and criticism. The student who struggles four terms to pass geometry will see the light and forsake the goal of becoming a civil engineer. The same student achieving continued success in mechanical trade courses will find an appropriate niche there and a sense of worth doing what can be done well, i.e., providing family and society will be willing to ascribe worth to that role and stop bemoaning how too bad it is that the individual never became a professional engineer.

Since religion is such a prominent institution as far as setting standards for human worth and value, one would expect some assistance for the individual from this resource. In this regard, as in many other instances of social ethics, "religion" does not speak with one voice.

✗ Some Sunday Schools used to give pins and bars for perfect attendance, awards for those who memorized the most Bible verses, and great approval for those who did well in programs and pageants. Sometimes the "failures" and below average were harshly judged. Those receiving the least attention and support were often the inconspicuous, average persons who did not stand out in excellence nor in disaster. Such child-rearing was in keeping with the so-called "Protestant Work Ethic" of works righteousness. One's human worth and achievement were identical.

✓ Others grew up in a religious context of grace where each individual was considered of inestimable worth as a child of God. Whether the person had a high or low IQ, were handsome or disfigured, were adept or uncoordinated regarding manual dexterity, were outstanding, mediocre, or below average; that person was accepted as a <u>person</u> and appreciated for whatever that personality possessed or could do. Needless to say that person would be less likely to develop what Adler referred to as an "inferiority complex." On the other hand, such an individual would also feel positive toward such religious influences and support, would turn to religious resources for help in time of need expecting strength and useful guidance.

While serving a parish of Danes, who were already burdened with enough Kierkegaardian gloom and self-deprecation, I reflected on my own disasterous Christmas Program experiences as a stuttering kid in a rural Norwegian church. Since it had been the custom to have memorized "pieces" with their assorted trap doors of failure opening up beneath below-average children, I thought it might be time for a change. Following J. L. Moreno's "Spontaneity Theatre," I encouraged the teachers to share the Christmas story for a month and then let little clusters of pupils tell the story in their own way. Different classes chose different roles in skits which grouped themselves around the traditional themes: Holy Family, Shepherds, Wise Men, etc. Each child spoke or acted out the story in his/her own way. The stutterer in the Shepherds group quite naturally decided not to assume a speaking role but to "tend the campfire and keep the coffee hot so that when his companions returned from their chilly mid-winter visit, they could warm themselves." The gift-bearing Wise Persons brought from home what was most precious to them. A child from a povertied family brought three pennies in a snuff box; another brought a Teddy Bear with one ear sucked to a point; and a third, from an affluent family, brought an expensive new doll that could even do things that were not permissible in a Danish Christmas Program. The children enjoyed

47

the freedom of "telling and doing the Christmas Story" in their own way. The teachers, on the other hand, were uncomfortable, because there was no way of keeping score, no way of measuring the success or failure of their individual classes.

At this point we should reflect on Erikson's first four stages of personality development and think about how religious factors may contribute toward the individual's positive upward growth in the spiral of life and those negative influences which may retard development or keep the individual down.

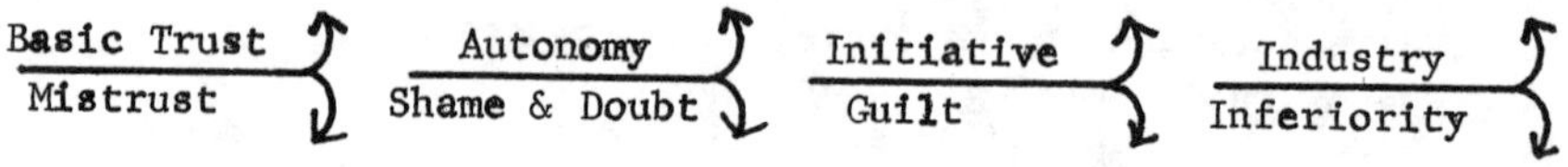

Basic Trust
Mistrust
Autonomy
Shame & Doubt
Initiative
Guilt
Industry
Inferiority

Fig. 8 First Four Stages

THE PSYCHOLOGY OF INDIVIDUAL DIFFERENCES

We need to consider more fully the individual differences referred to in the preceding section. Intelligence is one capacity which differentiates persons on the well known continuum of the normal curve thus:

100 I.Q.
Needs Custodial Care
Retarded
Average
Above Average
Genius

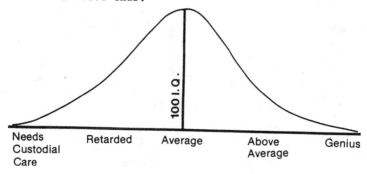

Fig. 9 The Bell-shaped Curve of the Intelligence Quotient

Intelligence is not the only aspect of personhood that ranges from low to high with a large proportion in the middle of the distribution. Height, weight, and somatotype lend themselves to similar comparison ranging from giant to midget, fat to thin, etc. Allport proposed a "Psychograph"[7] in which he paired, among other traits, the following:

symmetry	-	deformity
health	-	ill health
ascendance	-	submission
gregariousness	-	solitariness

(to which we could add)

wealth	-	poverty
upper class	-	lower class
educated	-	illiterate
musical	-	tone-deaf

We would end up with many axes upon which the same person may be rated high on one scale and low on another. The combinations and configurations are so numerous that no two would be the same, much like the uniqueness of each individual's fingerprints.

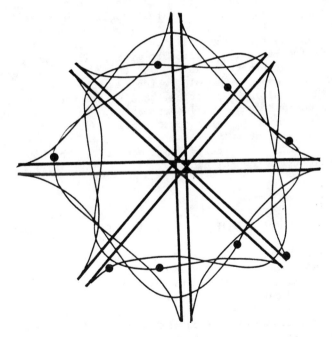

Fig. 10   Eight Factors Compared

49

Soren Kierkegaard was a philosophical genius but had a misshapen body; he was socially gregarious in some ways but reticent with Regena; wealthy and deeply religious, but sometimes a recluse and morbidly depressed. In short he was a mixture; and aren't we all? ✕

Add to the above varieties of temperaments and capacities the social factors of sibling order and the decade into which we were born (whether depression, war or post-war years, a period of peace and affluence or social unrest), national and ethnic grouping, rural-urban setting, and you begin to understand why Allport made a strong plea for the study of the individual in all his/her uniqueness. Practically every category listed in these last two pages has the potential for being considered by someone an asset, or by someone else, a liability, a stigma or a mark of distinction. One person gives thanks for an adversity because of its character-building effect upon the self, while another decries a great gift because it is such a "burden."

As it begins to dawn upon the pre-adolescent that he/she has the task of creating a unique identity out of all this myriad of inherited and socially acquired factors, it can be a little perplexing. This is the time for seeking out like-minded peers whether the common interest be basketball, school band or drama, Scouts or 4-H Club, church youth group, delinquent gang, or whatever. Whatever support religion is providing at this juncture, the time is near when support will be increased as the group of significant others seeks to help the youth shape an identity and think about some role, which can accommodate and utilize all the different capacities, skills, and resources that have been learned and can be called one's own. We are now ready to enter with the child into the period called adolescence. The young person who has not only believed that it was OK to be born, but also safe to be a child, must now cope with this transition from childhood to adulthood.

CASE ILLUSTRATIONS OF THE IMPACT OF CHILDHOOD

The following description of childhood was told by a priest. He felt the review and interpretation of these experiences helped him gain insight into his later adult behavior patterns. Notice the basically negative impact of this stage of life and how, unfortunately, his intense religious involvement was not functional for him. In preparation for our later discussion of sin in Chapter 7, we observe that he was not able to make effective use of the Catholic remedy for sin and guilt, the Sacrament of Penance. In speaking of religious scruples, he said, "I went to Confession weekly in the hope of purging my guilt, but I never spoke of the items which had caused me most guilt in my previous two years. My confessor was a patient person and a good listener. Though he gave me little specific direction, my scruples passed away in the course of that year." Unfortunately his sense of unworthiness plagued him long into adulthood.

Looking back on my childhood, I see it as an unhappy time. I feel that I emerged from Erikson's First Stage with a basic mistrust. My mother's anxiety and insecurity, coupled with the many demands made on her on the farm, made it difficult for her to communicate to me that I was in a warm and secure world where I could relax and feel sure I was loved and cared for. Having fared rather poorly in the First Stage, I did no better in the Second. Having only a little "basic faith in existence," it was dangerous to begin to exercise a choice. To make daring demands was out of the question lest I should lose the little love and security I had. It is likely then, that at this point shame and doubt found a place in my life: I was ashamed to assert some autonomy and "let go"' I was in doubt whether to assert a little autonomy or suppress it. I must have been keenly aware that my life was controlled extensively by authorities outside of me. I came out of this stage then with little freedom for self-expression and with little capacity for love.

Stage Three, Guilt vs. Initiative, was a decisive stage for me, and the Guilt came out on top. But I did have some initiative. I recall that as a boy of not more than three or four, I coveted a "pram" which a neighboring family owned. It became the most desirable toy I could hope to possess. So I decided I would take it. I crept secretly towards the owner's house, but the children were playing in the lawn and I had to withdraw. Here there was initiative, but I remember the incident because of the guilt, which the contemplated felony inspired in me. When I was slightly older I went to the creamery with my brother one afternoon, where we joined some of our school-mates. It made me feel good to be accepted as part of the group, until one of the boys broke a door knob, and all of us fled. For a time I lived in fear of being discovered and arrested as an accomplice to the crime. Another incident from childhood belongs here too, though I was eight years old when it occurred. One day I had a long and serious conversation with another boy; I felt happy that I could carry on a conversation as seriously as adults did. Then I related to my friend some scandal about a neighbor, which I had heard in an adult conversation. For a year afterwards I felt intensely guilty for having violated the Eighth Commandment. I say that this was a decisive stage in my life, because from that time forward guilt, secrecy and the fear of apprehension have been a major impediment to my emotional development.

In the Fourth Stage, Industry vs. Inferiority, I did a little better. In school, I found that I was intelligent; while I was never "the best in the class," seldom were there more than three in a class of twenty who were smarter than I. This was important to me in that it gave me a sense of worth and a source of pride. It is paradoxical that during all the years of childhood and adolescence when continuing guilt filled me with a sense of unworthiness, I consciously felt all the while that I was superior to most of my class-mates because I was more intelligent than they. On the farm too, there were many things I could do, since there were tasks to suit every age and size. But at no time did I feel very adequate on the farm; my brother was the strong one who could really help; I was the weak one who did his best. I was a poor athlete, footballer and boxer. I had only one fight in school. My adversary was smaller than I but I was afraid of him; I refused to fight because he was older than I. Then he rushed at me, and as I raised my fists as a last resort, I hit him on the nose. He withdrew bleeding, and I was acclaimed as the surprise warrior; I felt a hypocrite because I knew the truth.

I had two unhappy experiences in later childhood. One afternoon I was driving a donkey-and-cart on the wrong side of the road and became involved in a collision with a car driven by the local veterinary surgeon; a headlight of the car was broken, and the driver was very angry. I was too scared to tell my parents about the accident, and I lived in mortal fear from then on that my parents would find out about my crime. In the following year I took the Primary Certificate Examination to graduate from grade-school. In the course of the examination, another pupil gave me an answer to one of the questions, and the teacher saw us talking. I was publicly ordered to leave the room. This event I also kept from my parents, and now there were two terrible crimes to make me feel guilty. At no time did it occur to me to bring this guilt to the Church's Confessional, where I might have had it resolved. I lived in constant fear of being found out. The conviction that I was an unworthy person was deepened: I had committed crimes, but people still thought I was a good boy; I knew that I was a hypocrite. It may have been at this time that I developed my "unworthy man's" gait: I am told that today I walk with my shoulders bent forward and my head bowed a little.

My fourteenth year was a trying one; in that year I was one of three who were chosen to study for an examination which might win for us scholarships to finance our high-school education. Believing that knowledge can be imparted by force, the teacher would slap us on the hands, head and face, as part of our special preparation. Added to my heavy weight of guilt, this punishment took a heavy toll on my health. I became unhealthily compulsive: I could not sit in a room where there were papers on the floor, without having to pick them. This may well have been a neurotic attempt to put my life in order. My physical health left much also to be desired. From the age of four I had suffered from asthma: now at age fourteen, it became more severe; I would awake in the night, and sit gasping for breath for an hour.

I do not recall when religion began to play a large part in my life; at fourteen, it had already begun to do so. We were not a religious family; we had no family prayers, not even meal prayers. In church and school it was constantly repeated that every family should recite the Rosary together every night. So constant were the imperatives that even my strong brother began to feel guilty about our family negligence. I lived in the fear that one day our terrible ungodliness would become known to my classmates. Perhaps it was natural for me to turn to religion: I was a good boy who never got in trouble; it was fitting that he should be religious too. I turned to religion too in the hope that it would free me from my guilt and supply for my inadequacies. Immediately before the scholarship examination, our teacher recommended us to pray as a last resort. All summer, as I awaited the results, I prayed and prayed. It was the Marian Year, and I prayed to Mary over and over during the day's work. A priest began to influence my life at this time too. My brother and I served at Sunday Mass in our church from the age of eight; this priest took a special interest in me, and invited me to serve his Mass each day when he returned to our parish for his annual vacation. He was deeply convinced about the value of his own vocation, and felt that I would be a good candidate for his Order. He was a kind and considerate person, and invited me to ask him questions about anything I wished. He was more available to me than anybody else, but I never brought myself to reveal my secrets or anxieties to him.

Well, my prayers were answered, and I won sixth place in the examination. I was robed in glory; not only was I a good boy now, but I was also brilliant. I was ill at ease in glory, too.

* * * * * * * * * * *

Benjamin Franklin's pithy sayings resemble current religions of "positive thinking." "Early to bed and early to rise, makes a man healthy, wealthy, and wise." "God helps them that help themselves." He preached the virtues of industry, frugality, and thrift. He did not want to be restricted to any one sect and was bothered by narrowness in religious polemics. He held to a Puritan ethic but with a sense of humor and good nature. William James' category of "The Religion of Healthy-mindedness" could well be applied to Benjamin Franklin. Without getting involved in more specific doctrines, we can see his basic belief in Providence in these quotes:

> "Having emerged from the poverty and obscurity
> in which I was born and bred, to a state of af-
> fluence and some degree of reputation in the world,
> and having gone so far through life with a con-
> siderable share of felicity, the conducing means
> I made use of, which with the blessing of God
> so well succeeded, my posterity may like to
> know.....And now I speak of thanking God, I
> desire with all humility to acknowledge that I
> owe the mentioned happiness of my past life to
> His kind providence, which led me to the means
> I used and gave them success."

Benjamin was baptized on the day of his birth and raised by his parents in a stable home in the tradition of New England Congregationalism. He seemed to have had a positive outlook and self-confident experiences during his childhood. Let him speak for himself in these excerpts from his Autobiography:

> "I was put to the grammar-school at eight years
> of age, my father intending to devote me, as
> the tithe of his sons, to the service of the
> Church. My early readiness in learning to read
> (which must have been very early, as I do not
> remember when I could not read), and the opinion
> of all his friends, that I should certainly make
> a good scholar, encouraged him in this purpose
> of his. My uncle Benjamin, too, approved of

54

it, and proposed to give me all his short-hand
volumes of sermons, I suppose as a stock to set
up with, if I would learn his character. I
continued, however, at the grammar-school not
quite one year, though in that time I had risen
gradually from the middle of the class of that
year to be the head of it, and farther was removed
into the next class above it, in order to go with
that into the third at the end of the year.
But my father, in the meantime, from a view of
the expense of a college education, which having
so large a family he could not well afford, and
the mean living many so educated were afterwards
able to obtain--reasons that he gave to his
friends in my hearing--altered his first intention, took me from the grammar-school, and sent
me to a school for writing and arithmetic, kept
by a then famous man, Mr. George Brownell, very
successful in his profession generally, and that
by mild, encouraging methods. Under him I acquired
fair writing pretty soon, but I failed in the
arithmetic, and made no progress in it. At ten
years old I was taken home to assist my father
in his business, which was that of a tallow-
chandler and sope-boiler; a business he was not
bred to, but had assumed on his arrival in New
England, and on finding his dyeing trade would
not maintain his family, being in little request.
Accordingly, I was employed in cutting wick for
the candles, filling the dipping mould and the
moulds for cast candles, attending the shop,
going of errands, etc......

"I continued thus employed in my father's business
for two years, that is, till I was twelve years
old; and my brother John, who was bred to that
business, having left my father, married, and
set up for himself at Rhode Island, there was
all appearance that I was destined to supply his
place, and become a tallow-chandler. But my
dislike to the trade continuing, my father was
under apprehensions that if he did not find one
for me more agreeable, I should break away and
get to sea, as his son Josiah had done, to his
great vexation. He therefore sometimes took
me to walk with him, and see joiners, brick-
layers, turners, braziers, etc., at their work,
that he might observe my inclination, and endeavor
to fix it on some trade or other on land.....

55

"This bookish inclination at length determined
my father to make me a printer, though he had
already one son (James) of that profession. In
1717 my brother James returned from England
with a press and letters to set up his business
in Boston. I liked it much better than that
of my father, but still had a hankering for the
sea. To prevent the apprehended effect of such
an inclination, my father was impatient to have
me bound to my brother. I stood out some time,
but at last was persuaded, and signed the inden-
tures when I was yet but twelve years old. I
was to serve as an apprentice till I was twenty-
one years of age, only I was to be allowed journey-
man's wages during the last year. In a little
time I made great proficiency in the business,
and became a useful hand to my brother. I now
had access to better books. An acquaintance
with the apprentices of booksellers enabled me
sometimes to borrow a small one, which I was
careful to return soon and clean. Often I sat
up in my room reading the greatest part of the
night, when the book was borrowed in the evening
and to be returned early in the morning, lest
it should be missed or wanted.

"When about 16 years of age I happened to meet
with a book, written by one Tryon, recommending
a vegetable diet. I determined to go into it.
My brother, being yet unmarried, did not keep
house, but boarded himself and his apprentices
in another family. My refusing to eat flesh
occasioned an inconveniency, and I was frequently
chid for my singularity. I made myself acquainted
with Tryon's manner of preparing some of his
dishes, such as boiling potatoes or rice, making
hasty pudding, and a few others, and then proposed to my brother, that if he would give me,
weekly, half the money he paid for my board, I
would board myself. He instantly agreed to it,
and I presently found that I could save half
what he paid me. This was an additional fund
for buying books. But I had another advantage
in it. My brother and the rest going from the
printing house to their meals, I remained there
alone, and, dispatching presently my light repast,
which often was no more than a bisket or a slice
of bread, a handful of raisins or a tart from
the pastry-cook's, and a glass of water, had

the rest of the time till their return for study, in which I made the greater progress, from that greater clearness of head and quicker apprehension which usually attend temperance in eating and drinking.

"I had been religiously educated as a Presbyterian; and though some of the dogmas of that persuasion, such as the eternal decrees of God, election, reprobation, etc., appeared to me unintelligible, others doubtful, and I early absented myself from the public assemblies of the sect, Sunday being my studying day, I never was without some religious principles. I never doubted, for instance, the existence of the Deity; that he made the world, and govern'd it by his Providence; that the most acceptable service of God was the doing good to man; that our souls are immortal; and that all crime will be punished, and virtue rewarded, either here or hereafter. These I esteem'd the essentials of every religion; and, being to be found in all the religions we had in our country, I respected them all, tho' with different degrees of respect, as I found them more or less mix'd with other articles, which, without any tendency to inspire, promote, or confirm morality, serv'd principally to divide us, and make us unfriendly to one another. This respect to all, with an opinion that the worst had some good effects, induc'd me to avoid all discourse that might tend to lessen the good opinion another might have of his own religion; and as our province increas'd in people, and new places of worship were continually wanted, and generally erected by voluntary contribution, my mite for such purpose, whatever might be the sect, was never refused."[8]

NOTES

1. Erikson, Insight and Responsibility, pp. 118-119.

2. Tournier, Secrets, Richmond, Virginia: John Knox Press, 1965.

3. John Woolman, The Journal of John Woolman (John Greenleaf Whittier Edition Text), New York: Corinth Press, 1961,

p. 3.

4. Erikson, Toys and Reasons, p. 62.

5. Allport, The Individual and His Religion, p. 105.

6. Erikson, Childhood and Society, p. 260.

7. Allport, Personality: A Psychological Interpretation, p. 403.

8. Frank Woodworth Pine (Editor), The Autobiography of Benjamin Franklin.
   New York: Garden City Publishing Co., Inc., 1916. These and the following quotations are taken from pages 3-6, 13-14, 19, 22, 27-28, 142-143.

QUESTIONS AND PROBLEMS FOR DISCUSSION

1. What is the earliest experience of "shame" you can remember?

2. Have you seen shame in a young child recently at a family reunion, in a restaurant, or at a worship service?

3. What difference would it make in dealing with a child's self-image if one were to confuse guilt with shame in the diagnosis?

4. Indicate some criteria which would be useful in guiding a child to aim for the highest and best in behavior and ideals and at the same time be able to avoid destructive frustration and despair by knocking against the brick wall of reality.

5. What are the constructive and destructive potentials in the cultural value of competition?

6. In what way do you exercise play and humor as coping mechanisms for dealing with stress, maintaining self-regard, or facilitating interpersonal relationships? How is it working?

7. As you compare yourself with others and find yourself above average on some scales and below average in other characteristics, how do you handle this information?

8. Do you find it necessary to go against some generally accepted American culture norm to maintain your sense of worth? Give an illustration or two.

9. Do you find that certain current religious values or social expectations were helpful/hurtful as they impinged upon you in your pre-adolescent years? What were they?

10. Which descriptive type, in Figure 4, characterizes you most of the time? How do you feel about that?

CHAPTER 3

THE TRANSITION OF ADOLESCENCE: WHO AM I ?

The pre-adolescent sees upon the horizon two large question marks: Who am I? and Where am I going? Even the word "adolescence" means "growing toward" or growing up to something. That something, of course, is adulthood. Adultus is the participle form of the same Latin word from which adolescence is derived and means "grown," or, as a child may interpret it, "having arrived." Any transition raises the question of "what next?" Although all of life is change and transition, the increased tempo of change during puberty may be the reason that this stage of life is especially characterized in this way.

GROWING UP

Growing pains accompanied early childhood in special ways such as teething. Not all parts of the body grow at the same rate, causing tension and discomfort. During adolescence there are rapid growth spurts in different body systems such as the skeletal, muscular, and endocrinological. The gangling arms stick out of coat sleeves that seemed to have been the right length only months before. A period of physical awkwardness may be mirrored in embarrassment and social self-consciousness reminiscent of the younger child's wrestling with shame and doubt. It can be confusing to feel less co-ordinated and adept in junior high than one was in the lower grades. Fortunately, this condition is not permanent. Fortunate, also, is the adolescent whose parents and other significant adults are understanding and supportive in contrast to those who are chided with, "Why don't you grow up!"

The emerging sexual characteristics call for a reassessment of body image and new generative capacity. Not only has the shape of the body changed, e.g., breasts, but the distinguishing

61

appearance of pubic hair and beard set one apart from the childhood to which there is no returning. The onset of menstruation and the experience of nocturnal emission and penile erection signal a dramatic new power; the capacity to create another person.

A fourteen-year-old open heart surgery candidate was residing in a pediatric ward after having delivered her baby upstairs in the maternity ward. The nursing staff were quite disturbed by the fact that she was so pleased to have had the baby even though it threatened her life and there was no father to help support the child. The little mother, who had only recently played with baby dolls, was delighted to have a little doll of her very own. It was a case of a child having a child rather than a woman delivering a baby. The child entering puberty has all the anatomical potential for parenthood long before the emotional and social readiness, at least in contemporary American society.

The above case illustrates the concern of parents, adults, and society at large, that parenthood be delayed until the individual is fully ready for the responsibility. This calls for social controls, guidance, taboos, customs, commandments, even legislation to prevent pre-maturity in parenthood. Anthropologists have discovered a universal pattern in a wide variety of primitive and developed societies, namely: rites of passage and initiation ceremonies related to puberty. These may be perceived by some adolescents as oppressive and hostile regimentation and by others as helpful guidance. Sometimes the taboo against premature parenthood is exercised with such heavy-handed judgmentalism that the adolescent perceives of the entire sexual sphere as a disaster area; and even marriage does not remove the stigma, so that all sexuality is equated with shame and sin. This kind of destructive and immobilizing over-kill makes moral guidance non-functional.

X A religious interpretation of the physical body and its wonders as a positive gift of God can do much to aid the adolescent youth to gain self-acceptance and feel a kinship with the rest of nature. Religious education curricula and public school courses on family life and sex education have provided a context in which youth can mature, discuss, and ask questions as they make a gradual adjustment to their changing bodies. Yet our society is not of one mind on this matter, and many school districts have had to slow down these programs in response to a vocal opposition in the community. Each youth will cope with this change in his/her own unique way.

Conflict with authority figures is inevitable partly

62

because adult status is not generally handed to a young person on a silver platter; it must be earned through struggle. Father and son may wrestle on the living room floor in a playful manner when the boy is 8, 10, or 12; but if this keeps up long enough, the day will come when the son can pin the father. In a good relationship it is a wholesome contesting, a socialized re-enactment of the young, male seals who contend with the bull of the herd on the Pribilof Islands. Sigmund Freud attributed such seriousness to this competition between generations that he assumed deep seated guilt on the part of the son for subconsciously wanting to do in the "old man" in order to take his place in the adult world. The resultant Oedipus complex has been used by psychoanalysts ever since Freud to explain many later emotional disturbances and maladjustments.

The adolescent is caught in a bind, because the father, against whom he wrestles in many ways, is also the provider upon whom he is dependent for board, room, and clothing to say nothing of permission of various kinds until he reaches legal age. The following vignette illustrates the subtle ambivalence involved even in a very good father-son relationship. Having been invited to the home of a family for Sunday dinner after church, I had their sixteen-year-old son riding with me to show me the way. He began speaking about what a wonderful athlete his father had been in his college days. "He was a terrific outfielder until he broke his fingers and wrist making a stretch play. He was also a great base runner, but he got spiked several times. You should see his feet; they're a mess!" A perfect balance of achievement and depreciation. Some parents can take this in good humor, knowing that in due time they should graciously move over and make room for the next generation. Others find it so threatening that they must retaliate with put-downs and harsher discipline.

It has been my clinical experience that when a counselee is complaining about difficulty in getting along with a boss, supervisor, or some seemingly inconsequential regulations, one can often uncover a chain of other authority figures who have been that person's nemesis. There was also trouble with the dean of students or bandmaster, scoutmaster, swimming coach, and, finally, yes, a parent. It is not difficult to see how God the Father also gets roped into this authority conflict circus. Even when an authority conflict is based on logical reasons and objective facts, if there is an underlying unresolved authority problem with parents dating back to this adolescent period, the whole issue will be tinged with excess emotion and take on larger proportions than the case warrants. A small administrative matter may take on lofty dimensions of ethical principle and even end up in court.

63

Ideally, increasing responsibility is attributed to the youth in this age group. Meanwhile, external authority can gradually be relinquished so that by the time she/he is of legal age full adult status can be realized. The adolescent who is held down to a childish level throughout this period is confronted by two unfortunate alternatives: to rebel and take off on his/her own too soon, or to come to adulthood without experience in assuming authority for his/her own life. It is a later reenactment of the issue of autonomy vs. shame and doubt in an earlier stage. Thus the task of each stage is not completed once and for all. Rather it is as though each time an issue reappears the stakes are higher. As Erikson explains at the end of his chapter "Eight Ages of Man":

> "To leave this matter truly open, certain misuses of the whole conception have to be avoided. Among them is the assumption that the sense of trust (and all the other 'positive' states postulated) is an <u>achievement</u>, secured once and for all at a given state...The personality is engaged with the hazards of existence continuously, even as the body's metabolism copes with decay."[1]

DEVELOPMENTAL DISTORTIONS

Developmental psychology assumes that there is a certain sequence or schedule which serves as a norm. Although there may be a considerable leaway to allow for individual differences in rate of development, there is a sense in which too great deviation is pathological or at least likely to cause problems for the individual. Erikson describes what is appropriate for each of three stages by using an adjectival form of the stage name thus: childlike child, adolescent adolescent, and adult adult.[2] By this he means it is appropriate for a child to act in a childlike manner and for an adult to act in an adult manner. If we extrapolate from his original diagram, we discover that it is possible for each of the three stages to be distorted in four ways either by the person being precocious or too advanced, or by being retarded in development or behind schedule.

In Figure 11, the first space to the right indicates a child who is being urged or tempted to act like an adolescent, to date long before other children, to wear lipstick and a training bra several years before puberty, to want to hang around with teenagers while still in the lower grades. The "adult" child role is created when the father dies and others begin saying to the young boy, "Well, you're the man of the house now; your mother will have to depend on you since your father is no

64

longer here to do all the chores." Even when it happens out of economic necessity and not from anyone's ill will, such a person is likely to say, later in life, that it was too bad to have missed out on the carefree childhood that others enjoyed. Ascending in a vertical direction, the "childlike" adolescent is the one who has not progressed but is still fixated at the child's level. The "childlike" adult is even more extreme and uses tactics like temper tantrums, which would not be that remarkable for a two-year-old, to gain some desired end.

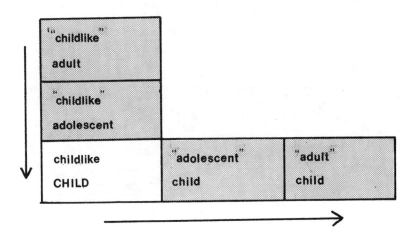

Fig. 11   Four Possible Distortions of Childhood

Turning to the level of adulthood, we also find appropriate and distorted adjustments (Figure 12). We have already alluded to the "adult" child who has been thrust into maturity before readiness. The "adult" adolescent has likewise jumped the gun. This ambitious person cannot wait for adult experiences with their attendant responsibilities, which are too difficult for the adolescent to assume. A bright student may skip a grade because of intellectual advancement but then miss out on the socializing experiences of an appropriate peer group. Unfortunately some teenagers look down upon their peers and develop a snobbish arrogance which is not good preparation for adult social relations. Overly ambitious parents may encourage this attitude under the assumption that it reflects favorably upon them to have a precocious offspring.

In Figure 12, in the first space to the left of the normal adult box, we find the "adolescent" adult who competes with her adolescent daughter and takes it as the greatest compliment to be mistaken for her daughter's sister. A middle-aged man may leave his wife for a teenager, dress in the current high school fashion, pretend to be completely at home in the youth's world of music, dance and entertainment, and be completely oblivious to the fact that the bald spot in the midst of his greying hair gives him away. We have already discussed the adult who resorts to childlike thinking and tactics. The method of transactional analysis has proven useful in helping such persons become aware of these distortions and exchange their child role for an adult identity.

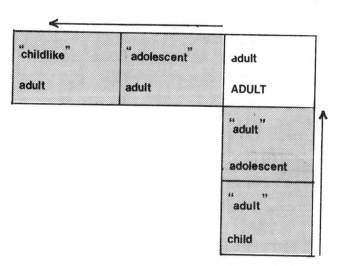

Fig. 12   Four Possible Distortions of Adulthood

Finally, on the middle step of this staircase, we find the
adolescent who is thinking, feeling, and behaving in generally
accepted adolescent fashion. One thing strikes us immediately
in Figure 13; the distortions can go in all four directions.
No wonder it is a confusing period; there are so many possibili-
ties. The boxes to the left and right have been discussed suf-
ficiently. What has intrigued me about our contemporary society
is the lack of definition of what is or is not appropriate
within the range of adolescence.

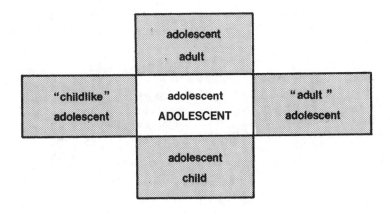

Fig. 13   Four Possible Distortions of Adolescence

Consider "delayed adolescence." Although we have outlawed child labor as such, there are newspaper carriers who earn enough money to buy expensive stereo sets and pay their way when the school French class decides to take a field trip to Paris. One marital dispute included disagreement as to whether a young child should be allowed to have the same $2,000 music center in her bedroom which the parents had in the living room. So much for prematurity. At the other end, there are professional trainees who must remain as "school boys" until their late twenties before they are licensed to enter upon their adult, vocational role in society. One is required to remain in school until age 16. Other bench marks of maturity are voting age, getting a driver's license, age at which beer may be consumed, etc. Society has been so confused about this definitional problem that some states who lowered the age of majority promptly repealed on second thought.

What a contrast between me and my rural cousin of the same age. He was married upon finishing high school and was immediately a householder and owner-manager of a sizeable farm alongside other adult men. When I became married and began my career as professor, his oldest child was in the fifth grade. (See the section on sacramental support, below, for further ramifications of this problem.)

A final footnote to this section on development is needed concerning a dynamic that closely relates personality development to religious development. It is the matter of dependency. In early childhood we are very dependent upon our parents; and one of the classic aspects of religion is dependency upon God as Provider. One might assume that the opposite end of the continuum would be independence; yet that is not the goal of mature adulthood, but rather the characteristic of adolescence. Much of the apparent rebellion of youth is the assertion of independence as a part of the struggle for identity. A functionally mature adult, however, is one who has ridden the pendulum back to a moderate mid-point, combining both traits into a co-operative working relationship of inter-dependence. Adults who feel 100 per cent independent are kidding themselves. If the "self-made businessman" thinks he has succeeded independently, it is only because he is oblivious to the associates, workers, customers, advisors, money lenders, etc., who have been integral to the development of his business. A distortion of the maxim: "It is more blessed to give than to receive" tempts a person to conceptualize independence and self-sufficiency as the ultimate good. Mutuality, sharing, co-operation, give-and-take, and acknowledgement of needs as well as strengths require the maturity of an adult who does not continually have to prove himself or herself. The independent heroic type refuses to admit need for help, such as medical treatment, and stoically endures pain until dragged into the hospital unconscious. The totally dependent adult passively awaits a miracle, since "everything depends upon God." The inter-dependent patient accepts help and advice, actively co-operates in the case history-taking, as well as the treatments or exercises, and prays for God's blessing upon the whole enterprise and seeks for spiritual resources such as patience, courage, and hope as needed.

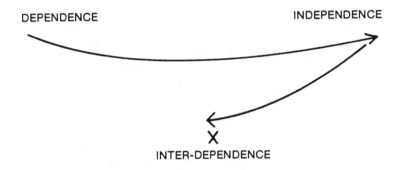

DEPENDENCE   INDEPENDENCE

X
INTER-DEPENDENCE

Fig. 14   Dependency Pendulum

When studying the personality development of any individual, it is useful to inquire how the person coped with the stresses and adjustments of adolescence. Was it traumatic, fun, a challenge, adventuresome, shameful, depressing, conflicted, or a time of optimism and idealism? Did this person pass through this transitional period on a schedule that suited or thwarted a wholesome progression from childhood to adulthood?

IDENTITY AS DESTINY

Leaving the security of childhood with its familiar patterns, youth enters upon an unchartered course. We have already indicated how many changes are going on within the adolescent. It is enough to make one ask seriously about one's identity.

What of this new, emerging self, and what is to become of it in the future? This puzzling period has been characterized as an "identity crisis." We shall discuss identity before destiny because before one takes a car out on the road for a trip one has to be sure of the machine. A young person may even call a moratorium on further progress in order, as the saying goes, "to get it all together." Erikson elaborates.

> "I have, for example, conceptualized within the stage of youth a <u>psychosocial</u> <u>moratorium</u>--a period when the young person can dramatize, or at any rate experiment with, patterns of behavior which are both juvenile and adult, and yet often find a grandiose alignment with traditional ideals or new ideological trends. A true moratorium, of course, takes the pressure out of time as it provides leeway for timeless values. If by definition it must end, it is expected to be followed by a period of energetic and goal-oriented activity. In the past, adults have often mourned the end of the moratorium as an irrevocable loss of potential identities sacrificed to the necessities of life."3

WHO ARE YOU?

A simple and self-revealing test of identity is administered in the following way. The subject is given a blank piece of paper and asked to answer in three or four sentences the brief question: "Who are you?" There are no clues or suggestions. It is amazing how a person's notion of self comes through in this exercise. Even the choice of categories is distinguishing. One uses statistical categories: age, height, weight, number of years in school, etc. (a value-free, objective description). Another refers to memberships: family, church, school, extra-curricular group, sports team, etc.--(I am the sum total of my memberships). Another goes into details about origins: ethnic and national heritage, religious background, change in socio-economic class from the last generation, etc. (I am the result of my inheritance and ancestry.) Occasionally someone will make a list of accomplishments, awards, honors, degrees, titles, elected offices held, etc. (My identity is equal to my work, and I plan to mention only my successes.) Still another adds many adjectives of value and meaning: the warm family, the exciting job, the frustrations and joys of personal experience (a subjective description of what my selfhood means to me!). When I gave this test to a group of ten clergymen, each one was unique, and one would have been hard pressed to have lumped them together in any group. Some revealed a concern for proving

70

something like masculinity, spiritual righteousness, or vocational worth. One of the ministers spoke of self almost exclusively in terms of being God's child, of salvation, dependence upon the Spirit, and Eternal Life--almost exclusively other-worldly.

Adolescents reinforce their identity by checking out their own perceptions with that of their peers--like looking in the multiple mirrors in a clothing store. Hence the opinions and judgements of others are very important to them. They may vacilate between striking out on their own with a unique idea or behavior, only to blend back into the crowd of conformity when it gets too lonely out there.

In the late 60's and early 70's it was common to hear youth claim their right to do their "own thing." Rebellion against the establishment and the demand for freedom to be oneself marked their search for identity. Giving up memberships in their parents' established religious groups, they wandered rootless for a while, only to grasp onto new identities in communes, Eastern cults, and charismatic sects. Some found an expanded and intensified identity through consciousness-raising drugs and hallucinogenic agents. Alcohol may loosen the inhibitions of a youth and provide a sense of greater self-confidence in social situations. Meanwhile, each adolescent has always had to exert some effort and struggle in the search for an identity, some with greater and some with less success. A "delayed adolescent" may never find a satisfactory identity in an entire lifetime.

LOOKING AHEAD TO FUTURE ROLES

> "The sense of ego identity, then, is the accrued
> confidence that the inner sameness and continuity
> prepared in the past are matched by the sameness
> and continuity of one's meaning for others, as
> evidenced in the tangible promise of a 'career'."[4]

Erikson has indicated that the failure to discover or create an acceptable identity can lead to "role confusion." In response to the Who-Are-You question, some persons begin promptly with what they consider their primary role. "I am a nurse;" "I am a housewife and mother;" "I am a contractor." It was not that long ago that a man's very surname signified his vocational role: Mason, Carpenter, Shoemaker, Smith, Cartwright, Cooper, and Baker, to name only a few. Will the adolescent be able to claim a number of roles as his/her own identity?

A basic bio-socio-emotional role choice is that of male or female. These roles used to be considered quite distinct and were supported by distinctive and characteristic ways of acting, dressing, thinking, feeling, and being. It was assumed that boys should be aimed toward masculinity by playing with mechanical toys and engaging in sports like boxing and hunting. Girls should play with dolls in preparation for motherhood and also play house in preparation for wifery. Vocational roles of nurse and school marm were acceptable. Erikson was roundly criticized by feminists for his interpretation of children's play with blocks and objects, since he assumed that boys and girls had inherently different ways of perceiving of space as symbolic of their own bodies.[5] The classical psychoanalytical explanation was that a round space represented the womb and a tunnel the vagina, whereas long, narrow objects, towers, etc., represented the penis.

Currently there has been a thorough-going re-evaluation of sex roles. They are not to be set against one another as of yore. There is a wider range of vocational roles open to both sexes and a greater lattitude of behavior and temperament granted to each. Men are more free to become nurses and women are entering formerly perceived masculine fields such as engineering, law, and ministry. Clothing and hair styles have become somewhat unisex.

Perhaps the most significant change has been the decision of the American Psychiatric Association to drop the category of homosexuality from their list of deviant disorders. Another has been the gradual acceptance of sex-change surgery. This is confusing to a person who has been brought up to believe that you have only two choices--all-male or all-female. We need to wait a couple generations before we can determine whether these recent developments are inclining adolescents toward role confusion.

By mid-adolescence adult, vocational roles are also becoming an increasingly pressing choice question. Vocational guidance counselors are trying to help students sort out their long range goals: the trades and manual arts route or the collegiate/professional track. Each year that goes by adds urgency. Adult role models are important at this stage as young people choose whom they want to be like, whom they wish to emulate. Again, autonomy comes into play with one person feeling more free to choose than another. Parental expectation can be a strongly coercive force to fulfill the ambitions of another generation's dreams. I had a cousin whose mother had dreamed of being a concert pianist. The daughter was urged on to a very successful career, playing solo piano with some outstanding symphony orchestras. Then she got married and gave up the piano, which she would just as soon have done at age 10 if she had had her choice.

72

A young boy of six years was brought to an eye-ear-nose-and-throat doctor for treatment of adenoids and related matters. He idolized this wonderful, warm-hearted doctor and wanted to be like him some day. As he progressed in school there was never any question what he should study or what courses he should take. Just give me whatever will make me an eye-ear-nose-and-throat doctor. It was not a choice as much as a steady progression toward his goal: pre-med, medical school, internship and specialization. You guessed it! He began his practice as a junior partner of this same wonderful doctor who treated him when he was six years old; and when the old doctor retired, there stood his protégé exactly in his footsteps treating little six-year-olds. Crystal clear identity with almost zero role confusion!

Just as in the sexual roles, so in other social relationships roles are reciprocal. One cannot fulfill the role of storekeeper without customers, nor the role of buyer without a seller. One cannot exercise leadership without followers, nor be an effective sadist without someone whose role it is to submit to abuse. Indeed, adolescents learn by trial and error what roles they might be best suited for in adult life. It is for this reason that extra-curricular functions serve as a useful arena for experimentation. As with each of the stages on life's way, some succeed and progress constructively on to the next learning task while others get hung up in a revolving door; their spiral of life neither widens nor ascends on schedule.

IDEOLOGY: BELIEFS RE-EXAMINED

So far it may sound as though the adolescent's tests are limited to the bio-socio-emotional spheres. There is more to it than that. By mid-adolescence the student is being confronted by many new facts and theories in both the physical and social sciences. Literature and history of other eras and other cultures broaden the youth's outlook and may increase conflicts within his/her mind. Christian theologians argued on both sides of the slavery question using the same Bible for their source. The teacher of social studies may assign readings which go against what the student's parents believe concerning race, social ethics, sexual morality, and political party. A person from a fundamentalist religious persuasion may be upset by teaching about evolution or other topics from the biological sciences or anthropology, which are considered heresy in his/her church. It is a time when many beliefs and understandings are re-examined.

Although the rebellious youth of the past decade were sometimes referred to as "uncommitted" insofar as they were disenchanted with the ideology and policies of the American establishment, they were not without a great hunger for an ideology. At anti-war rallies they would wave red copies of <u>Quotations From Chairman Mao Tse-tung</u>, promise allegiance to the non-violent doctrines of Dr. Martin Luther King, Jr. and sing "We Shall Overcome," quote from their favorite existentialists philosophers, and in other ways show that they were as concerned about theory as practice. Some strains of thought were religious and traditional, others were secular and innovative, but all contributed to the quest for ideology which gave the movement an identity.

Human beings have the capacity to see relationships, to see how various parts of life and experience hang together, also to understand why there is conflict and dissonance in society as well as within the self. The maturing person needs to make sense out of life, to find meaning and purpose beyond the self. Possessing what Allport called a "unifying philosophy of life" makes it easier to cope with change, conflict, problems, and needs. As soon as the youth has announced that he/she plans to be a photographer or pharmacist, someone asks, "Why do that?" It is reassuring to be able to give some reasons, a rationale for one's identity and destiny. The responsible person provides a cognitive house to live in as well as a physical shelter. Religion is close at hand to provide meaning in terms of stewardship, vocation, mission and the "orders" or structures of society and some way for each individual to find an appropriate niche. We will return to this theme in the next chapter dealing with vocation and status.

As the simple life of childhood is outgrown, there is a need for a larger system which can encompass pain and pleasure, good and evil, justice and freedom. Santa Claus must be replaced by larger conceptions of giving and receiving gifts, as the naive beliefs of childhood have to be revised and stretched to include more variables. God as Santa Claus no longer works.

A viable ideology or theology gives the adolescent something to hang on to, a dependable standard against which to judge decisions, a road map for the journey into adulthood. That is one reason why adolescents are such inveterate talkers, discussing and arguing at great length. They are testing out their ideas and notions, shaping their philosophy.

Idealism, heroism, and visions seem popular among youth. Movie idols, pop singers, and athletic super stars are dreamed about as the young person wonders vicariously about fulfilling some such idealized role. For the vast majority somewhat more mundane roles are settled for, but the value of the dreaming was the impetus which it gave to push ahead and carve out a place for oneself. Not moving ahead would be to stagnate. The physical, emotional, and visionary turmoil of adolescence needs to be purposeful, and when the religio-social resources of society are functional the teenager is aided in passing through this transitional period into a constructive adulthood.

RELIGIOUS EXPERIENCE AND SUPPORT

One of the great contributions of William James was his distinction between two types of personalities and the respective kinds of religious experience which they have, and hence the kind of support that they need. In his _Varieties of Religious Experience_, he devoted two lectures to "The Religion of Healthy-mindedness" and two lectures to "The Sick Soul." The former is basically happy and optimistic about things: "God's in his Heaven and all's well with the world." The latter broods about trouble, sin, and the possibility of being rescued from damnation.

Two religious leaders represent these two approaches. The first, Horace Bushnell, taught that the child should be brought up from the beginning knowing God's love and blessing, never to have thought of himself as anything other than a child of God. Such a child sees God's hand in the sunset and the rainbow, the beautiful flower and the fresh rain. It is a positive approach and assumes gradual development on the part of the child. The second leader, also a Congregationalist minister from New England, but a century earlier during the Great Awakening, held a sterner view. In his famous sermon, "Sinners in the Hands of an Angry God," he threatened his listeners with their precarious situation, as dangerous as a spider hanging over a fire by a thread. Only a dramatic conversion experience could save them from the fire and brimstone of Hell.

GRADUAL DEVELOPMENT AND CEREMONIAL SUPPORT

The "Healthy-minded" type of approach to religious development assumes that there will be a steady progression from one insight to another, an evolutionary process of unfolding. This is typical of the universal or state church pattern. Everyone in the community is automatically baptized as a very young child. It is assumed that they will be swept along in the developmental process of acculturation and socialization. Religious instruction will begin early and progress each year until Confirmation, which traditionally came during adolescence in many of the state churches of Europe. One was confirmed because he/she was developmentally at that stage of life when it was time to take on adult membership status, to begin receiving Holy Communion, and in general, to be responsible for one's own behavior. The bar mitzvah ceremony of Judaism, already referred to, also came at a certain chronological age rather than being related to some inner emotional state. As such, this typology follows the pattern of puberty rites around the world. It was just part of growing up, a landmark on the journey.

In earlier times, and especially in European cultures, the period of adolescence was more sharply defined and shorter in duration. For example, there was the switching from the informal to the formal mode of address--from "du" to "Sie" in German, and from Master to Mister in England. Perhaps boys now wore long trousers for the first time. The young person would be apprenticed or go to some other service around sixteen years of age and shortly thereafter become married and launched upon adulthood. Bar mitzvah or confirmation would mark this transition from childhood to adult responsibility within the congregation. Thus moral, social, economic, and psychological aspects of the "rite of passage" were more closely co-ordinated than today. This is partly due to our pluralistic and secular society in which there is less agreement on the meaning of and manner of signalizing, the trasition of puberty or adolescence.

Religious instruction is intensified prior to such a ceremony, and there is a general sense in the community that this is the natural and inevitable process through which all young adolescents should pass at a given age. The greeting and one of the prayers used in a typical Order for Confirmation illustrate the nature of this ceremony.

> "Dearly Beloved: In Holy Baptism you were received by our Lord Jesus Christ and made members of his holy Church. In accordance with our Lord's command, you have been instructed in the Word of God and led to the knowledge of his will and of his gracious Gospel, and you now desire to make public profession of your faith, and to be confirmed......"

(The candidates profess their faith in the words of the historic Apostles' creed. This is followed by the Blessing and prayer:)

> "The Father in Heaven, for Jesus' sake, renew and increase in thee the gift of the Holy Ghost, to thy strengthening in faith, to thy growth in grace, to thy patience in suffering, and to the blessed hope of everlasting life.....
>
> "Almighty and merciful God, heavenly Father, who only workest in us to will and do the things that please thee: Confirm, we beseech thee, the

work which thou hast begun in these thy servants;
that, abiding in the communion of thy Church
and in the faith of thy Gospel, no false doctrine,
no lusts of the flesh, nor love of the world
may lead them away from thee, nor from the truth
which they have confessed; but that in joyful
obedience to thy Word, they may ever know thee
more perfectly, love thee more fervently, and
serve thee in every good word and deed, to the
blessing of their fellow men, the edification
of thy people and the glory of thy Name; through
Jesus Christ, thy Son, our Lord, who liveth and
reigneth with thee, and the Holy Ghost, one God,
world without end. Amen."[6]

It is doubtful if this kind of ceremony has the same kind
of impact in our pluralistic society of today as it did when
more significance was attached to it culturally. Nevertheless,
it is not uncommon for special family celebrations to accompany
such an event, and, at least it has the potential of being a
support for the adolescent in a period of uncertainty.

Ceremony, ritual, and liturgy symbolize security and community consensus. The adolescent who belongs to a group in
which such a transitional rite is used routinely has public and
moral support for this stage of life. Re-inforcement of an
emerging status, and acknowledgement of growth and development
up to this point is thus signified and confirmed. It implies
that an accepted level of religious knowledge and moral growth
entitles the youth to new responsibilities and privileges within
the religious community, to take a new role in worship such as
receiving Holy Communion, perhaps to hold office or in other
ways share organizationally. Naturally, the rite has the amount
of emotional impact and social power and religious significance
which significant others, family, peers, and adult members at-
tribute to it.

CRISIS, CONVERSION, AND MYSTICAL EXPERIENCE

We now turn to the "sick soul" type as described by William
James around the turn of the century.[7] In that same decade the
new field of psychology of religion was turning its attention to
the study of conversion experience. Starbuck was the first one
to use a questionnaire to explore the nature of this religious
phenomenon by drawing upon the self-report of those involved.[8]
Meanwhile, G. Stanley Hall wrote a major book about the nature
of adolescence.[9] The consensus of research in that decade was
that most conversion experiences occurred during the height of
adolescence, around age 16. Secondly, it was found that where

77

ceremonial provisions were not made by the church for a "rite of passage" such as confirmation, a more dramatic experience of conversion seemed to fulfill the same need from a psychological point of view. For the purposes of our discussion we are by-passing the theological and doctrinal implications of either confirmation (or bar mitzvah) or conversion experiences.

The "sick soul" mentality does not come about accidentally but is carefully schooled in the theology of pessimism, the continual focusing upon human depravity, sin, failure, suffering, despair, punishment, unworthiness, and death. Preaching in such groups aims to convict of sin, to break the proud spirit which is enjoying itself too much and feeling complacent. The stiff-necked generation should exchange its arrogance for a broken and a contrite heart. Rather than help a child feel from little on that he/she was a child of a loving God in a beautiful world, revivalistic preaching strives to make sinners aware of their lost and fallen condition. Children live under this threat until the pressure builds up and finally a great explosion takes place in the psyche and the person is born again, freed from the awful power of sin, at last able to rejoice in the love of God. After forsaking self-righteousness and other sins, and throwing themselves on the mercy of God, such converts make a dramatic decision to live a new life of faith and obedience. The new believer may be baptized by immersion or otherwise be inducted into the Kingdom of God. It is this conversion experience which has been found to be frequently occurring among adolescents, especially in groups where such commitment is expected in that age group.

One explanation is that the conflict and turmoil characteristic of adolescence (struggling with issues of identity, ideology, sexuality, guilt, vocation, dependency, authority, and growing pains in general) cry out for resolution. An emotional outburst like an exploding boiler or an upheaval like an earthquake is the consequence. The greater the expectation of drama and emotionalism, the more likely the subject is going to fulfill this expectation, especially if it is prerequisite to adult membership in good standing. Often such a person can point to the day and the hour of the awakening, the re-birth.

We have now considered two "types" of religious transition and have deliberately set them forth in bold relief. There are many gradations in between the extremes of stoical, matter-of-fact ceremonial liturgy and convulsive conversion experience. We reiterate that each person's experience is unique. It is also true that if a person of light-hearted optimism belongs to a group which expects a doleful outlook up until conversion time, that one may leave the group completely and join another denomination more congenial to his/her personality traits. I have seen some persons whose needs were not met by the gradual religious development route who felt warmly attracted to a charismatic leader who promised dramatic and emotional religious fulfillment in another sect.

Some youth choose a third option; casting aside both the gradual and the sudden form of religious development, they simply declare a moratorium on religion in general and use secular substitutes to fulfill the functions which traditional religious resources were designed to supply. (We will take up that possibility in Chapter 13.) Others return to religion when they are married and looking for support in rearing the next generation.

A word needs to be said about the appeal of mystical experience. Like conversion experience it tends to be more emotional than rational. Mystics claim to have acquired spiritual knowledge unobtainable by reason. Like the one undergoing conversion experience, they have been swept away by a power beyond their control; their main stance was one of passive reception of a great gift or blessing rather than active accomplishment of some goal. Like conversion it is a very personal and solitary experience, whereas ceremony usually implies a social setting and group involvement. Mystical experience may also follow a period of stress and bring a corresponding sense of resolution much like conversion experience. Both religious experiences also have a sense of immediacy and transiency. Like the disciples on the Mount of Transfiguration, persons having these experiences wish they could prolong the event or return to it again and again.

However the teenager handles the transition of adolescence, he or she must sooner or later come down into the valley of practical necessity and plan for the future roles of adulthood. One of the more universal of these necessities is the seeking and claiming of a vocational role. Society expects it; and by the end of adolescence the young person may also be impatient to take up some worthy task.

EXAMPLES OF ADOLESCENT STRUGGLE

The following account involves an adolescent's identification with an older sibling as role model. When this example is withdrawn by death, this youth is thrown back upon his own resources. He finds much support and guidance in the religious teachings and inspiration of some classic religious leaders, and he also finds a new and unique identity, which is his own and not simply the incorporation of the idealized brother.

Doug entered the adolescence stage, which Erikson labels, Identity versus Role Confusion, with an underlying feeling of inferiority. As he saw his childhood identity slip away, he feared the future. Had he not failed to meet even some of the easier problems of childhood? How then could he possibly expect to meet the difficulties of this new confusing stage in life? Again, Doug found little help from institutional religion. He had already been confirmed an adult member of the church at the age of twelve when he was still in the childhood stage. Since he was considered an adult member of his church, Doug and his family saw little need in more formalized religious instruction.

Failing to find religious institutional help, Doug again turned to his brother Tom. Tom was to Doug a perfect example of an individual with firm ego identity. He was not only a brother who had shown understanding before in times of need, but he was now a popular sports figure. Doug needed someone to identify himself with, and Tom was the ideal figure. The name Tom Fisher was fast becoming the biggest name in track in Siouxland. Doug was not disappointed by his efforts to seek help from Tom, for together they soon developed plans to meet all challenges jointly. Doug recalls that they even planned to run in the Olympics together.

When Doug began his track career he faced a mighty image to equal, but he didn't mind because he had Tom right by his side to help him. With Tom's help he set a new city freshman mile record, and by his sophomore year was ranked as one of the state's top five cross country runners. Tom, too, was progressing rapidly to their joint goal to be Olympians, for, as a sophomore in college, he was already rated an All-American cross country runner.

It was just as everything seemed to be going so smoothly that Doug received the most severe blow of his life. His brother Tom was killed in a car accident while on his way back to college after the Spring vacation. Doug was struck not only with deep sorrow over the loss of his closest friend, but he now had to face his adaptation to adolescence alone. Encouraged by Tom's college coach, Doug decided to continue running, but he never again possessed the race determination that he once had. Before finishing high school, Doug became the number one cross country runner in the state; but he never challenged Tom's mile records. While Doug's failure to assault his brother's records may have been due to physical inferiority, Doug's feeling of sacredness for Tom's records may very well have played a subconscious role in his failure to set new standards. Because these records were set by one who had always been available in time of need, and he was no longer around to defend them, it would hardly seem right that they be taken from him.

Doug continued to follow the lead left by Tom, and entered State University. It was during this period that he found the now famous image of his brother impossible to imitate. Remembering his need to prove himself scholastically and seeing in this path a means of establishing a new, completely independent ego identity, Doug Fisher began to place more and more emphasis on his scholastic success and less on running.

With this change in emphasis, Doug soon found himself finishing last instead of first in time trials. He began making fewer athletic trips. Regardless of the growing importance of studies, track was still an important part of Doug's life, and failure to succeed resulted in extreme depression. Now Doug was ready to turn to God or religion for help. He began praying to the God that he had been told would listen to his troubles. He began also to read many religious books which often referred to conversion and mystical experiences. The lives of Bernadette of Lourdes and St. Francis of Assisi aroused Doug to seek the perfect life. Ignited by a need for aid in a time of distress and strengthened by appropriate literature, Doug found God through a mystical experience in a chapel on the State University Campus. Doug describes this experience as one of great elation and a true feeling of inferiority to an all powerful deity. This experience was so profound that Doug thought seriously of entering the priesthood; but urged by parents and friends to regain his track image, Doug set out to become a great track star with God's help.

He set out on a rigorous training program followed only by a few of the world's greatest track stars. He began running 100 miles a week. He soon became the equal of any State distance runner. Just as Doug began to run with the best of them, he developed a rare intestinal disorder brought on by his rigorous training schedule. He was now faced with the difficulty of abdominal pains in many of the most important races. Turning to God for help, Doug found the true meaning of religion. He became aware of the fact that God is more than a dispenser of favors. By reading many of the works of Saint Augustine, Doug began to recognize the existence of two worlds--one of the flesh and one of the spirit. He began to feel that the desires for success and power in this world should not be sought unless they be according to the will of God. While he still possessed some feelings of frustration when he was forced to the sidelines in a big race, he found real comfort in his belief that such was the will of God. He learned to thank God for the few good races which were granted him from above.

* * * * * * * * * * *

The adolescent conflict with the father is beautifully illustrated by the excerpts from Carl Gustav Jung, the psycho-analyst who was fascinated by the meaning of symbolism. He was the son of a Swiss protestant pastor. The rigidities of the Victorian times were also evident in his home and community. An example of the role of religion in his early childhood is this bedtime prayer:

> "Spread out thy wings, Lord Jesus mild,
> and take to thee thy chick, thy child.
> 'If Satan would devour it,
> No harm shall overpower it,'
> So let the angels sing!"

> "Lord Jesus was comforting, a nice, benevolent
> gentleman like Herr Wegenstein up at the castle,
> rich, powerful, respected, and mindful of little
> children at night. Why he should be winged
> like a bird was a conundrum that did not worry
> me any further. Far more significant and thought-
> provoking was the fact that little children were
> compared to chicks which Lord Jesus evidently
> 'took' reluctantly, like bitter medicine. This
> was difficult to understand. But I understood
> at once that Satan liked chicks and had to be
> prevented from eating them. So, although Lord
> Jesus did not like the taste, he ate them any-
> way, so that Satan would not get them."10

This is just one example of how this introspective child rumi-nated on matters of religion. There were other ominous things connected with his father's religion—the black-frocked men who carried the box or coffin and placed it in the grave periodical-ly. Whenever this happened one more church member was never seen again. He was troubled with strange dreams and imagina-tive thoughts related to religion and his father's God. In early adolescence this precocious minister's son had an experi-ence which reminded me of the young pastor's son's put-down of his father, referred to previously in this chapter (see section entitled GROWING UP).

> "One fine summer day that same year I came out
> of school at noon and went to the cathedral
> square. The sky was gloriously blue, the day
> one of radiant sunshine. The roof of the ca-
> thedral glittered, the sun sparkling from the
> new, brightly glazed tiles. I was overwhelmed
> by the beauty of the sight, and thought: 'The
> world is beautiful and the church is beautiful,

82

and God made all this and sits above it far
away in the blue sky on a golden throne and...'
Here came a great hole in my thoughts, and a
choking sensation. I felt numbed, and knew only:
'Don't go on thinking now! Something terrible
is coming, something I do not want to think,
something I dare not even approach. Why not?
Because I would be committing the most frightful
of sins. What is the most terrible sin? Murder?
No, it can't be that. The most terrible sin
is the sin against the Holy Ghost, which cannot
be forgiven. Anyone who commits that sin is
damned to hell for all eternity. That would be
very sad for my parents, if their only son, to
whom they are so attached, should be doomed to
eternal damnation. I cannot do that to my
parents. All I need do is not go on thinking.'"11

Obviously repression was at work keeping some dark and socially unacceptable thought from coming to awareness. Jung
describes his youthful struggle. The outcome reminded me of the
youth who indirectly denigrated his athlete father.

"I gathered all my courage, as though I were
about to leap forthwith into hell-fire, and let
the thought come. I saw before me the cathedral,
the blue sky. God sits on His golden throne,
high above the world--and from under the throne
an enormous turd falls upon the sparkling new
roof, shatters it, and breaks the walls of the
cathedral asunder."12

So much for everything young Carl's father stood for, the
preaching, even the church itself: God defecates on it all and
smashes it to pieces with a giant turd. One could hardly conceive of a more grotesque depreciation of a father. Remarkably, young Carl explains this experience as a revelation of
God's grace. He now understood that the living God stands
above the Bible, tradition, and the Church. This is what his
rigid father had never grasped.

Jung's interpretation that this experience was a message of
grace seems like gilding the lily. Grace should fill one with
joy. Jung found this an oppressive secret because, as I suspect, he did not want to focus on the obscene vision of God's
rejection of his father's authority--not an uncommon occurrence
among preachers' kids.

"My entire youth can be understood in terms of this secret. It induced in me an almost unendurable loneliness. My one great achievement during those years was that I resisted the temptation to talk about it with anyone. Thus the pattern of my relationship to the world was already prefigured: today as then I am a solitary, because I know things and must hint at things which other people do not know, and usually do not even want to know."[13]

NOTES

1. Erikson, _Childhood_ and _Society_, pp. 273-274.

2. _____, _Insight_ and _Responsibility_, p. 137.

3. _____, _Life History_ and _the Historical Moment_, pp. 199-200.

4. _____, _Childhood_ and _Society_, 261-262.

5. _____, See Chapter 2, "The Theory of Infantile Sexuality," in _Childhood_ and _Society_, and Chapter 7, "Womanhood and the Inner Space," in _Identity, Youth_ and _Crisis_, as well as his restatement or response to the criticism of the woman's movement in Part Three, Chapter 2, "Once More the Inner Space" _Life History_ and _the Historical Moment_.

6. _Service Book_ and _Hymnal_, Minneapolis: Augsburg Publishing House, 1958, pp. 245 and 247.

7. James, William, _The Varieties of Religious Experience: A Study in Human Nature_, New York: Longmans, Green & Co., 1902, Lectures IV - X.

8. Starbuck, Edwin Diller, _The Psychology of Religion_, New York: Charles Scribner's Sons, 1899.

9. Hall, G. Stanley, _Adolescence_ (2 volumes), New York: D. Appleton & Co., 1904.

10. Jung, C. G., _Memories, Dreams, Reflections_ (recorded and edited by Aniela Jaffe and translated from the German by Richard and Clara Winston, Revised Edition), New York: Pantheon Books, a Division of Random House, 1963, p. 10.

11. Ibid., p. 36.

12. Ibid., p. 39.

13. Ibid. pp. 41-42.

QUESTIONS FOR YOUTH AND ADULTS ABOUT ADOLESCENCE

1. Why do you suppose Erikson focuses on identity instead of sexuality in his discussion of adolescence? Would you?

2. You may have come through adolescence by either the conversion (dramatic) or ceremonial (e.g., confirmation) route. Is it difficult for you to imagine what the other route would be like or to have empathy for someone of the opposite religious life style? What could you do to grow in ecumenical appreciation of persons different from yourself in this regard?

3. Considering some individuals in particular (yourself, relatives, and friends), can you cite examples of persons who are of the "healthy-minded" religious type and belong to a religious group which assumes conversion and even requires it for membership? What kinds of conflicts have been involved? On the contrary, do you know of someone who is of the "sick-soul" type who found it necessary to change denominations in order to belong to a group more congenial to his/her temperament? What implications do you find in these conflicts for the ecumenical movement among religious bodies? What kind of research should be pursued in the psychology of religion to clarify this issue in ecumenism?

4. Were you subject to any developmental distortions (precocity or retardation) of personality development through the transition of adolescence? If so, what were the adjustment problems deriving therefrom? Perhaps you felt that not being "on schedule" had its benefits. What were they?

5. You may disagree with Figure 14. Explain why and how you would draw a different diagram.

6. If you were given the "Who-Are-You" test, how prominent would religious factors be in your answer? Explain.

7. How does the current debate about sex roles (from MS Magazine to TOTAL WOMAN, from militant feminist to traditionalist) affect you? How has this discussion of masculinity-femininity influenced your own identity? Has it led to a feeling of self-assurance or role confusion? As this book

goes to press it is anyone's guess whether ERA (Equal
Rights Amendment) will be crystalized into legislation.
How has religion been used to support one side or the other
of this debate?

8. Do you agree that adolescence is a period concerned about
   ideology? Could this be one reason for the attraction of
   cults among youth?

9. Have you known anyone involved in the charismatic movement
   (speaking in tongues)? Does anything from this chapter
   relate to that phenomenon?

10. What cultural factors in our society may be taking over the
    role which confirmation or bar mizvah fulfilled in assist-
    ing youth pass through the adjustments of adolescence?

CHAPTER 4

VOCATION OR VACUUM

By the end of adolescence, a person should be equipped with the capacity and potential to enter the adult world of meaningful work. With tens of thousands of jobs to choose from, the opportunities are staggering. It was not so in medieval society. One vocational expert judged that there may not have been more than thirty or forty occupations available, and many of them were exclusive according to rank and station in life. But just as there were religious meanings to practically everything in those days, so the entering upon a work had its ritual side. Kings were crowned, knights were knighted, clergy were ordained, craftsmen were admitted to guilds, and even the lowly vassal or serf took an oath of fealty (faithfulness or loyalty) to the lord of the manor. Could the existential vacuum present in many young adults today stem from a role confusion in regard to finding for themselves meaningful work? Many clients suffer from "ennui"--a feeling of boredom, lack of interest, and this just when they should be getting launched upon a career.

ROLE, CAREER, AND WORK

One's role in society is more complex than simply the job at which he/she works for an hourly wage or monthly paycheck. A newly married physician may be highly respected for his skill by peers and patients; but if his wife does not consider him an adequate "man," whatever she means by that, he may subjectively feel a failure as much as if he were dropped from the hospital's staff. In studies of job satisfaction, it has been discovered that what one's spouse thinks of one's job is as significant, if not more so, than such tangible rewards as salary and working

87

conditions.

As youth move into adult vocations, they continue to fulfill several roles: worker, citizen, son, sister, bowling
league member, church or synagogue member, cross country skiing
enthusiast, etc. A person may take a job in which he/she has
very little interest simply for financial support so that the
more important roles will be possible. Another one finds the
job all-consuming, which serves as work, income, family, recreation, religion--everything. ("He's all wrapped up in his
job.") Whether these roles are central or peripheral, large,
conflicted, transitory, etc., is diagramed in Figure 15.

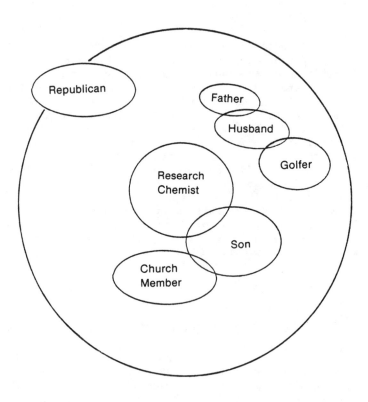

Fig. 15   Significance and Relationships of Roles

Here we see a young man, Bill, whose work in the chemistry laboratory is absolutely central in his life. His father, a chemistry professor, dotes on his son's accomplishments and takes great pride in his career progress. We note that Bill's role as son is larger than either his own role of father or husband. He is also equally involved in his golf, which he plays regularly with his wife, as he is in his role of father to his own child. Bill continues membership in the family church, although this is not a commitment shared with his wife. Meanwhile, he has some very peripheral interests such as a general interest in the Republican Party, but only sporadic involvement. The wife is not much interested in Bill's chemical career, but is pleased that it provides a good income, which makes it possible for them to live in an above average home.

How differently one would diagram the roles and relationships of Jack, who is owner-manager of a large gas station. His wife has for years spent each morning in the office keeping the books, making out the bills, and sending in orders for parts, etc. On their day off they routinely take their camper down by the river to go fishing. They have no children. Both enjoy singing in the church choir and have not missed a rehearsal for seven years.

A recovered alcoholic also runs a gas station. As a member of Alcoholics Anonymous, he views his station as a source of employment for alcoholics who want and need a second start in life. He becomes their big brother sponsor in the local AA chapter, takes great interest in their rehabilitation, etc. His entire staff are AA members. One might say that his primary role in life is AA worker and therapist, with the gas station as only a means to that end. Meanwhile, his wife is very glad to play a supportive role alongside this busy man even though he is often away from the home, because she appreciates having a sober and worthwhile husband once again. They are both faithful members of the Roman Catholic parish, practically their only other interest.

Dissident youth on our campus wrote these words on a wall: "They teach us how to make a living but not how to live." These two, however, do not need to be mutually exclusive. As we have seen from the above three descriptions of Bill, Jack, and the AA member, job role and life style are often inextricably interrelated.

Contemporary career patterns are markedly different from those of past generations. Previously, it was thought that one should ideally follow one line of work or even stay with one firm or institution for a lifetime. That was stability, security, honorable. Today it is not uncommon for persons to change careers entirely every decade: from school teacher to salesman to business manager of a large parish; from priest to social worker to free lance consultant. There is more freedom of choice and more flexibility within the range of choices.

If you want to write a case history of an individual, you should look for any red thread which runs through that life concerning career. It may be that what seems to be a disjointed jumping from one job to another can be understood as part of a larger pattern or search. One's hobby may turn into a full-time business and finally a state-wide campaign as the individual becomes Chairperson of the State Arts Council. Only part of this series of activities will have been compensated financially or actually called a job. You will want to ascertain the meaning behind these activities and these assorted kinds of work. Is it a growing sense of mission, a crusade? Another person may be headed in the opposite direction of the career cone. He/she is looking for less and less responsibility, a more specific work and private life style, less hassle with authority and bureaucracy.

A vocational guidance counselor in Minneapolis indicated that many workers find their identity vicariously by being associated with a prestigious firm even though they are not necessarily proud of their specific task. He explained, it is as though the worker would say, "I work for Honeywell (but don't ask what I do there)." Another is willing to immerse his/her own identity in a larger whole: "Let's all work together to build up this department." During World War II, workers were proud to be associated with a company which received a pennant and citation from the President for their contribution to the war effort. Rosie the Riveter might be just an assembly line worker, but she knew she was as important as her brother overseas. The psycho-dynamics of this role satisfaction is not unlike that of the vassal or serf in medieval times who basked in the reflected glory of his lord or duke.

A final comment on roles is necessary at this point. They divide into two categories which must be understood to avoid role confusion. There are "universalistic roles" and "personalistic roles." Examples of the former are dentist, ditch digger, priest, school teacher, mailman, etc. If one drops dead another can easily be found to take his/her place. If your favorite dentist is in Europe on a month's vacation when your filling falls out, another dentist in town, who has been trained in the same school, licensed by the state and in possession of nearly the same set of instruments, is supposed to be able to treat your tooth according to the same professional standards as your

family dentist. Likewise the Sacrament is as valid if administered by Father McCarthy, who is tall and handsome, as if it
were administered by Father Lynch, who is short and ugly. Likewise, one husky day laborer should be as able to dig a ditch as
the next. In short, universalistic roles are interchangeable.
Examples of personalistic roles are mother, son, aunt, grandfather, close friend, etc. You may love your mother or never
speak to her again, but you can only be born of one mother. You
may even someday have a step-mother, but it is different from
changing dentists.

Problems accompany confusion of these two kinds of roles.
The pastor who was consoling a widow for months after the funeral
of her husband found himself slipping from a professional role
into a personal one, and it blossomed into romance and the demise
of his own marriage. Another pastor could not believe that the
interim pastor would be able to do justice to the grief work,
funeral, and pastoral care of a favorite family of the parish he
had left three months ago in Minneapolis; so he flew all the way
back from Seattle to carry out these functions. On the other
hand a husband may treat his wife, and the marriage generally,
in such an impersonal and routine manner that it ends up being
not a personalistic but a universalistic role. Sure enough, he
finds out he is as interchangeable as a dentist or ditch digger
while the next man takes over his role as husband. Thus we see
that the adolescent issue of identity vs. role confusion has implications for the adult handling of vocation and work roles.
All of this is important for a person to know how and where he/
she fits into society.

STATUS AND SOCIETY

Status refers to one's standing in society, one's relationship to those above, below, and alongside oneself in the social
order. Americans have looked with contempt upon the caste system of India and have considered any abolition of such rankings
as enlightened progress. Democracy supposedly favors an egalitarian society. Communism is ideally characterized as a class-
less society. The significance which any society places upon
class, status, rank, and other categories of power, prestige,
financial income, social influence, cultural level, etc., will
provide the individual with a relatively more or less difficult
task of "fitting in" and "finding one's place." Members of
various groups were supposed to "know their place" whether they
be blacks, women, children, or a variety of minority or immigrant
groups. Such status is heavily value-laden and often supported
by religious teachings and implicit social ethics.

91

How this works out in practice can be illustrated by the personnel categories, pay grades, and classifications of jobs in any large institution or corporation. Figure 16 shows part of one of the many pages describing over 350 job classifications in a large university under the merit system (non-academic) together with the 16 incremental salary steps for each position. From this we are led to believe that a GF75 is worth exactly $162 more per year than a GA68; and it boggles the mind of PHOTO TECH I to discover that she is worth exactly $6 per year less than PKG MAINT WK I, until she realizes that she is only on step 3, whereas her friend is on step 5. If Satan were to work out a plan for tempting persons to violate the Commandment, "Thou shalt not covet," he/she would devise a plan of closely graded caste distinctions very similar to this one.

CLASS	TITLE	GDE	1	2	3	4	5	6
			PAY SCHEDULE					
GA60	PHM MF TECH II	407	9360	9542	9802	9984	10244	10452
GA61	PHM MF TECH III	109	10452	10686	10946	11206	11466	11752
GA67	PHOTO SPEC I	407	9360	9542	(9802)	9984	10244	10452
GA68	PHOTO SPEC II	409	(10452)	10686	10946	11206	11466	11752
GA69	PHOTO SPEC III	113	12584	12896	13156	13520	13832	13962
GA64	PHOTO TECH I	402	6604	6734	6942	7072	7228	7410
GA65	PHOTO TECH II	404	7696	7904	8060	8242	8450	8632
GA66	PHOTO TECH III	406	8788	9022	9126	9360	9542	9802
GB44	PHOTOCOPY OPER	103	7228	7410	7566	7696	7904	8060
GG74	PIPEFITTER	210	11056	11290	11524	11758	11992	12252
GG75	PIPEFITTER LD	210	11056	11290	11524	11758	11992	12252
GF70	PIPEFITTER TR	210	11056	11290	11524	11758	11992	12252
GE61	PKG CNTRL SUPV	108	9802	9984	10244	10452	10686	10946
GB40	PKG CSHR ATTD	103	7228	7410	7566	7696	7904	8060
GB41	PKG CSHR SUPV	108	9802	9984	10244	10452	10686	10946
GE60	PKG ENFMNT OFF	303	7516	7654	7820	7958	8123	8289
GE62	PKG MAINT WK I	206	9132	9340	9444	9626	(9808)	10016
GE63	PKG MAINT WK II	208	10016	10198	10432	10614	10822	11056
GE64	PKG MT WK II LD	208	10016	10198	10432	10614	10822	11056
GG76	PLASTERER	209	10614	10822	11056	11290	11524	11758
GF75	PLASTERER TR	209	(10614)	10822	11056	11290	11524	11758
GE68	PLT HSE ASST	406	8788	9022	9126	9360	9542	9802
GG77	PLUMBER	210	11056	11290	11524	11758	11992	12252
GF77	PLUMBER-TR	210	11056	11290	11524	11758	11992	12252
CE56	PNT TRNS COORD	112	12012	12258	12584	12896	13156	13520
GG78	PP ASST CHF OPR	210	11056	11290	11524	11758	11992	12252

Fig. 16.   Classification of some workers
             by class, grade, and salary

During a counseling session with a distressed person, I have found it sometimes productive to ask where the client fits into the vocational status structure of the rest of the family and relatives. The law student whose father is a political science professor and mother a school principal, whose brother is a certified public accountant and sister an orthopaedic surgeon, is surrounded by professional and educational peers. This person finds little problem in vocational-status acculturation. On the other hand, a young woman who is completing her research for a doctoral dissertation in Islamic Studies and is aspiring to be a professor some day may feel "out of it" at the family reunion, for she is the only one of the entire relationship who has gone beyond high school. It is not certain she would feel alienated from her siblings and cousins, but the potential for a problem is there. Much depends upon how she developed her sense of worth over the years. (See Erikson's stages of "autonomy vs. shame and doubt" and "industry vs. inferiority.") Will she count on her vocational role and the academic status that goes with it to give her a sense of personal worth and identity? She may need to feel superior. On the other hand, she may not place any premium upon her intellectual achievements, but view her vocation as neither higher nor lower than that of the construction workers and day laborers who comprise her extended family. Yet even if she holds one view about her career, that does not mean that others may not impute to that work status-significance of their own choosing.

A preacher was once trying to reinforce the spiritual and moral worth of lay vocations, since in that denomination the ministry was considered holy and above the level of secular work. "A person may serve God just as fully by being a doctor or lawyer, a social worker, etc." But when his list was ended it included only persons with at least a bachelor's degree and some graduate or professional training beyond that. No wonder many workers feel unsupported concerning their status in society. In spite of the women's movement, one will hear a person describe herself as "just a _____."

In a society noted for upward social mobility, there are many who feel compelled to become over-achievers or follow the Peter Principle--getting promoted to the level of their incompetence where they finally remain in a stressful and unsatisfactory position. Pressure prevents a person from following Saint Paul's experience: "...I have learned, in whatever state I am, to be content." (Philippians 4:11b) On the contrary one is told that discontent is more likely to lead to creativity and progress. Contentment smacks of complacency. Each maturing adult entering upon a vocation needs to come to grips with the issue of status and how to regard it as personality continues to develop.

Thus far we have spoken of status as though it had to be negative, a sign of the sin of pride and great source of conflict. Actually, in social organization a certain heirarchy of authority and status can be useful for purposes of administration of a complex work force. In such an instance it is not used for ego-support but for clarification of functions and coordination. Persons may subordinate themselves to supervision and evaluation to accomplish a goal efficiently. It is possible for self-confident and mature adults to accept roles at different levels of status and responsibility and still accept one another as human beings of equal worth and value. This congenial state of affairs may continue peacefully until the end of the month when suddenly they are reminded through their paychecks that some are more equal than others. Whether one likes it or not, adjusting to this harsh bit of reality is one of the issues confronting the young adult entering the work force. Several options are open: to accept it, to challenge the system and rebel, to work to change it, to become cynical and depressed, _____, and _____(add other options of your own).

VOCATION AND STEWARDSHIP

Religious meanings of work have had a pervasive influence on its place in personality formation. Consider the ramifications of the doctrine that work shall forever be odious for mankind because of the primordial sin.

> And to Adam he said,
> "Because you have listened to the voice
>   of your wife,
>   and have eaten of the tree
> of which I commanded you,
>   'You shall not eat of it,'
> cursed is the ground because of you;
>   in toil you shall eat of it all the days
>   of your life;
> thorns and thistles it shall bring forth
>   to you;
>   and you shall eat the plants of the
>   field.
> In the sweat of your face
>   you shall eat bread
> till you return to the ground,

for out of it you were taken;
you are dust,
and to dust you shall return."
(Genesis 3:17-19)

If a rigid adherent of the Protestant Work Ethic thinks he/she can gain a blessing out of the curse of work, certainly that person is in a double bind. It would be irreverent to find work as fun or interesting when it has been decreed a curse. The person who says, "I hate my damn job," is right on target; it is condemned exactly as he says.

The famous parable of the talents views work differently. A servant is to be responsible and make the most of his opportunity to do productive work. This parable is frequently cited as an example of righteous stewardship.

"He who had received the five talents went at once and traded with them; and he made five talents more.....His master said to him, 'Well done, good and faithful servant; you have been faithful over a little, I will set you over much; enter into the joy of your master." (Matthew 25:14-30 contains the entire parable.)

Here it is possible to be blessed by responsible work, and it is not a curse. The curse lies in poor stewardship of one's capacity and abilities, because the servant who simply buried in the ground one talent given to him received a rebuke: "So take the talent from him, and give it to him who has the ten talents." Neither should one hide one's light under a bushel.

Religious teachings and values are always assimilated by individuals according to their own unique perception; and regardless of the preacher's intention or the text's actual message as properly exegeted, the hearer picks out certain parts like a magnet drawing out minerals which have an affinity for it. The person with an inferiority complex or the "down-and-outer" says AMEN to verses 29 and 30 of the above text of Matthew:

"For to every one who has will more be given, and he will have abundance; but from him who has not, even what he has will be taken away. And cast the worthless servant into the outer darkness; there men will weep and gnash their teeth."

Remembering the child who felt like a "nobody" and hence was entitled to do "nothing," the unworthy person who now should be entering the productive work force can read a heavy predestination from this passage. What starts out as inadequate failure is doomed to get worse.

The "healthy minded" person tends to take a positive attitude, whereas the "sick soul" dwells on the curse of work. (Compare the previous discussion of "Religious Experience and Support" in Chapter 3.)

Chairman Mao Tse-tung praised the vocational motivation of Dr. Norman Bethune, a Canadian surgeon who volunteered to serve the People's Liberation Army.

> "Comrade Bethune's spirit, his utter devotion
> to others without any thought of self, was
> shown in his great sense of responsibility
> in his work and his great warm-heartedness
> towards all comrades and the people.....the
> art of healing was his profession and he was
> constantly perfecting his skill.....With this
> spirit everyone can be very useful to the people.
> A man's ability may be great or small, but
> if he has this spirit, he is already noble-
> minded and pure, a man of moral integrity
> and above vulgar interests, a man who is of
> value to the people."[1]

On October 11, 1944, Mao gave a brief memorial address for a common soldier who had died while making charcoal, due to the sudden collapse of a kiln. The title of this address, "Serve the People" became a famous motto throughout the land and may be seen written over gates to factories and on walls in rural communes. There was a massive campaign to dignify all useful work. Note the stress on ceremonial and social significance ascribed to the worth of any worker. (We will return to this issue in Chapter 13, SECULAR SUBSTITUTES FOR TRADITIONAL RELIGION.) He concluded the funeral sermon with these words:

> "From now on, when anyone in our ranks who has
> done some useful work dies, be he soldier or
> cook, we should have a funeral ceremony and a
> memorial meeting in his honour. This should
> become the rule. And it should be introduced
> among the people as well. When someone dies
> in a village, let a memorial meeting be held.
> In this way we express our mourning for the
> dead and unite all the people."[2]

The clearest instance I know of vocation (a calling) motivated by a combination of intrinsic religious faith and a personal sense of stewardship of talents is that of an eighty-year-
old Danish tailor. During one of our visits, while he was re-
cuperating from his heart attack, he began to reminisce about
how he began his life work shortly after confirmation in the
Church of Denmark.

> "Before I cut on the wool with the big shears,
> I thought about what all this meant. God had
> cared for the sheep out in the meadow, and shep-
> herds had worked hard to guide them and finally
> shear them. Then in the woolen mills the weavers
> had to be careful around the whirling machinery.
> Yes, much had gone into this bolt of cloth; and
> now it was in my hands. So before I cut on the
> wool I folded my hands and prayed that God would
> bless my work so that I could suit the man."

One senses here a meaningfulness and significance of work that
makes it far more than a job or a task. It became clear to
me why orthopaedic surgeons and others dealing with handicapped
and misshapen bodies should refer their clients to "Tailor
Jensen." He would make a sincere effort to suit each one. In
all the years I knew him, I never heard him wonder about his
worth, his identity, his status in society, or any of the many
anxieties that plague the neurotics of our day. There was an
ego integrity and a quiet peace of mind that was refreshing. He
was also realistic enough to cut back considerably on his work
load since he had his heart attack at age eighty, but he was
still available if needed.

Vocation is the meeting place of integrity and integration:
integrity in being true to oneself in choice of work and life
style; integration of the self into a larger society as service
meets the needs of others as well as the self. Even the most
individualistic free lance writer or photographer has a need to
be needed, is glad when a magazine buys the articles or pictures.
A merchant needs customers and needs to provide products these
customers want, or the store soon ceases to exist. The ideally
functional vocation is one in which the worker has found a task
which needs to be done in the real world, which makes use of the
capacities and unique abilities of the worker, and which the
worker finds satisfying in terms of enjoyment, challenge, or
fulfillment. Such vocation enhances personality development and
adjustment. It fosters good mental health.

Most vocations toward the end of the twentieth century are
set in a complex and sometimes de-personalized society. Each

individual is challenged with the task of finding a meaningful work and life style which can accommodate both personal needs and unique character within the larger society of institutions, classifications, policy and procedure manuals, rules and regulations.[3] Religion serves many persons as a resource for bringing meaning to vocation.

VOCATION IN THE LIFE OF FLORENCE NIGHTINGALE

O'Malley's biography of Florence Nightingale is helpful in providing case material because it draws heavily upon her own diary, personal notes, journals and correspondence.[4] Her life extended from 1820 to 1910.

It was not easy for a woman of the upper class in England, born in the early part of the nineteenth century, to exercise autonomy over her vocation in life nor to create an identity other than that role which society prescribed. That role was to marry according to your station or continue as an elegant hostess and lady of leisure in your parents' mansion. Florence was repelled by marriage because she was afraid she would lose her identity thereby, and the usual entertainments and teas of society seemed frivolous to her compared with the needs in society to which she felt called to minister. She wondered why one could not simply have good friendships with men as well as women without the sex roles of marriage complicating the scene. The tragedy of her ambivalence was that Richard Monckton Milnes, who wanted to marry her, could not settle for friendship, could not relate to her on her terms. Meanwhile, she had her own strong sense of integrity and autonomy. She chose to carry out her "generativity" (Erikson's term, see Chapter 5) through vocation instead of family life.

Florence was an admirer of Catholic nuns who had social approval for remaining single and giving themselves wholeheartedly to a career. While in Rome she became a friend and counselee of a Mother Superior, went on a spiritual retreat in a convent, and struggled with the possibility of going that route. She was disillusioned with the passivity of the Church of England for its lack of spirituality. O'Malley describes her dilemma.

> "Religious opinion was, she saw, apt to fall into patterns like political opinion, and in this case she had not been born into any definite pattern. She had no wish to return to the Unitarianism of her forefathers: it seemed arid to her, and gave no place for her longings

99

after what was called the supernatural--
though it might only be another development
of natural law.

The Unitarian picture did not, in fact, show
the upper floors. But what could be said of the
Church of England in which she had been brought
up? It appeared to her as at once rent by
faction and spreading itself in comfort. The
Puseyites had put forward a harsh doctrine of
authority; they were avowedly opposed to every
kind of liberalism; they were ready to stake
their souls and the souls of their people on
forms and ceremonies. The Evangelicals were
not less narrow. They idolized the Bible and
condemned everyone who did not accept every word
of it literally to Hell Fire; they spent their
time distributing tracts to starving people who
could not read them...."[5]

Florence seemed to be drawn by compassion to help the sick
and needy. The story goes that when she was quite young, she
nursed back to health a dog on her father's estate. She was
concerned for their dying housekeeper. She assisted three dying
persons in the village that was near the palatial family estate.
As she did this she realized how much more useful she could be
if she had some training in a hospital. Her family was horrified that she would degrade herself by stooping so low. Women
who worked in hospitals were of a low class and rough character--
certainly no place for a "lady."

(Relatives thought that Florence's) "inability
to find contentment in the delightful surroundings provided for her, and her perverse desire
to go off to Salisbury Hospital, were nothing
after all but a sign of the times...Both parents
felt their daughter's proper place was in her
home.

Florence could not agree. 'If our Saviour
walked the earth now and I went to him, would
he send me back to the life I am leading?'
she asked herself again and again; and the
answer was always the same: 'No, he would say
to me 'Do this.' He would send me to work
for him.' It was agony to her not to obey
the call...."[6]

"Life is in a much truer form in London than

100

in the country--in a much stronger form certainly. In an English country place, everything
that is painful is so carefully removed out of
sight, behind those fine trees to a village
three miles off, and all the intercourse with
your fellow-creatures is that between the land-
lord and his tenant, the dependent and the
dependee, the untruest possible.

In London, at all events if you open your eyes,
you cannot help seeing in the next street that
life is not as it has been made to you. You
cannot get out of your carriage at a party
without seeing "what is" in the faces making
a lane on either side and without feeling
tempted to rush back and say 'Those are my
brothers and sisters.'

Ought not one's externals to be as nearly as
possible an incarnation of what life really
is? Life is not a green pasture and a still
water as our homes make it. Life is to some
a forty-days' fasting moral or physical, in
the wilderness; to some it is a fainting under
the carrying of the Cross; to some it is a
crucifixion, to all a struggle for safety which
convulses our lives."[7]

At age 30, Florence visited Kaiserswerth in Germany, where
Pastor Fliedner gave her an orientation to the hospital, orphan-
age, kindergarten, and other works of mercy which his Lutheran
Deaconesses carried on. Here was a model of service that inspired her greatly. After this fortnight visit was over, she
returned to the family estate, which seemed even still further
removed from the vocation to which she felt increasingly called.
Florence returned to Kaiserswerth a year later, not as a visitor,
but as an apprentice, which role she fulfilled admirably, according to Fliedner. Her family did not seem moved by the
poignant plea for understanding in a letter from which this quote
is taken.

"'Give me time, give me faith. Trust me, help
me,' she wrote. 'I feel within me that I could
gladden your loving hearts which now I wound.
Say to me 'Follow the dictates of that spirit
within thee.' Oh, my beloved people, that
spirit shall never lead me to anything unworthy
of one who is yours in love. Give me your
blessing....."[8]

The rest of her story is well known history. She studied
further and pioneered the modern profession of nursing. The
British soldiers wounded in the Crimean War called her affec-
tionately "the lady with the lamp" as she made her rounds super-
vising their care. She had the strength of her convictions and
religious faith to sustain her as she doggedly and painfully
carved out her unique career

A CONTEMPORARY NURSING STUDENT'S LAMP FLICKERS

A high school graduate left home to learn nursing in a
school attached to a very large city hospital. There was no
such department in the state university in her home town.
Throughout her adolescence she had been an active member in the
Presbyterian youth fellowship and felt that much of her motivation to go into nursing had been derived from her religious experiences in that group. She was referred to me for counseling
by her local minister. The presenting problem was that she had
been expelled from nursing school for violating dormitory rules
by spending the night in a male medical intern's room. (Such
regulations may, indeed, have been lifted since then.)

We had not gotten far into the counseling relationship before it became quite apparent that the episode represented status
more than sex. She wanted desperately to marry a doctor. Her
father was a doctor, and through his connections she made many
friends among the country club set. Her father (divorced from
her mother and now practicing medicine in New Orleans) had offered to pay her entire expenses, plus sorority dues and lovely
clothes, at Tulane University. But she was inspired by a religious experience at a youth camp to want to help the sick and
needy. Her mixed motivation, of which she was unaware at the
time, allowed her to study nursing, marry a doctor, and have the
best of both worlds: service and status.

When I asked what her stepfather's occupation was, she replied in an off-hand way, "He heats and cools the university."
I assumed he was either an electrical or mechanical engineer with
enormous responsibilities. Perhaps he was Vice President in
charge of Plant Operations. Sheepishly she admitted that he was
"only a janitor," and sometimes turned up the thermostat or
opened a window to "heat and cool the university." Actually she
was embarrassed about his job and hoped none of her friends on
the other side of town would ask about him. Meanwhile, he was
a very good father and faithful husband. He was paying the tui-
tion for her to go to the nursing school, and, in many other
ways was a perfectly decent and responsible citizen, quite unlike

her affluent but immoral biological father. Herein lay the conflict: she had to choose between these two and found herself torn, ambivalent, and feeling guilty.

This case could have been cited under Chapter 7 as well as under "Vocation," because she was deeply involved in sin. She was surprised to discover that her primary sin was one of social snobbishness. Theologians have maintained that PRIDE is a kind of root sin that proliferates out into many directions to destroy persons and relationships. Sexual acting out was a spin-off. The reason for her expulsion was sex; but who ever heard of anyone being expelled from a school for the sin of pride? She also went through an attitude pendulum swing from adoration to hatred for her father when she realized how she had been taken in by his sophisticated ways and financial bribery attempts. Finally, she levelled out and saw both father and stepfather for what they really were. She began taking a more adult attitude (after all she was 21 years of age by now). She could forgive her father and accept him more realistically as a person with strengths and weaknesses who was trying hard to be what he thought was a "Successful American," the kind of person who made our country great. Meanwhile, she was able to appreciate her stepfather without condescension, and finally said, "I no longer think it is a disgrace to carry your lunch in a bucket and wear coveralls with 'Physical Plant' embroidered on the breast pocket."

Our more mature and seasoned penitent recovered totally from the anxiety state and depression into which she had sunk. She felt forgiven and reconciled, at peace. She found a new meaning in the well-worn term "fellowship." As she returned to the nursing school to resume her studies, she realized that her attitudes and motivation toward her own vocation were inextricably related to how she felt about other occupations and roles, what status meant and how not to misuse it. She wrote to me from her nursing school that she could appreciate the many types of workers at the hospital in ways that were not open to her before. Whether she marries a doctor or a man who "heats and cools the hospital," I had the warm feeling that she would be another "lady with the lamp," and that she would not hide it under a bushel.

NOTES

1. Selected Works of Mao Tse-tung, Volume II, Peking: Foreign Languages Press, 1967, pp. 337-338.

2. <u>Selected</u> <u>Works</u> <u>of</u> <u>Mao</u> <u>Tse-tung</u>, Volume III, Peking: Foreign
    Languages Press, 1967, pp. 177-178.

3. See the author's treatment of how to live in a depersonal-
    ized society in <u>Alone, Alone, All, All Alone</u>, Saint Louis:
    Concordia Publishing House, 1972.

4. O'Malley, I.B., <u>Florence</u> <u>Nightingale</u> <u>1820-1856</u>: <u>A study of</u>
    <u>her life down to the end of the Crimean War</u>, London: Thorn-
    ton Butterworth, Limited, 1931.

5. <u>Ibid</u>., pp. 76-77.

6. <u>Ibid</u>., p. 115.

7. <u>Ibid</u>., pp. 149-150.

8. <u>Ibid</u>., p. 185.

DISCUSSION ABOUT THE ETHICS AND MEANING OF WORK

1. What motivated your father (or mother) to pursue the major
    career he/she followed? What attitude did the spouse take
    toward that vocation?

2. Are some jobs (scientist, judge, dentist) more value-free
    than others (businessman, priest, artist)? On what ratio-
    nale did you base your answer?

3. Florence Nightingale seemed to have been caught in an impos-
    sible dilemma. How else might she have resolved it? What
    factors in her personality or her circumstances would have
    to have been different for such an alternative as you sug-
    gested to be workable? If she had come to you for counsel-
    ing, what would you have considered helpful?

4. Perhaps you disagree with the interpretation or approach
    used with the nursing student who was expelled. That's OK;
    it's a free country. Does it sound like a simplistic in-
    terpretation? By the way, I did refer her for vocational
    guidance, and the test scores were shared with her and me
    by the clinical psychologist. Why was that important? What
    role should such test results have played in the therapeutic
    relationship?

5. Is it possible to separate out personal, human worth in vo-
    cation from the issue of financial reward? Or, to put the
    same issue in other words: How in the world (especially the

third world) could persons be motivated to work without unequal financial incentives?

6. Is it fair to give an across-the-board raise of 5% to high and low paid workers in an institution or factory?

7. Rate the following vocation-oriented concepts on a scale of 1 - 5, with the ideal being 1 and the least desirable 5.

_____ (a) From everyone according to his/her ability, to everyone according to his/her need.

_____ (b) Those who don't work don't eat.

_____ (c) By their fruits ye shall know them.

_____ (d) From everyone according to his/her ability, to everyone according to his/her work.

_____ (e) He who has much should be given more.

Discuss how each of the above concepts relates to motivation, personality adjustment, self-regard, enhanced interpersonal relations, and mental health (if relevant).

8. How could the meaning and personal value of work be enhanced in a meat packing plant, automobile factory, secretarial pool in a large corporation, police force, hospital, elementary school, postal service, etc.? On the other hand, what options does the individual worker have in this regard if "others," "society" or "management" fail to enhance the value of a given work role?

CHAPTER 5

LOVE AND CREATION

"The strength acquired at any stage is
tested by the necessity to transcend it in
such a way that the individual can take chances
in the next stage with what was most vulnerably
precious in the previous one. Thus, the young
adult, emerging from the search for and the in-
sistence on identity, is eager and willing to
fuse his identity with that of others. He is
ready for intimacy, that is, the capacity to
commit himself to concrete affiliations and
partnerships and to develop the ethical strength
to abide by such commitments, even though they
may call for significant sacrifices and compro-
mises."[1]

Thus Erikson begins his section on "Intimacy vs. Isolation."
Intimacy, like the term "love," deals with much more than sex.
It includes the capacity to have warm friendships, to be willing
to reach out and trust other persons in meaningful relationships.
This is increasingly possible in proportion as the earlier
stages have represented wholesome and positive experiences. On
the other hand, the young adult, who began life in an atmosphere
of mistrust, never developed a sense of autonomy or individual
worth, was burdened with excessive inferiority feelings, and
has floundered in adolescent role confusion; that young adult is
not well equipped for mature intimacy, certainly not marriage.
It is only natural that religion universally has been deeply
involved in this important adjustment.

GOD AS CREATOR--PERSONS AS CO-CREATORS

The _Genesis_ account of the creation of Adam is closely followed by the need for intimacy, which is fulfilled by the creation of Eve. "Then the Lord God said, 'It is not good that the
man should be alone; I will make him a helper fit for him.'"
(_Genesis_ 2:18) Hence, from the beginning of time, creation, procreation, and family life were closely linked. Ironically, this
happy estate was also to be the center of pervasive trouble,
because it was not long before they were to lose their innocense,
become ashamed of their bodies, and were driven from the Garden
of Eden with a curse. Just because they had this wonderful
potency to be co-creators of Cain and Abel did not mean they
were _omni_potent like God the Creator. Human beings as co-
creators or procreators are still creatures in their own right.
Only God is the Creator who is not a creature. God is uncreated
from all eternity. Thus the Judeao-Christian Scriptures have
circumscribed the identity and role of human beings. (More of
this in Chapter 10, where the Biblical view of human nature is
discussed.)

The Islamic scripture combines the creation of man from
clay, presumably a reference to the _Genesis_ account, with the
description of the reproductive process.

> "Man We did create
> From a quintessence (of clay);
>
> Then We placed him
> As (a drop of) sperm
> In a place of rest,
> Firmly fixed;
>
> Then We made the sperm
> Into a clot of congealed blood;
> Then of that clot We made
> A (foetus) lump; then We
> Made out of that lump
> Bones and clothed the bones
> With flesh; then We developed
> Out of it another creature:
> So blessed be Allah,
> The Best to create!"[2]

A contemporary Swedish theologian, Gustav Wingren, claims
that it would be constructive to re-emphasize creation theology,
to put more stress on the First Article of the Apostles' Creed:
"I believe in God, the Father almighty, creator of heaven and

108

earth." This would provide a proper perspective for sexual relations and procreation.

> "Intercourse between man and woman is an act that
> is willed by God and one through which he now
> creates. It is not the case that God was once
> Creator and is now something else. According
> to Luther, he is Creator today. And the act
> of Creation in intercourse leads directly to
> the nourishment and care of the child.....in
> the service of the Creator, who chooses life
> over death."3

Indeed, it is crucial whether a person approaching the challenge of intimacy regards it as in keeping with God's plan or sinful by nature. If the former, sexuality and reproduction can be ego-enhancing and fulfilling; if the latter, sexuality exists under a cloud of guilt and intimacy and is seen as the first step on the slippery slope to sin.

MALE AND FEMALE AS COMPLEMENTARY

The notion that masculinity and femininity represent complementary parts of a whole life pattern is an ancient one nowhere more neatly illustrated than in the Chinese Yin and Yang symbol shown in Figure 17.

Fig. 17   Yin and Yang

"The Yang is the positive force in nature:
male, heat, the sun, land, dry. Yin is the
negative aspect: female, cool, shade, the
moon, the sea. The two forces are not in conflict but continuous, harmonious interchange
and interaction, symbolized by the circle
equally divided by a curving line, so that the
two parts represent a constant balanced flux.....
Too much Yang will bring drought and fire, and
too much Yin causes floods and unseasonable
rain."[4]

Much of this doctrine is quite unacceptable to us in post-
liberation society, especially about the cause of drought and
floods; and the "positive" and "negative" sound too pejorative
for our ears. Some would challenge the idea that it takes two
to make one whole. "Can I not be a whole man or a whole woman
without a partner?" What impresses me as a model for marriage,
however, is the inter-dependent nature of the symbol. They fit
together along the entire curving surface. There is no part of
their relationship which is not contributed to by one or the
other; more in this area by one partner, more in another area by
the other person. Here is equality of contribution to the union,
"harmonious interchange and interaction." Yet each partner is
clearly distinctive and there is no loss of identity in the
merger.

The reason Erikson took up the theme of identity before
intimacy is instructive. Fullfledged sexual union is threatening
to an immature person who is in danger of loosing his/her fragile
identity by merging the self with another. This is seen in the
frantic and insecure adolescent who rushes into a liaison in
order to solve all youth's problems only to discover that the
relationship takes as much or more out of one as it gives back.
Thus one should not seek intimacy or marriage in order to become
a worthwhile person; rather a person should understand oneself
to be an autonomous person of worth with a rightful identity and
calling of one's own. Then one is ready to merge this wholesome
and legitimate self with another self in the kind of union described in the words of Jesus and frequently quoted in marriage
liturgies:

"God made them male and female. For this reason
a man shall leave his father and mother and
be joined to his wife, and the two shall become one. So they are no longer two but one.
What therefore God has joined together, let
not man put asunder." (Mark 10:6b-9)

Another instance of inappropriate motivation for marriage

is the woman who marries an alcoholic to reform him. Nor should a strong, compassionate person marry a deformed and inadequate person out of pity. Mutual strengthening may well be the result of a good marriage, but it should not be on the basis of one bringing all the assets and the other only liabilities. It is in this sense of mutual interdependence that the Yin and Yang symbol serve as a thought-provoking model of marital intimacy.

If marriage did not provide the immature person with enough therapeutic help, the second, even more unfortunate place to seek value as a person of worth is in parenthood. Then having a baby is supposed to save the marriage, which in turn was supposed to have saved the "adolescent" or even "childlike" adult. Marriage is an adult vocation involving intimacy, and, of course, much more.

SEX: POWERFUL DRIVE WITHIN THE SOCIAL ADJUSTMENT OF MARRIAGE

Let us be more explicit about the nature and meaning of sexual relations as one of the most intense and all-encompassing experiences of intimacy. It is an exceedingly strong instinct which guarantees the preservation of the species as such. In this regard it is not unlike the reproductive force which creates generation after generation of cattle, dogs, potatoes, flowers, and the proverbial birds and the bees. There's a Yin and a Yang in all of them--the male and female principle at work, which we refer to as sexual attraction. Whatever the courtship dance of the pair of birds or the wanderings of the bull and cow, sooner or later the two mates have to co-operate enough to copulate, to contribute their respective germinal cells to form the new life. The physiological attraction may be augmented by sights, sounds, smells, touch, etc. Among civilized humans, social significance and values are richly embroidered upon this bio-logical fabric. Sex becomes also personally and emotionally characterized as <u>love</u>. What we said at the beginning about the "spiral of life" is here again evident. As one's circle of outreach is immeasurably increased by early adulthood, so these early stirrings of sexual awareness become increasingly complex and morally socialized as one ascends the spiral.

"It must be an important evolutionary fact
that man, over and above sexuality, develops
a selectivity of love: I think it is the
<u>mutuality</u> of <u>mates</u> <u>and</u> <u>partners</u> <u>in</u> <u>a</u> <u>shared</u>
<u>identity</u>, for the mutual verification through
an experience of finding oneself, as one loses

111

oneself, in another. For let me emphasize here
that identity proves itself strongest where it
can take chances with itself. For this reason,
love in its truest sense presupposes both identity and fidelity. While many forms of love
can be shown to be at work in the formation of
the various virtues, it is important to realize that only graduation from adolescence per-
mits the development of that intimacy, the
selflessness of joined devotion, which anchors
love in a mutual commitment. Intimate love
thus is the guardian of that elusive and yet
all-pervasive power in psycho-social evolution:
the power of <u>cultural</u> <u>and</u> <u>personal</u> <u>style</u>,
which gives and demands conviction in the shared
patterns of living, guarantees individual identity in joint intimacy, and binds into a 'way
of life' the affiliations of procreation and
of production."[5]

VULNERABILITY AND CARNAL KNOWLEDGE

"Carnal knowledge" is by now a quaint expression. The folk
wisdom of the phrase goes back several thousand years. "Now
Adam knew Eve his wife, and she conceived and bore Cain..."
(<u>Genesis</u> 4:1a) (The verb for coitus in Hebrew being the same as
"to know.") From a psychological point of view the kind of
knowledge about another person derived during sexual intercourse
goes far beyond the cognitive understanding gained from discussion. The community may consider Mr. John Doe a generous person
because he has served faithfully on the United Fund campaign and
tithes at church, but, I dare say, his wife knows through sexual
intercourse whether he is <u>really</u> generous or selfish in a more
profound way than the community at large. There is an essential
nakedness here which cannot be covered up with status, vocational
prestige, titles, nor the rank of authority. In this basically
defenseless posture one has only one's intrinsic personhood to
rely upon. Hence, one is known essentially and not superficially
in the sexual encounter.

There is a totality of involvement of the individual. There
may be words and commitments, morals and values that are commonly shared by this mutually related diad; but feelings and
emotions are also powerfully involved. The various senses propel
the couple with increasing momentum in the direction of union,
which is the goal of this basic instinct of sex. Even those who
thought to enter into sexual intercourse in a casual way,

according to the advice of <u>Playboy</u> magazine, find that they have become more involved than they had intended. One or the other of the couple suddenly realizes that the other feels hurt that the relationship had been considered casual by the other person when he/she had begun to "get involved" at a deeper level of commitment. Partly because of this unpredictability of the human sexual relationship, it has been culturally assumed that sexual intercourse should be carried out between persons with long term commitments. The problem with trivializing sex is that one thereby misrepresents a fundamental bio-psycho-social aspect of personality. It is an adult responsibility to deal with this reality; and to handle these powerful forces in a childlike or adolescent fashion can be disruptive to personality adjustment and create social problems for others.

MODESTY AND PORNOGRAPHY

It is not fair to take a swipe at <u>Playboy</u> or other skin magazines without further discussion. Modesty has fallen on hard times because it represents to so many a kind of body-denying, Victorian rigidity and repression which has become associated with neurotic and non-functional personality. A humorous example of an adult denying sexuality while trying to talk about it is the case of the theological student who was requested to write a lesson plan for confirmation students dealing with the Commandment: Thou shalt not commit adultery. He was a married, thirty-year-old with several children, who had also been a reporter for the <u>Milwaukee Journal</u>, supposedly not naive about the subject. He explained that adulteration meant dilution or mixing things that ought not to go together--like if a farmer diluted his milk supply by adding water, a misrepresentation of the product. I presume his pupils learned from this hyper-modest explanation that commiting adultery is a violation of the Federal Food and Drugs Act of 1906. This is a fearful false modesty, hesitating to discuss reality openly under the assumption that it is too dangerous to bring up to consciousness.

Going to the other extreme we have pornography (from two Greek words meaning writing about harlots), which likewise fails to deal realistically and appropriately with reality. It is usually a distortion about one or another body part related to sexuality such as breasts, penis, etc. The problem lies in the misrepresentation or excessive stress rather than in the subject matter. C.S. Lewis illustrated the problem by means of the following analogy. Suppose that some creatures from outer space arrived in their spacecraft and came upon a large building with hundreds of human persons sitting in rows cheering and screaming for "more," MORE, as veil after veil was parted before the

113

gasping and drooling audience. Finally, the music comes to a climax as the last curtains are pulled back; and there, on center stage, is a card table with a plate of ham and eggs upon it. The visitors could only assume that an enormous concentration of time and energy and value were being ascribed to this one instinct. We might even say it was a distortion. I do not know if it would be misleading to call it pornography if a person subscribed to several magazines picturing only elbows or toes. If the reader began to think that elbows or toes were all that was important about persons or to focus on them to the neglect of the rest of the person, we could call it distortion.

One of the legitimate complaints of the women's movement is that women have been exploited as sex objects, which is depersonalizing. They would rather be perceived as subjects than objects. One cannot deal realistically with a person unless all facets of personality are taken into account: physical, emotional, intellectual, cultural, aesthetic, attitudinal, moral, vocational, etc., in short, the many modes through which this individual expresses a selfhood. Moderate and modest both come from a common cognate: modus (Latin), meaning "manner." Perhaps the connection is that a modest or moderate life style is one that does not distort or exaggerate one part over another. Thus the manner in which we view persons in a wholistic way runs the least likelihood of distorting or misrepresenting the person as he/she really is.

The significance of this dynamic for intimacy is profound. A married person may relate in a pornographic manner to the spouse by not being concerned about the whole person but only about one sexual body part. This is repulsive to the other person and demeaning. It is not long before true intimacy wanes and the offended party withdraws into isolation; the couple drifts apart. How adolescents have learned to understand and appreciate sexuality as a part of their total makeup will be influential in preparing them for adult intimacy. One wonders how sexual intimacy will work out for one young adolescent who came home from school crying because a sex education class had explained menstruation to both boys and girls in her grade. She wept to her mother, "Now the boys know that about us." Where did she get such a mode of modesty? What does religion contribute to this whole sexual sphere of personality adjustment? We turn to that next.

MARRIAGE AS RELIGIOUS SUPPORT

We now come to another "rite of passage," a passage from the single role to the couple role with the implications of family responsibility. It is practically universal that every

114

culture and every society seems to have needed some way of legit-
imatizing procreation within some kind of family structure and
publicly certifying that relationship by a ceremony of marriage.
It is as though a power so socially significant and with so
many ramifications could not be left to chance or private interest. The consequences of childbearing and childrearing affect
the whole tribe or community economically, socially, and politi-
cally. The prolonged period of dependency of the human infant
and child implies that the procreators will have a joint responsibility not only to sustain the physical life of the children
born of this union, but also to bring such children psychologically and morally to adulthood--one full generation.

The Russian Communists suspected that the family was used
by the entrenched establishment to foster privacy in attitudes
as well as property; therefore, they deliberately set about
weakening family ties, minimizing the need for marriage, making
divorce as easy as sending a post card to your mate, etc. From
1917 until 1944 this massive social experiment was carried out
with devastating results. Regardless of the adequacy of physical and nutritional care within state nurseries, it was discovered that the young needed a primary group for identification
and for learning such primary precepts as loyalty, self-worth,
morality, etc. One of the dynamics of sociopathy is that the
person thus stunted in moral development does not feel that he/
she has any significant or intimate relationships to lose. As
discussed in Chapter 2, this deficiency of character is partly
caused by the lack of close ties in early childhood. In the de-
personalized state nurseries of Russia this was missing. They
were rearing a generation of sociopaths who could not commit
themselves to anyone or anything. That is pretty risky for a
society. They restored marriage to a place of prominence again
and even re-instituted liturgies for the marriage ceremony. (See
Chapter 13, SECULAR SUBSTITUTES FOR TRADITIONAL RELIGION.)

The wedding ceremony of any denomination is likely to include prayers for the new couple that their relationship will
be blessed. The congregation is supportive of their role of
parenting. Full approval is given to their sexual union ("one
flesh" Genesis 2:24-25). If the religious group has had prohi-
bitions and taboos against sexual relations up to this point,
the couple is now fully released from such proscriptions. When
proper preparation through pre-marital counseling and education
has been provided by the religious body and minister, this
transition works very well. The sexual instinct urging union
is reinforced by the social approval of parents, friends, and
precisely that religious agency of moral education and guidance
representing the Ten Commandments and all the other values which
the group upholds. Since sex is frequently heavily laden with
moral overtones, it is important that this transition be blessed

by the guardians of that moral order. Even persons who have drifted away from their family's religion frequently return for this ceremony to a religious agency rather than the secular officer at the Court House. They seek a "blessing."

Another feature of the wedding is vows--promising fidelity throughout their lifetime. Some vows are less ambitious, and the couple promises to stay together "as long as love lasts." Some vows are practically job descriptions; others are more or less explicit about the roles they plan to fulfill. Friends and attendants witness these vows and sign documents to that effect. Social festivity, party-like atmosphere, and celebration follow the religious ceremony as congratulations are offered. The covenant vow provides the security of knowing that the spouse will be willing to continue in a supportive role during the lengthy period of child-rearing, through vocational tasks and on into the later years. The couple make a promise in the context not only of divine blessing and socio-moral sanction but in the presence of a community of significant others. When religious support of sex and marriage is functioning positively, personality adjustment is enhanced.

As a pastor I found pre-marital counseling, weddings, and ministering to families rewarding. Nowhere did religion seem more relevant. But to be impartially fair, it must be admitted that sometimes religion is not supportive but oppressive, providing a negative view of sex and an arbitrary attitude toward the institution of marriage. At least that is how Molly perceived it in her town. The following literal quotation from a student's term paper expresses the mood of such a negative community. The reader should not assume that this is the norm of this particular ethnic denomination, but, rather, simply how it was in one community. Similar instances could be cited from other towns, ethnic groups, or congregations.

> "While many people see the Irish as light hearted
> with high spirits, and while they perhaps can
> tell a good joke they really tend to be a sullen
> and bitter people. At least this was much the
> case in Molly's community. There is a feeling
> that all the world is bearing down on them.
> The most stressful moments of life are the ones
> the community dwell on constantly. Typically
> these life concerns are birth, marriage, and
> death. The church is central to them all.
> From her society Molly learned that birth was
> a secretive and cruel thing. Rarely will the
> Irish woman say her pregnancy and delivery were
> average or, considering it all, normal. They
> will worry about a small bone frame, or heredity

or other problems that they are sure will bring
them close to death in childbirth. Molly's
mother always feared her pregnancies with this
common dread, and Molly, as the oldest and a
daughter, learned to dread her mother's pregnancies as much as her mother. It would not be
until she had children of her own that Molly would
begin to see how the beliefs of the Catholic
Church helped making having children such a seemingly unhappy experience. Thus the new child
entered Molly's world surrounded by misappre-
hension. As Molly matured she also began to
perceive that while the Irish Catholic women
had many children, their sex lives were generally not the healthy side of marriage that would
be desirable. From as early as she could remember she saw that the woman's attitude toward
pregnancy was, more or less, 'He did it to me.'
On the other hand, for a woman not to marry and
not have children was viewed as an abnormalty
and even a threat to the society. Marriage was
the bedrock of the community; it was the one
thing that everyone had to do. Marriage was
much more important than love.....

"Jim did offer some romance and Molly enjoyed
him as a friend. WWII had started and Jim joined
the Air Corps and left for four years in Burma.
They had been married two months, and Molly was
pregnant. As was traditional in this community,
Molly feared she would die in childbirth. The
doctor told her that she would be okay, but the
women warned her of her small bone frame. Because of the war there was much talk of death
and dying already. Jim was in a particularly
dangerous area. Again Molly went to a priest,
concerned over her own future and Jim's. She
was sternly lectured. Many people were suffering because of the war, and she should pray and
be thankful that the situation was not worse,
the priest said. He also told her that Catholic
women looked to their children with joy, not
dread. Now Molly knew perfectly well that few
children she knew had been looked forward to
with joy, but hearing the priest say this somehow
made her feel that she was different and had
done something to be ashamed of by fearing
childbirth. Molly was confused, and saw herself
as completely weak and a failure as a Catholic.
She vividly remembers going into the empty church

for one last effort at comfort through prayer. As she reached a front pew and tried to genuflect, her knees would not bend. Molly was shaken and believed this had something to do with her pregnancy. She tried again, but simply could not make her legs move. She then crossed herself and ran from the church. She quit going to mass every day, and when she went on Sundays she would attend the most crowded mass and stand throughout, in the rear of the church. The ushers were always trying to find her a seat, but she was afraid to move too far into the sanctuary. Molly could no longer feel a deep sense of security in the church. She felt she had known it, but now she was disappointed and distant. Then she came to the conclusion that she was really like everyone else, needing the church and what it represented, needing the traditions on which the society was built, but that there was no way to have a personal relationship with an institution."

Another student wrote more positively about the role of religion as a healthy support of marriage:

"Actually, I believe the resources of religion can strengthen marriage when used with wisdom and compassion. It has been established that most people with marital difficulties seek help first from their pastors. Thus, it is important that pastoral counseling sees the difficulties of sexual adjustment as an expression of underlying anxieties. As Erik Erikson points out, avoidance of experiences of intimacy and close affiliation may lead to a deep sense of isolation and self-absorption. On the other hand, these experiences must become subject to the ethical sense which is the mark of maturity, and which includes mutual trust with a loved partner, leading to the goal of 'generativity.' It is there that the church can be of great importance and value."

This section on marriage may be fittingly concluded with the words of a psychiatrist, who also had a keen interest in religion, Gotthard Booth.

"Marriage offers, in theory at least, the ideal opportunity for the physical expression of love, since social conventions and legal protections concur in keeping the anxieties of unconventional relations away from the partners. Those living in a religious marriage furthermore may find in faith security against anxiety which no worldly forms of protection can equal."

THE CHANGING FAMILY

I used the above quotation from Booth in a chapter entitled "Marriage and Creation Amidst Family Life" in 1963.[7] At that time my wife was a full-time homemaker with three young children to care for, ages 8, 6, and 4. She was married to a 41-year-old husband, who is now 56. The eight-year-old will finish law school in a year, and the other two "kids" are college students. Today my wife is a full-time professional librarian in a large law college library. I have changed from a seminary professor to a university professor. You would be correct to say that that is hardly the same family at all. We began with a family of two, a couple. Our first child was born into a family of three, and our last was born into a family of five persons. Our first child had naive parents; our last child had at least somewhat more experienced parents. Our economic circumstances have changed, and much more. Yet there is a continuity which runs through the whole enterprise so that we are in another sense the same family over the years--growing and changing, but very much the same family in a fundamental sense. In this "empty nest" phase, my wife and I are back to being a couple again, but last Christmas vacation the "family of five" was very much in evidence.

The above personal example illustrates the obvious fact that "this holy estate" is not simply a status, nor an accomplished fact, but rather a dynamic process of becoming something new and different continuously. Remember our discussion of adolescence and how adult means literally "having arrived"? That could be misleading. Also, a certain sense of relief in "settling down" to marriage can lead to complacency and stagnation, settling into a rut. Erikson indicates that in mid-life the alternatives are generativity vs. stagnation. Marriage partners cannot be supportive of each other if one continues to grow and the other atrophies--they drift apart.

Typical of the rapid change of family models is the annual conference on "The Changing Family" conducted at the University of Iowa, which in some years has attracted an attendance of 1,500. They come to hear about single parent families, extended families, "open marriage," nuclear families, divorce-and-remarriage, communal substitutes for the traditional family, mobility and the family, the family in transition, etc. It is only the most recent development of the evolution of the family from the days of Solomon's many wives, and the handmaiden arrangement of Abraham, the dowry and bride price, the lady fair of knighthood days, parental choice of spouses for their children, down to the democratic and uni-sex mores of our day.

In one's marriage relationship and family life can be found clues to how a given adult is handling or coping with the issues of self-worth, initiative, identity, authority, status, as well as the more obvious intimacy and generativity. Here values and beliefs find their most intimate expression or exposure. On the stage of the microcosm of the family are acted out the issues of society, which, in the macrocosm of the larger world are seen as government, education, law, war-and-peace, art, medicine, religion, culture, etc. The numerous combinations of temperaments and personality traits combined into millions of marriages and family patterns are perhaps as unique and idiosyncratic as the fingerprints of the partners. Each bears the stamp of unique personalities in combination.

CREATE OR STAGNATE

When Sigmund Freud was asked what essential things a person with a normal, healthy personality should be able to do, he replied: _Lieben_ _und_ _arbeiten_ ("to love and to work"). Producing children is certainly not the only form of creativity. Jane Addams created the social settlement Hull House in the slums of Chicago, and the compassion she had for child laborers, and the energy she invested in the child welfare movement could surely be characterized as maternal. Many an unmarried nurse has nurtured sick children as though they were her own. Others have created poetry, music, mechanical inventions, works of art, educational programs, factories, theories, etc. Works of mercy, so called, literally combine Freud's dictum--to love and to work--in one enterprise. In other instances, the two functions seem less related, as in the case of a person who is "all business" at work and then changes roles when relating socially with friends and companions in a personal and very warm manner. All of this could certainly take place without marriage, sexual relations, or family connections.

The famous priest-palaeontologist-philosopher, Pierre Teilhard de Chardin, not only contributed to scientific knowledge by his research work in China, not only developed mind-expanding theological concepts and theories; but he also formed warm friendships with women as well as men. This celibate individual not only could be intimate, but was able to resist bitter isolation when his writing ministry was severely circumscribed by the Church of Rome. When his creativity was frustrated he did not stagnate nor lose his motivational momentum. He maintained his integrity and inner vocational clarity while still not breaking fellowship with the Church, which often did not understand or appreciate his contribution to modern theology.

Maslow referred to "growth motives" leading to "self-actualization."[8] This implies that the individual is moving toward some future goal, the very activity of which, in turn, makes it possible for that person more nearly to reach his/her full potential. The person's selfhood is enhanced and expanded in this positive process. The person who has to spend too much energy on "deficit motives," overcoming basic drives like hunger and self-preservation, may not achieve maturity, but be fixated at the level of infantile complexes. Reflecting on our "Dilemma of the Will," could we push this line of reasoning one step further? A person who thinks his/her primary needs are not being adequately met may also remain at this simpler level and not be able to focus on self-actualization. I cite myself at this present moment as a case in point. Today I have had three perfectly adequate meals and need no nourishment whatsoever, physically speaking. But as I type these lines, I am plagued with the notion that I should go to the kitchen and get something to nibble on. Clearly, finishing this chapter would lead to fuller self-actualization than consuming a few cookies, especially since I am trying to control my weight.

Gordon Allport championed the idea of willful, positive motivation which one could claim as one's own. This was to counter-balance what he believed was a too heavy emphasis on determinism of the behaviorist and positivist schools.

> "Let us take note of the large number of crucial terms in contemporary psychology that start with the prefix re: receptor, reaction, response, reflex, repression, repetition, reward, reinforcement, regression--to name some but not all .....We hear much of reaction but seldom of proaction."

> "Terms commencing with re connote againness, passivity, being pushed or maneuvered. Terms with pro suggest futurity, intention, forward thrust."[9]

121

The creative inventor, the initiator of new methods of doing his/her job, the individual with a purposeful vocation--all of these could be characterized by Allport's "pro" prefix. The person with the "calling" has a vocation which attracts and draws him/her toward a goal in the future. The stagnator resists new ideas, resents new assignments, retreats into familiar patterns of behavior and work. The person exhudes a mood of resignation.

In the mid-life period from 40 to 55 a person may once again grapple with identity vs. role confusion issues. Am I in the right job? Will I ever really be successful? Are my peers passing me by with promotions and achievements? Is it too late to start over in another career? Maybe I've hit my peak at 40 and it's down the old toboggan slide from here till retirement (oh, oh! another re word). I'm torn between generativity (success at the office as a workaholic) and intimacy (more time and closeness with my spouse and children). Mental health workers find some persons in the mid-life crisis so confused that they cannot distinguish between the two: love and work.

> "A new partner for sex seems to promise relief, often without awareness of the nonsexual origin of the desire. When a businessman falls in love with his secretary, my usual experience has been not that she is more attractive than his wife, but that his business is failing."10

Gail Sheehy has written a provocative and witty description of the challenges that confront adults at various stages of intimacy and generativity.11 It is undergirded by research and peppered with interview cases illustrating various strategies and methods of coping with adulthood. A bit of the dialogue with a General Motors businessman in Detroit should tempt the reader to dip into Passages further.

> "Age is starting to be a factor," he told me. "Right now, it's to my advantage. But if you look at the people driving to the top, you have to move fast, or usually you die before you get there."
>
> I asked this unpretentious man, whose personal style runs to black shirts and white ties, if he had always had the idea of "running for president" in the back of his mind.
>
> "Absolutely not."

"And now?"

"Now, yes, I want to be Number One. The bonus
potential is what makes any executive perform
--up to a certain level. Then, they tell me,
they're motivated by just wanting to be Number
One. President or chairman of the board.....Once
people have got all the money they want, they
become philanthropic. The older guy who's all
for the good of humanity has already made his
million.".....

"I'm not the best father; that bugs me a little
bit. I try to do things to make up for that.
Like this year, I contemplated a four-week vacation. But I only took one week because I'm
limited as to how long I can be away from the
plant. It's probably not true, but I feel that
way.".....

"The next thing is to get to general manager
level. It's got to happen in six years if I'm
going to get all the way to the top. If it
doesn't happen by the time I'm 44 (giving himself
two years grace), rather than getting into a
mess with my family or giving up, I would try
self-employment. I've always thought farming was
rewarding. That's what I came from"[12]

As this man implies, if you are lucky, you will live through
the ulcers, hassles, and dangers of the rat race which he considers mid-life to be. Whether one has created a life style of
peace of mind and balanced love-work ratio, whether one has become a workaholic, a hero, a drone, an over-achiever, a failure
or a success; one thing is for sure, old age is just around the
corner. Toward the end of the career, as one's own children are
establishing their families, anywhere from the early or mid-
fifties until actual retirement in the sixties, the person's
spiral of life takes another turn and can move up to the next
level, aging and finally the last task of all, dying.

THE NEAR MARRIAGE OF JOHN WESLEY AS REPORTED IN HIS SAVANNAH JOURNAL (excerpts)[13]

In the evening we landed on an uninhabited island, made a fire, supped, went to prayers together, and then spread our sail over us on four stakes, to keep off the night dews. Under this on one side were Miss Sophy, myself, and one of our boys who came with me from Savannah; on the other, our boat's crew....

(Oct. 29, 1736) It was not without some difficulty that in the afternoon we landed on St. Katherine's again. Observing in the night the fire we lay by burning bright, that Miss Sophy was broad awake, I asked her, "Miss Sophy, how far are you engaged to Mr. Mellichamp?" She answered, "I have promised him either to marry or to marry no one at all." I said (which indeed was the expression of a sudden wish, not of any formed design), "Miss Sophy, I should think myself happy if I was to spend my life with you." She burst out into tears and said, "I am every way unhappy. I won't have Tommy; for he is a bad man. And I can have none else."......

(Oct. 30) In the afternoon we landed on Bear Island and walked together for near two hours. Here again Miss Sophy expressed the strongest uneasiness, and an utter aversion to living at Mr. Causton's, saying, with many tears, "I can't live in that house: I can't bear the shocks I meet with there." I said, "Don't be uneasy, Miss Sophy, on that account. If you don't care to be at Mr. Causton's, you are welcome to a room in our house; or, which I think would be best of all, and your aunt once proposed it, you may live in the house with the Germans." She made little reply.....

(Nov. 1) She was eighteen years old. And from the beginning of our intimate acquaintance till this day, I verily believe she used no guile: not only because even now I know of no instance to the contrary, nor only because the simplicity of her behaviour was a constant voucher for her sincerity; but because of the entire openness of all her conversation.....Such was the woman, according to my closest observation of whom I now began to be much afraid. My desire and design still was to live single; but how long it would continue I knew not. I therefore consulted my friends whether it was not best to break off all intercourse with her immediately. They expressed themselves so ambiguously that I understood them to mean that I ought not break it off. And accordingly she came to me (as had been agreed) every morning and evening.

The time she spent at my house was spent thus. Immediately after breakfast we all joined in Hickes's _Devotions_. She was then alone till eight. I taught her French between eight and nine, and at nine we joined in prayer again. She then read or wrote French till ten. In the evening I read to her and some others select parts of Ephrem Syrus, and afterwards Dean Young's and Mr. Reeve's _Sermons_. We always concluded with a psalm.

This I began with a single eye. But it was not long before I found it a task too hard for me to preserve the same intention with which I began, in such intimacy of conversation as ours was.....

(At this point in his journal, Wesley explains his dilemma about whether he should stay on in Georgia or go back to England since his original purpose of preaching to the Indians was not working out and he did not feel obliged to continue as a minister in Georgia among the settlers.

"But though I had no other obligation not to leave Savannah now, yet that of love I could not break through; I could not resist the importunate request of the more serious parishioners 'to watch over their souls yet a little longer till some one came who might supply my place'." (Nov. 23)

(Jan. 31, 1737) After having been detained several days on Sapolo Island by mists and contrary winds, at last I came to Savannah. Finding Miss Sophy was with Mrs. Musgrove at the Cowpen, a place where I doubted she would learn little good, I went up thither the same evening. She took boat and came down with me immediately, as it was not her custom to deny me anything. For indeed from March 13, 1736 the day I first spoke to her, till that hour, I cannot recollect so much as a single instance of my proposing anything to her, or expressing any desire, which she did not fully comply with.....

(Feb. 3) I was now in a great strait. I still thought it best for me to live single. And this was still my design; but I felt the foundations of it shaken more and more every day. Insomuch that I again hinted at a desire of marriage, though I made no direct proposal. For indeed it was only a sudden thought, which had not the consent of my own mind. Yet I firmly believe, had she (Miss Sophy) closed with me at that time, my judgement would have made but a faint resistance. But she said "she thought it was best for clergymen not to be encumbered with worldly cares, and that it was best for her too, to live single, and she was accordingly resolved never to marry." I used no argument to induce her to alter her resolution.

Upon reflection, I thought this a very narrow escape; and

after much consideration, I went to Mr. Toltschig, the pastor of the Moravians, and desired his advice, whether I had not best, while it was yet in my power, break off so dangerous an acquaintance. He asked, "What do you think would be the consequence if you should?" I said, "I fear her soul would be lost, being surrounded with dangers, and having no other person to warn her of and arm her against them." He added, "And what do you think would be the consequence if you should not break it off?" I said, "I fear I should marry her." He replied short, "I don't see why you should not."

I went home amazed to the last degree; and it was now first that I had the least doubt whether it was best for me to marry or not, which I never before thought would bear a question.....

(March 8.....After some serious conversation interposed, I said, "I hear Mr. Williamson pays his addresses to you. Is it true?" She said, after a pause, "If it were not I would have told you so." I asked, "How do you like him?" She replied, "I don't know; there is a great deal in being in the house with one. But I have no inclination for him." I said, "Miss Sophy, if you ever deceive me, I shall scarce ever believe any one again."....."Of one thing, sir, be assured: I will never take any step in anything of importance without first consulting you."

She went, and I saw myself in the toils. But how to escape I saw not. If I continued to converse with her, though not alone, I found I should love her more and more. And the time to break it off was past....."

(No wonder it came as a great shock to Wesley to discover that the very next night she became engaged to Mr. Williamson--and they were married within only four days, a year from the time Wesley and Miss Sophy had met, almost to the day. The editor of this diary relates in a footnote that Wesley referred to her as "Miss Sophy" henceforth. Surely this is a classic case of ambivalence, being torn between intimacy and isolation; or, as Wesley saw it, between marriage and vocation.)

NOTES

1. Erikson, Erik H., Childhood and Society (Enlarged and Revised), New York: W.W. Norton, 1963, p. 263.

2. Ali, A. Yusuf, An English Interpretation of the Holy Quran With Full Arabic Text, Kashmiri Bazar Lahore, Pakistan: Sh. Muhammad Ashraf, 1975, p. 478 (Sura XXIII. 12-14).

3. Wingren, Gustav, Creation and Gospel: The New Situation in European Theology, New York and Toronto: The Edwin Mellen Press, 1979, p. 108.

4. Heren, Louis, et al, China's Three Thousand Years, New York: Collier Books, A Division of Macmillan Publishing Co., Inc., pp. 22-23.

5. Erikson, Erik H., Insight and Responsibility: Lectures on the Ethical Implications of Psychoanalytical Insight, New York: W.W. Norton & Company, Inc., 1964, p. 128.

   See also the author's treatment of sexuality in several contexts: Belgum, David, The Church and Sex Education, Philadelphia: Lutheran Church Press, 1967; Why Marry? Since You Don't Need a License to Love, Minneapolis: Augsburg Publishing House, 1972; and Engagement, Saint Louis: Concordia Publishing House, 1972.

6. Booth, Gotthard, "The Meaning of Sex--Psychosomatic Aspects of Love," in Sex and Religion Today, edited by Simon Doniger, New York: Association Press, 1953, pp. 133-134.

7. Belgum, David, The Church and Its Ministry, Englewood Cliffs, New Jersey: Prentice-Hall, Inc., 1963, Chapter 9.

8. Maslow, A.H., Motivation and Personality, New York: Harper, 1954, Chapter 5.

9. Allport, Gordon, W., Pattern and Growth in Personality, New York: Holt, Rinehart and Winston, 1961, pp. 206 and 550.

10. Booth, Gotthard, Op. cit., p. 134.

11. Sheehy, Gail, Passages: Predictable Crises of Adult Life, New York: E.P. Dutton & Co., Inc., 1976.

12. Ibid., pp. 274-275.

13. Curnock, Nehemiah, <u>The</u> <u>Journal</u> <u>of</u> <u>The</u> <u>Rev.</u> John Wesley, A.<u>M</u>., London: The Epworth Press, 1909, centinary issue, 1938, excerpts from pages 289-337. I believe the excerpts are true to the issue which they are intended to illustrate; but the reader would get a fuller understanding of this matter by reading the entire section. Wesley was unlucky in love later also when he almost married another woman who might have been good for him. The woman he finally married in mid-life turned out to be a shrew.

THOUGHTS FOR DISCUSSION

1. By and large, does the religious group within which you have been brought up deal with sexuality from a positive or negative point of view? Or both? Explain concretely.

2. Why do you suppose that such a large proportion of mental health problems are either caused by, or have a bearing upon sex? Can you think of examples?

3. Comment on the statement: Sex is a private matter; what goes on between two consenting adults should be no concern of society.

4. Give your own personal response to the Yin and Yang symbol.

5. What was your reaction to the "Molly" story? Are such experiences rare? What other instances could you cite in which the socio-cultural setting has been unhelpful or at least perceived negatively by some member of a religious group?

6. What does celibacy mean to you?

7. Hinduism and other interpretations of life, such as pietism, give the impression that there is a quantifiable amount of life force or psychic energy at a person's disposal. If this energy is dissipated or drained off through sexual intercourse, the person has less energy to do more important work. Mahatma Gandhi took a vow of celibacy (brahmacharya) after having been married for many years. He wrote in his biography: "As I look back upon the twenty years of the vow, I am filled with pleasure and wonderment.....In about a month of my returning there, the foundation of Satyagraha (the policy of passive resistance) was laid. As though unknown to me, the <u>brahmacharya</u> vow had been preparing me for it." Comment.

8. Sigmund Freud thought the sex drive, if not expressed directly, would find other outlets in art, work, etc. What does this notion have in common with that in item Number 7, above?

9. Was Wesley's religion a help or hindrance to him in the struggle he had with Miss Sophy? Realizing the paucity of case material provided, let it simply be a jumping off point for your discussion.

10. What should have been said about divorce in this chapter?

CHAPTER 6

AGING AND DYING

When one lives in a youth-beauty-health oriented society,
it should not be too surprising that there is not much support
for aging and dying roles. It has not always been so. In the
antiquity of Moses' day, elders were sought out for counsel and
the very term "patriarch" still implies a respectable role in
society. "You shall rise up before the hoary head, and honor the
face of an old man..." (Leviticus 19:32a) "...and do not
despise your mother when she is old." (Proverbs 23:22b) And even
today, in spite of our stress on youth, we realize that certain
functions require the wisdom that only a long life can accumulate.
Thus, we have known of young prodigies teaching mathematics while
still in their teens; but we find white haired senior citizens
on the Supreme Court bench. This is the difference between com-
putational brain power and seasoned judgment. Aging and dying
are also linked by anyone who pays attention to the insurance
statistics and actuarial tables. As my elderly landlady used to
say when she thought I was getting too cocky, "The old must die
-- but the young may die."

ASPECTS OF AGING

Aging is not a static concept but is culturally structured.
Consider the rapid extension of longevity alone. The geron-
tologist, Sir William Ferguson Anderson, claims that we are
going to have a massive increase of persons 80 years and over
(96% increase).[1] Contemporary culture allows and even encour-
ages denial of aging. If one uses Grecian Formula hair coloring,
it is possible to darken white hair to a younger grey. Use a
little more and all that is left of the grey is just the sug-
gestion of it in the sideburns for a "distinguished look." A
bit more and the sixty-year-old can re-capture the vigor of
forty-five, etc. Could it be that the mature adult might

131

actually wish to look like a youth? Such distortion should be
properly labelled "regression." Or if old age is feared, it may
be denial. If it is true that so many of us will live to an
old age, it is important for us to accept the reality of this
stage of life just as it has been important to accept adolescence
and puberty, mid-life, menopause, and all the other realities
of the life cycle.

SENILITY AN UNHELPFUL MYTH

Sir William Ferguson Anderson, a geriatric physician from
Scotland, wishes that people should stop stereotyping aged persons and attributing all their problems to their advanced age
as though that in itself were a pathology.

> "People tend to take ill when they're older but
> mainly with remediable disease. One can do
> something for almost anybody with cardiac failure.
> One can help most of the people with anaemia.
> One can improve those with urinary symptoms.
> About 12% of the people in our country who come
> with deafness, have got wax in their ears, and
> failing sight can be remedied very frequently
> by getting proper glasses or by a change of
> glasses, or sometimes by a fairly minor opera-
> tion. So it is not a hopeless proposition.
> You can do so much for older people. People
> don't get to be 80 unless they are made of good
> material.....(In "functional mental illness") it
> is important to assess why the brain has failed
> rather than assume that there may be fewer
> neurons. Acute brain failure may be caused by
> fever which may upset the brain temporarily, and
> of course, that is completely remedial.....No
> mother would be happy if you said, 'Your child
> is having convulsions because he is three years
> old.' So nobody, especially no relative, should
> feel happy if the doctor says 'Your mother of 85
> is falling because she is 85."[2]

It has been easy and convenient to lump the aged together without regard for their individual differences, and to let the
syndrome of senility serve as a catch-all for whatever ails
them.

Professor Malamud contended that a series of autopsies
performed on supposedly senile patients at Worcester State
Hospital did not reveal anatomical abnormality. It was his
guess that aged persons were often not expected to use their
senses, and thus their alertness in a given area was diminished

132

by lack of motivation or attention. If no one speaks to you or believes you would be interested in hearing anything, there is not much incentive to exercise the sense of hearing. A contrary incident illustrates the point in reverse. Peter S. was one of my 80-year-old parishioners who was classified generally as hard of hearing. One Sunday, after shaking my hand at the door following worship, I noticed that he had stopped at the foot of the stairs (about ten steps) with his head cocked to one side as if listening. The lady who was at that moment talking with me was one who always had some weird thing to say, often about symptoms of a sexual nature. Peter wouldn't want to miss that for anything and could hear juicy gossip perfectly well. Another elderly person, an arthritic "shut-in" was totally confined to her cold water flat in the slums for the four years I had known her. Unexpectedly she appeared at the 50th anniversary banquet of the congregation, which was being held in a fashionable hotel ballroom. She entered on the arm of the cab driver whom she paid out of her old age assistance money. Yes, we still have much to learn about aging.

TIME AND MEANING

Time means something different at the various stages of life according to William Clemens.[3] Youth considers there is much time left in life and most of their orientation is in the future. Middle aged persons are literally in the middle. The focus changes from time elapsed to time remaining. Hence they think in terms of the present tense and present productivity. "In early old age persons appear to have a sense of time which involves a long interval of past time and an uncertain interval of future time. They tend to find meaning in the past. "Old age is oriented instead to a sense of the 'now'..." The former categories of time can be suspended; that is the luxury of old age. The "now" is different from the "present" of task oriented middle age vocation because one has retired from all that busyness. There is freedom from scheduling and time constraints. In the perspective of the "now" one can meditate and simply experience life. This concept is a heuristic one in that it partakes of what theologians have described as "eternity," which is also devoid of the time categories of past, present, and future; and it also provides the unhurried opportunity for meditation and wisdom (wisdom being distinguished here from informational knowledge, which is so often oriented toward problem solving).

"This radical opportunity for growth which stems from...the 'now' found in old age is often overlooked because of the pain and threat which is associated with its coming. Because of the tendency to identify with achievements and past

roles, moving into the 'now' means giving up
the known, the secure and that meaning in life
which has been earned.....

"Clearly then, the 'now' of old age does not
necessarily become identified as a period of
stale inactivity in which one merely recapitu-
lates what was sown in the developmental crises
of earlier ages. Instead, the inadequate justi-
fications past are experienced as empty and
devoid of meaning.....(and this) enables the
spark of creative growth to emerge continually
as a gift."[4]

This kind of self-acceptance in the experience of old age is
what is meant by grace apart from the "works of the Law."
Erikson would say it is related to the kind of basic trust
with which life hopefully began.

EGO INTEGRITY VS. DESPAIR

As in all of Erikson's ages of man, there is the option of
a positive or negative perspective. This is how he explains the
choice of old age:

"Only in him who in some way has taken
care of things and people and has adapted himself to the triumphs and disappointments adherent to being, the originator of others or
the generator of products and ideas -- only in
him may gradually ripen the fruit of these
seven stages. I know no better word for it
than ego integrity.....It is the acceptance of
one's one and only life cycle.....
"The lack or loss of this accrued ego integration is signified by fear of death: the one
and only life cycle is not accepted as the
ultimate of life. Despair expresses the feeling
that the time is now short, too short for the
attempt to start another life and to try out
alternate roads to integrity.....
"Webster's Dictionary is kind enough to
help us complete this outline in a circular
fashion. Trust (the first of our ego values)
is here defined as 'the assured reliance on
another's integrity,' the last of our values. I
suspect that Webster had business in mind rather
than babies, credit rather than faith. But the
formulation stands. And it seems possible to
further paraphrase the relation of adult integrity and infantile trust by saying that

healthy children will not fear life if their elders have integrity enough not to fear death."[5]

At harvest time, in old age, we reap the results of the growing season whether it be a cultivated optimism or a nurtured pessimism. Has this long life been a blessing or a mistake? Accepted or abhorred? Religious literature is full of the symbolism of this dichotomy: wheat and weeds, sheep and goats, light and darkness. Old age bears in itself the culmination of the motives, thoughts, feelings, values, and life style of many decades. The grumpy oldster very likely did not become crotchety over night. Remember "Tailor Jensen"? He had laid the foundation for ego integrity as he entered positively upon his career as a young confirmand and had pursued that goal in a straight line until the day I visited him as an eighty-year-old man. Saint Paul put it this way: "...whatever a man sews, that he will also reap." (Galatians 6:7b)

The spirit of ego integrity is warmly illustrated by the following letter from the eighty-year-old Bishop Dibelius of East Berlin. Note how his years of struggle within a totalitarian state had not created despair, realism but not cynicism. This Christmas letter was written to an aged pastor friend in America who was dying of cancer.

December 15, 1966

My dear Brother,

Thank you for your letter. Everything you write has a certain melancholy undertone. I sympathize greatly with you.

Our old age brings the parting from the life-work closer and closer. And to adapt oneself to this parting is not always easy. In this time of ours the things of the world run in unpleasant confusion. We imagined so many things altogether differently.

But indeed one cannot demand of nations and churches that, in a period of worldwide crises, they could have happier thoughts for the future. Whoever simply reads the newspapers could, as a German, be pleased that today the problems of the church occupy a wide space in the press. But yet, if one considers the actual situation, a withdrawal of public interest into the innermost

differences of opinion can be observed, since
for the time being the conditions are not to be
externally changed. Everything that is written
on new efforts in the political sphere is only
talk. And the withdrawal into the inside is also
only talk. Only the hope remains to us that
God's government of the world still lasts and
that such times of general decline will one day
yield to a new orientation. The gap between our
modern theology and the life of the individual
Christian becomes bigger and bigger. But in
spite of that we will celebrate Christmas in
joyful trust. And I wish you such a Christmas
from my heart.

At our age one can no longer count on the
recovery of one's strength. Even in one's
prayers one doesn't speak of that anymore. For
us only the request for a blessed hour in which
to die is fitting -- as our fathers said, when
their hour of departure had come.

Greet your dear wife. May God make the
last short stretch of the road easy for us.
May He let His blessing be active upon the life
of our children and grandchildren. This is
more important than that which still remains for
us. I myself am still busy with a final contribution to overcoming the conflicts in our
Christian church. That I can do something effective in this, I must consider out of the
question. But I would like to do my duty until
the last moment!

                              In old friendship,

                              Your faithful
                              Otto Dibelius[6]

Contrast with this sentiment the remarks of the retiring
Dean of a theological school. Usually such a person responds
at the testimonial banquet with a warm glow about what a
privilege it has been to serve all these years. This salty
old soul, however, said simply and abruptly, "If I'd have known
then what I know now, I'd have stayed in the lumber business."
In short, this whole career has been a sordid mistake. The
sadness about that is that it is also too late to start over.

THE MATURE RELIGIOUS SENTIMENT

At this stage is the appropriate place to discuss religious maturity. As Erikson said, "...the fruit of these seven stages" should have ripened. Bear in mind that a person may not necessarily have attained maturity simply because he/she has lived four score years. The personality may have been stunted or fixated at any one of the earlier stages -- childhood, adolescence, or early adulthood. The term "mature religious sentiment" comes from the third chapter of Allport's book, The Individual and His Religion. He listed six criteria which characterize mature religion: "(1) well differentiated; (2) dynamic in character in spite of its derivative nature; (3) productive of a consistent morality; (4) comprehensive; (5) integral; and (6) fundamentally heuristic."

(1) A mature person should be able to discriminate and discern various aspects of life and see them in relationship. The bigot sees issues in over-simplistic and rigid categories. Hence the quip about certain doctrinaire liberals who pride themselves on having forsaken their earlier fundamentalism. Lo, the latter state of that person is as arbitrary as the former. "You can take the boy out of the farm but you can't take the farm out of the boy (substitute rigid fundamentalism for farm and theologian for boy)." Allport explained that "...the very subjects who accept religion unreflectively and uncritically tend to react in an equally unreflective way to their parents, to political issues, to social institutions." I knew one such person as a theological student. His search for heretics was an obsession. Later he transferred to a denomination which was more pure doctrinally until he discovered that many there also could not be trusted with "The Word." He transferred once again only to discover that his new church home was also not safe and it became necessary to excommunicate dozens of theologians and hundreds of theological students and pastors. He saw things as either black or white; but went further, distinguishing between black squares, black triangles, and black dots. Review again our Figure 2 and the differences between the "naive belief" and "mature faith." Mature religion is ecumenical, willing to see value in a variety of patterns and traditions and experiences.

> "If I speak in the tongues of men and of angels, but have not love, I am a noisy gong or a clanging cymbal. And if I have prophetic powers, and understand all mysteries and all knowledge, and if I have all faith, so as to remove mountains, but have not love, I am nothing.....When I was a child, I spoke like

a child, I thought like a child, I reasoned
like a child; when I became a man, I gave up
childish ways." (I Corinthians 13:1-2 and 11)

(2) Mature religion is dynamic and growing, increasing in
ever expanding relationships. Allport said it well:

"Immature religion, whether in adult or
child, is largely concerned with magical thinking, self-justification, and creature comfort.
Thus it betrays its sustaining motives still
to be the drives and desires of the body. By
contrast, mature religion is less of a servant,
and more of a master, in the economy of life.
No longer goaded and steered exclusively by
impulse, fear, wish, it tends rather to control
and to direct these motives toward a goal that
is no longer determined by mere self-interest."[9]

Whatever is organic and alive is always growing. Mature religion should help a person move from the self-love and concern
about one's own identity (adolescence) to the willingness to
share with others, to move toward others in intimacy and concern, compassion and service. This is not a pietistic rejection
of the self, but a social use of the self in a dynamic and
ever-expanding sphere. To refer again to our "spiral of life"
(Figure 1), what is alive grows upward and outward; what is
dying withers and shrinks -- the spiral is reversed and becomes
a whirlpool drawing downward and inward in a constricting
pattern.

(3) Religious ideas are closely linked with behavior; and
the person with a mature religion finds his/her faith and value
system providing constructive moral guidance for behavior.
There is a consistency between theory and practice. The
opposite is likely to draw the chiding "Why don't you practice
what you preach?" One of our doctoral students, Mark Pett,
did his dissertation research on the role of religion as a part
of the decision-making process of those women confronted with
the option of abortion in our University's Early Termination
of Pregnancy Unit.[10] One of the perplexing discoveries was
the statistical fact that the percentage of Catholic women who
had abortions was very nearly the percentage of Catholic women
in the State of Iowa. There seemed to be little correlation
between the stated beliefs, legislative lobbying, etc. on the
one hand and the actual behavior on the other. Perhaps decisions were actually made on the basis of expediency. This
paradox fosters a split personality syndrome, or at best
hypocrisy. (See Chapter 7 on morality and mental health.)

(4) What does it take for religion to be comprehensive enough to embrace sorrow and joy, life and death, success and failure, sin and righteousness, past and future, self and society, etc.? Allport would say it needs to be mature and would function as a "Unifying Philosphy of Life."[11]

> "Religion is the search for a value underlying all things, and as such is the most comprehensive of all possible philosophies of life. A deeply moving religious experience is not readily forgotten, but is likely to remain as a focus of thought and desire. Many lives have no such focus; for them religion is an indifferent matter, or else a purely formal and compartmental interest. But the authentically religious personality unites the tangible present with some comprehensive view of the world that makes this tangible present intelligible and acceptable to him. Psychotherapy recognizes this integrative function being aided by the possession of a completely embracing theory of life."[12]

A person with such a unifying philosophy of life or theological system is not bowled over by unexpected events or a disappointing relationship. To be betrayed by a friend is indeed painful; but the person with some workable doctrine of sin has a better chance of "getting a handle" on the problem. One's theology needs to be comprehensive enough to handle the tragic fact that one's child dies in spite of the sincere prayers of many. Others have need to make sense out of unexpected blessings. The religiously mature person can also live with paradoxes and mystery.

(5) The terms "integral" and "religion" have an interesting relationship. An integer is a whole number as distinguished from a fraction, meaning literally, in the Latin, "untouched, hence, undivided, whole," according to The Random House Dictionary of the English Language. Religio means literally "to bind again" or tie together. A mature religious sentiment is one which helps to keep a person whole or restore one to wholeness if fragmented for a time. Perhaps this is why recent youth who have wanted "to get it all together" searched for religious answers and solutions -- if not in traditional forms then in occult sects or mystery religions. Freud saw immature religion as splitting personality apart: reality vs. illusion and reason vs. fantasy. Since he saw mostly disordered mentation among his patients, he did not have much occasion to see healthy religion at work fostering wholeness and integration of personality.

139

(6) A heuristic stance is one which holds a position or belief with the full realization that a deeper understanding or broader vision may be in the offing. It is the kind of attitude Paul took in his chapter on love. "For now we see in a mirror dimly, but then face to face. Now I know in part; then I shall understand fully, even as I have been fully understood." (I Corinthians 13:12) Faith means not having to know. As I continue to think and act on my beliefs, my experience, insights, and perspective enlarge; my faith grows deeper and more comprehensive. When I was engaged to be married, I believed that I loved Kathie very much indeed; but now, after twenty-five years of marriage, that love has broadened and deepened, been seasoned by experience and sharing a family life. An increasingly mature love has this heuristic aspect that while one claims that love with full conviction, he/she is open to the possibility that it may grow into something richer and more complex. This is what Allport meant by characterizing mature religion as heuristic. "It is characteristic of the mature mind that it can act whole-heartedly even without absolute certainty."[13]

Some persons arrive at maturity sooner than others. For some it takes a very long lifetime before they attain the kind of wisdom that Allport called a "unifying philosophy of life," which they can experience in their "now." It especially stands them in good stead when they contemplate the end of their living as they have always known it, i.e., when they face their dying.

FACING ONE'S DYING

"Then Jacob called his sons, and said,
'Gather yourselves together, that I may tell
you what shall befall you in the days to come.
Assemble and hear, O sons of Jacob,
and hearken to Israel your father.....
Then he charged them, and said to them, 'I
am to be gathered to my people; bury me with
my fathers in the cave that is in the field
of Ephron the Hittite, in the cave that is
in the field of Machpelah, to the east of
Mamre, in the land of Canaan.....When Jacob
finished charging his sons, he drew up his
feet into the bed, and breathed his last
and was gathered to his people." (Genesis
49:1-2, 29-30a, 33)

Here we have ego integrity, voluntary informed consent, destiny, acceptance, autonomy, death with dignity, social

140

support of the dying role; just about everything we moderns
are trying to recover, and maybe could have if it were not for
progress. Concomitant with our dramatic twentieth century
medical progress in curing disease and staving off death, we
had become a death-denying society. Flushed with the success
of so-called wonder drugs, organ transplants, and new medical
technology, we no more wanted to face death than a winning
football coach wants to discuss possible defeat. We began
using military terms for combatting disease, conquering polio,
mounting and all-out attack on cancer, and, of course, defeating
the final enemy, death. The warfare rose to such heights that
it was assumed by some that any death was pathological. Death
was no longer assumed to be a normal part of the life cycle like
it was in the days of Jacob.[14]

A DECADE OF DYING IN FIVE STAGES

The massive public campaign to talk about dying began when
four theological students sought out a psychiatrist to help them
with a research project on "crisis in human life."[15] Dying
seemed like the ultimate crisis; and if these young seminarians
could come to grips with that problem, they would not so likely
be thrown for a loss by lesser stresses of their future
parishioners. Dr. Ross, their mentor, was stumped by the unwillingness of physicians, in the large research hospital at the
University of Chicago, to talk about their dying patients. They
were willing enough to share their patients as "teaching
material" for all kinds of case conferences -- but not dying.
Dr. Ross was puzzled because in her native Switzerland there
was not this taboo, dying had been taken as a matter of course
and many, especially aged persons, died in their own beds at
home, surrounded by family and friends. What a strange reversal:
death had replaced sex as a taboo subject.

From such small beginnings a seminar was created, which was
attended by first curious and then eager health professionals,
for down deep physicians and nurses knew they needed help with
the personally threatening dilemma of death. When Dr. Ross'
seminar hit Life magazine and her book, On Death and Dying,
hit the stands in 1969, she was swamped by television inter-[16]
views, pressing requests to lecture throughout the country.
When this seemingly frail, unimposing woman spoke in her powerfully soft way to over-flow audiences, the effect was electri-
fying. Dying was no longer a taboo subject. Proof that dying
had re-entered our culture came when the famous television star,
Dr. Marcus Welby, had a patient who died exactly according to
the five stages of Ross' book: anger, denial, bargaining,
depression, and acceptance. And a major medical textbook for
students of family practice published in 1977 devotes a 31-page

141

chapter to "Care of the Dying Patient" with a humane and socially conscious attitude.[17]

Perhaps it is typical of our activist culture, but wouldn't you know, an educator has now proposed that there should be continuous "death education" from kindergarten through the twelfth grade. So we go from taboo to over-kill in a little more than a decade.

You may well hope that when you become terminally ill you would not be strung out on a lot of machinery but quietly come down with pneumonia like in the olden days when that condition used to be called "the old man's friend." You could slide into a coma and die in your sleep causing a minimum of agony and expense to your family and friends. Unfortunately death is not always that smooth nor as easy as it seemed for Jacob. Not many dying persons are able to sit on the edge of their bed and give a speech as long as Chapter 49 of Genesis just before they draw their feet up into their bed and die. Shakespeare also has his heroes come center stage and declaim a long soliloquy, often the best speech of the play, just before falling over dead. In the past people hung on a dying person's last words, hoped for a deathbed testimony of faith, or in other ways assumed that this would be his/her finest hour.

Death can be ugly, disgusting, painful, smelly, bloody, grotesque, agonizing. The unattractiveness of dying would be enough by itself to account for the stigma attached to it. We usually attach a stigma to anything that repels us or makes us feel uncomfortable whether that be leprosy, crime, mental illness, serious handicap, odd looking defect, or inadequacy. Who is more inadequate or less productive than the average person in the end stage of a terminal illness or a person gradually dying in advanced age? It would be a perfectly natural reaction to be repelled by such a person and attracted to another friend who happens to be healthy, vigorous, and good looking. It calls for a spiritual grace to do the unnatural thing and draw close in intimacy to the unattractive and threatening, to accept the unacceptable and to love the unlovely. But here we are speaking about how others might relate to you or me when it is our turn to die.

How you have been handling your own personal stigmas thus far in your life may be partly determinative in how you will handle your growing inadequacy in your last hour. Have you relied on beauty, perfection, approval for accomplishment, etc.? What will you do when these are withdrawn or disappear? How have you handled rejection in the past? Now we see how life style is preparatory for style of dying. The behavior observed by Elisabeth Ross was not all that attractive: denial after the physician worked hard to come up with a diagnosis; anger and hostility vented on those who come near, like nurses, physician, and family members; bargaining, which often sounds like whining and self-pity; depression with its negativity and turning inward. Only "acceptance" remains as an attractive and positive response, which is not so likely to turn others away and leave the dying person isolated and alienated, a condition, which studies have shown, the dying dread sometimes more than the death itself -- the fear that they will be abandoned. No wonder Bishop Jeremey Taylor thought it useful to write two meditations: <u>Rules for Holy Living</u> and <u>Rules for Holy Dying</u>. "To die well," "To come to a good end," "To die in a state of grace"; these were goals of an earlier era.

"LAST RITES" OR PREPARING FOR THE LAST JOURNEY

For centuries the Roman Catholic Church offered a special ministry to those "in extremis," extreme unction. Viaticum provided spiritual nourishment for the journey to the life beyond. Although current stress is placed upon the "Sacrament for the Sick" as a prayer of healing, there is still the use of sacramental support as time of death approaches. Less used than formerly, some Protestants had an "Order for the Commendation of the Dying" with prayers for special strength to make up for the believer's own failing powers and with some admonition such as "Depart, o Christian soul unto Eternal Life with God." There were opportunities to rid the soul of any burdens of sin still left unconfessed, support in this significant crisis by the use of Scripture, e.g., "Lord, now lettest thou thy servant depart in peace, according to thy word; for mine eyes have seen thy salvation...," the words of the aged Simeon. (<u>Luke</u> 2:29-30) The dying believer may so identify with the words of the Twenty-third Psalm that he says it along with his minister or rabbi:

> "Even though I walk through the
>   valley of the shadow of death,
>   I fear no evil;
> for thou art with me;
>   thy rod and thy staff,
>   they comfort me." (<u>Psalms</u> 23:4)

Religion can provide the resources for a person to tie loose ends together, to have a positive sense of closure to the tasks and issues of life, to help a person become reconciled to unfinished business, to conclude relationships with some deliberateness and ego integrity. I have deeded my body to the College of Medicine Anatomy Department for teaching and research purposes, and my pastor has a copy of my wishes and suggestions for my funeral when the day comes. This has been done even though I am in excellent health and fifty-six years of age.

Rather than deny death and repress that existential anxiety of what Tillich called "non-being," a testimony of my finiteness, I have found it salutary to bring it up to consciousness and deal with it. There is even a sense in which contemplating one's own end makes the stewardship of one's living more purposeful and deliberate. It has been said that one of the characteristics or capacities which distinguishes humankind from animals is the person's capacity to contemplate his/her own death.

One of our young patients dying of lymphosarcoma over a prolonged period took the time to write his memoirs for the benefit of his family, the hospital staff members, and anyone who might wish to share his thoughts and experience.[18] He wrote thoughts for each sibling and for his father and mother (though she had already died). He was a faithful Roman Catholic and used this medium to draw his life to a close meaningfully. He described two lists of priorities in his life: one before he came down with his terminal illness and the other when he knew he was dying. He was twenty years of age.

Priorities Before Terminal Illness	Priorities after Learning of Terminal Illness
1. To finish school (B.A.)	1. Appreciate life and its beauty
2. To teach or counsel	2. Finish the book on dying
3. Get M.A. in psychology	3. Finish school
4. Get married	4. To teach
5. Get a Ph.D. in psychology	5. To get married
6. Work with troubled people	6. Become a psychiatrist
7. Be thankful to be alive	7. Help people who need you

He admitted some goals in the right hand column were unrealistic but he had to keep some hope as long as he lived. He chose the eight pall bearers for his funeral and commented on some of their reactions to being asked (choked up, couldn't believe it, accepted, or used denial). Finally, he even summoned humor, which Allport said has this in common with religion that it puts things into perspective. "I know my last physical remains will be in good hands. I mean -- hell -- I don't want to be dropped down the stairs in front of the church." He was concerned to put the stamp of his own unique personality upon this last stage of life, his dying. At least he faced his own dying head on.

LIVING WITH GRIEF

Although we will die only once, we will each face many losses. How many have you already faced? The death of a grandparent, classmate, or neighbor? Many of the same dynamics faced in dying are also present in a significant loss. There is the "I can't believe it" and the upset anger; and one may go through considerable depression (some say an average of six months) before finally accepting the loss and getting back to normal equilibrium. A widower came to the conclusion that every marriage ends in sorrow. Divorce is sad, and so is death.

BEREAVEMENT AS VICARIOUS DYING

When you lose something a bit of you dies. If a leg or breast is amputated, a part of you has died, never to return. And it would be perfectly natural to grieve over that loss. If your wife dies you lose the role of husband; the same is true of a daughter, parent, or anyone significant -- you lose that relationship.

Mourning has been called <u>grief</u> <u>work</u> because there is much effort and struggle in making the adjustment to the loss. Especially if the relationship has been very meaningful and intimate, there is a lot of emotional material that has to be worked through before one comes out of the woods, that vague feeling of being lost or at loose ends. The package of life will have to be tied up again and it never will be the same.

So far it sounds as though a person only loses good things through the death of a significant family member, especially spouse. One can also lose something bad, an abusive parent, a wife beating husband, an oppressive relationship. One of my Danish immigrant parishioners lost her husband of forty years. Everyone in the congregation worried about her for she had always been so dependent on her husband, had never learned to drive the car or go shopping on her own. She had always spoken highly of her husband and seemed appreciative of his constant help and support. The surprise to us all was the fact, which became quickly evident, that she was like a bird let out of a cage. Suddenly she was quite competent, quite capable of selling her husband's plumbing tools and car for a good price. She quit buying $40.00 worth of medicine a month since she wasn't going to "waste any of <u>her</u> money on that stuff." And she began going about visiting the sick in the parish. Even a bad marriage takes a lot of adjustment. The spouse may have lost a sparring partner and now has no one to fight with, no one against whom to test his or her strength or worth. Almost universally, bereaved persons need help, and that often turns out to be religious in nature.

Erich Lindemann did for grief what Elisabeth Ross did for dying.[19] He happened to be a psychiatrist at Massachusetts General Hospital when the disastrous Coconut Grove night club

145

fire left so many burn victims in its wake. He was alert to the fact that some burn patients did not seem to recover on schedule, and that the one variable which distinguished them from normally recovering patients was their inability or unwillingness to express their emotions of shock or talk about their sorrow that their spouse or good friend had died in the blaze while they themselves had been spared. It was as though their wounds wept for them. Perhaps a husband felt guilty about not having saved his wife from the flames and may even have cajoled her into going to the night club against her wishes that evening. He deserved to suffer as a form of atonement. Lindemann perceived that it was unhealthy to repress this anguish and observed that patients who cried, spoke of the tragedy, and in other ways expressed their grief progressed much faster in their recovery and healing. His article on the management of the normal acute grief reactions opened up a wide discussion and altered many mistaken notions about bereavement. In other words, those who seemed to "bear up so well" after the loss of a loved one could be in a precarious position; and the one who breaks down or "goes to pieces" should not really have come as a surprise since Sigmund Freud had demonstrated the power of repressed negative emotion and the therapeutic value of its expression in catharsis.

THE FUNCTION OF THE FUNERAL

It is precisely the folk wisdom of all societies that has been the basis for providing ceremonial and social support for the mourners in the form of some kind of funeral or its equivalent. Usually this ceremony has a religious base or sponsorship. Even a family that has not been actively involved in any religious worship for many years will very likely have some "reverend" conduct a service or say a few words at the grave. Somehow there is the intuitive assumption that no person should have to do grief work in isolation. Such funeral ritual will very likely heighten the possibility of the expression of grief because it focuses so specifically upon the fact of death and loss. But, according to Lindemann and the further researches which his investigation stimulated, that would be a desirable result and helpful for mental health.

Considering what was said above about the earlier part of the twentieth century being a death denying epoch, it was only to be expected that grief expression should also be repressed. Evelyn Waugh, in his satire, The Loved One, pointed out how artificial and cushiony the modern morticians had made the funeral. It was epitomized in Forest Lawn which is so peaceful and beautiful that couples go to one of many chapels to be married. Loved ones rest in slumber rooms. Babies are in Lullaby Land. There is very little to symbolize the cold fact that the dead are actually buried there and that the following liturgical passage would have any place on the premises: "...we therefore commit his/her body to the ground; earth to earth, ashes to ashes, dust to dust." Some funeral chapels even have a special "family room" area set off by louvers so that they can see the minister but the congregation would not be able to see the family members weep or express any other unseemly emotion. The mortician may also make up the countenance so that the corpse appears less dead. When a service is announced for such a person, it is because he has "passed on" or "has gone to be with Jesus"; it is not because he died. Euphemisms, cosmetics, landscaping, architecture, customs, and etiquette have all been marshalled at one time or another to deny the reality, the harsh reality, of death.

When I conducted my first funeral in Boston, the funeral director leaned toward me at the graveside and asked if I wished to use earth or flowers for the commital service. I said earth, whereupon he handed me a salt shaker of sterilized white sand. There was also no way of perceiving that there would be a burial because flowers were tucked around the casket to obscure the hole, and the artificial grass was greener, if anything, the closer to the casket one approached.

How different were the funerals I observed my father conduct in rural Minnesota. The bell tolled the number of years the person had lived. The procession from the church to the graveyard was only a short walk and the tomb stones were in clear view every Sunday as we entered the church. Four farmers would grasp the four ends of two ropes which were used to lower the casket into the grave. My father took out his pastor's spade, which was a small one used to shovel dirt into the hole on top of the casket three times at the recitation of the liturgical words (1) "earth to earth," (2) "ashes to ashes," and (3) "dust to dust." Clunk, clunk went the clods of earth upon the casket. This was reality. The person was really dead and was really being buried. If the widow or other family member repressed grief till now, the floodgates usually opened and even the stoical Norwegians cried out their true feelings. Then everyone adjourned to the church basement for a lengthy lunch and much talk about the person who had just died and what a breech or gap had been created by the fact that he/she would no longer be among them. It may have seemed harsher, but it was far healthier than the Forest Lawn scene or the Boston salt shaker program.

Currently, clergy and morticians are more aware of the need for grief work and the usefulness of the expression and socializing of sorrow. Once again we must be aware of the fact that a person or family cannot suddenly turn on a program of good mental health for special occasions like birth, adolescence, marriage, and burial if the overall ethos of their life is one of

repression, alienation, hypocrisy, pretence, fear, and denial.
There needs to be a reservoir of health and strength to draw
upon in the community or church, in the family and friendship
circle, in a unifying philosophy of life and positive value
system. A religion of law, guilt, and punishment was represented by the parochial school teacher who asked two elementary
students if they hadn't been pretty bad since God had had to
take away their father in such an untimely death. Personally,
I find N. F. S. Gruntvig's seasonal hymn much more helpful both
theologically and psychologically. It is earthy, reality-
oriented, expressive of negative emotion, and positive in attitude toward God's love and providence.

> "The leaves are falling everywhere,
> And now the feathered legions
> That filled with song the summer air
> Have left for milder regions.
>
> Where waving fields of golden grain
> Have filled the hearts with gladness
> There only stubbles now remain
> As marks of death and sadness.
>
> But He who feeds the roaming bird
> And clothes the fading flower,
> Is ever with us in His Word,
> The Word of Life and power.
>
> To Him we give our thanks and praise
> For everything He gave us,
> For harvest joys and gladsome days,
> For what He doth to save us.....
>
> For harvest here, and harvest there,
> To God we thanks are giving,
> Who will with us His heaven share
> As Father of the living.[20]

Unfortunately there are losses for which there is no
liturgy and not much social support.

> divorce: the couple may not even be present in the
> Court House, just their lawyers or proxy
> losing one's job: even retirement
> losing friends: one out of four Americans change
> residence each year
> losing status: without a leg to stand on
> losing the Fatherland or the Mother tongue: immigration
> losing one's faith: excommunication?
> losing one's home: fire, flood, or windstorm

```
losing one's property:  through theft
losing one's reputation:  imprisonment or other shame
losing one's health:  invalidism
losing one's youth, beauty, strength, money, _____,
                _____, _____, etc.
```

As with all the stages and tasks of life, we see that there are
many ramifications beyond the obvious. Dying and grieving are
no exception.

We have now concluded all the predictable and chronologi-
cally scheduled tasks of personality adjustment from the cradle
to the grave. There are some stresses and issues which may
befall us at any time along the way, which will be taken up in
the next two chapters.

THE DEATH OF AN OLD PROFESSOR[21]

A woman in Finland has shared a touching account about the
death of her aged father, a retired professor of internal
medicine at the University of Helsinki. He had respiratory
and coronary problems, which understandably slowed him down at
his advanced age (80).

During the physician's long practice, he had granted the
wishes of his aged and terminal patients that they not have
extra-ordinary therapies or heroic measures carried out. He
followed the same plan for his life and felt that it was not
worthwhile to have extensive and expensive diagnostic procedures.

The aged and alert gentleman slowed down with dignity. He
sent home his dark dress suit which was no longer needed, but
requested that three new pairs of pajamas, "as stylish and beautiful as were available," be brought instead.

The daughter refers to his final fever in much the same way
as pneumonia has been described as "the old man's friend." She
writes, "Therefore, it was a triumph for him when his temperature climbed one day to 40 C (104 F). The fever was permitted
as in ancient times, to go on unchecked."

It is toward this kind of acceptance of death at the end of
a long life toward which we are striving to move in America

through the hospice movement, death with dignity legislation, the living will, and widespread discussions about aging and dying.

NOTES

1. Sir William Ferguson Anderson gave several lectures in the medical center at the University of Iowa during the first week in November, 1978, both at the College of Medicine and the College of Dentistry. A central theme was the need to regard aged persons as persons and not merely typical of a category. (See also Anderson's Practical Management of the Elderly, [3rd edition], Oxford: Blackwell Scientific Publications, 1976.) (See also Growing Older: Things You Need to Know About Aging, by Margaret Hellie Huyck [Englewood Cliffs, New Jersey: Prentice-Hall Inc., 1974], for a popular but comprehensive paperback on the subject.)

2. Ibid., pp. 2, 5, and 8 of an unpublished transcript of the above cited College of Dentistry lecture.

3. Clements, William, a lecture given at the College of Medicine, November 1, 1978, entitled "Thoughts on a Theology of Aging: Time and Meaning in the Second Half of Life." See also his article, "The Sense of Life Time in Human Development," scheduled to be published in Journal of Religion and Health, Volume 18, Number 2, April 1979.

4. The above quotes are all taken from Clements' lecture cited above.

150

5. Erikson, Erik H., _Childhood_ and _Society_, pp. 268 and 269.

6. As far as I know this Christmas letter was never published, though it was shared with friends.

7. Allport, Gordon W., Chapter 3, "The Religion of Maturity," from _The_ _Individual_ and _His_ _Religion_, New York: The Macmillan company, 1950. The quote is from pages 64 and 65.

8. _Ibid._, p. 67.

9. _Ibid._, p. 72.

10. Pett, Mark, _Religion_ and the _Abortion_ _Patient_: _A_ _Study_ of _Anxiety_ as a _Function_ of _Religious_ _Belief_ and _Participation_ and the _Decision-Making_ _Process_, Ph.D. Dissertation, The University of Iowa, 1975.

11. Allport uses this title for a section of his 1961 book, _Pattern_ and _Growth_ in _Personality_, pp. 294-307; and in his earlier version of this textbook, _Personality_: _A_ _Psychological_ _Interpretation_, 1937, pp. 225-231.

12. Allport, _Personality_: _A_ _Psychological_ _Interpretation_, p. 226.

13. Allport, _The_ _Individual_ and _His_ _Religion_, p. 81.

14. For previously published thoughts of the author on this subject see _His_ _Death_ and _Ours_: _Meditations_ on _Death_ _Based_ on the _Seven_ _Last_ _Words_, Minneapolis: Augsburg Publishing House, 1958; "Is Peaceful Death a Victim of Progress?", _The_ _University_ of _Iowa_ _Spectator_, Volume I, Number 3, March, 1968, p. 2; and _When_ _It's_ _Your_ _Turn_ _to_ _Decide_, Minneapolis: Augsburg Publishing House, 1978.

15. Ross, Elisabeth, "The Dying Patient as Teacher," _The_ _Chicago_ _Theological_ _Seminary_ _Register_, Volume 47, Number 3, December 1966, pp. 1-14.

16. Kübler-Ross, Elisabeth, _On_ _Death_ and _Dying_, New York: The Macmillan Company, 1969. (See also a readable paperback by Glen W. Davidson, _Living_ _with_ _Dying_, Minneapolis: Augsburg Publishing House, 1975. He worked for a time with Chaplain Carl Nighswonger in the "Program on Death and Dying" in the same Chicago hospital to which reference was made above.

17. Rakel, Robert E., _Principles_ of _Family_ _Medicine_, Philadelphia: W. B. Saunders Company, 1977, Chapter 12.

18. Van Heck, Timothy J., <u>Thoughts</u> <u>on</u> <u>Death</u>: <u>Dying</u> <u>and</u> <u>Living</u>, edited by David Belgum and published by the Clinical Pastoral Education Program, University of Iowa Hospitals, Iowa City, Iowa, 1972.

19. <u>The</u> <u>Annals</u> <u>of</u> <u>Surgery</u> devoted an entire issue to "Management of the Cocoanut Grove Burns at the Massachusetts General Hospital," Volume 117, Number 6, June 1943, pp. 801-965. Stanley Cobb, M.D., and Erich Lindemann, M.D., wrote "Neuropsychiatric Observations" in this issue, pp. 814-824. But the article that is best remembered and most often cited is Lindemann's article, "Symptomatology and Management of Acute Grief," in <u>The</u> <u>American</u> <u>Journal</u> <u>of</u> <u>Psychiatry</u>, Volume 101, September 1944, pp. 141-148.

One who interpreted these insights for clergy was Edgar N. Jackson in <u>Understanding</u> <u>Grief</u>, New York: Abingdon Press, 1957. A more recent work is <u>The</u> <u>Dynamics</u> <u>of</u> <u>Grief</u>: <u>Its</u> <u>Source</u>, <u>Pain</u>, <u>and</u> <u>Healing</u>, by David K. Switzer, also published by Abingdon, 1970.

20. _____, <u>Hymnal</u> <u>for</u> <u>Church</u> <u>and</u> <u>Home</u>, Blair, Nebraska: Danish Lutheran Publishing House, 1938, Hymn #59.

21. Kerppola-Sirola, Irma, "The Death of an Old Professor," <u>Journal</u> <u>of</u> <u>the</u> <u>American</u> <u>Medical</u> <u>Association</u>, Volume 232, Number 7, May 19, 1975, pp. 728-729. (Translated from the Suomen Lääkäritehti, 28:2662, 1974.)

PERSONAL PROJECTS

1. Visit an aged man or woman in a nursing home three times; then answer the following questions:

   (1) To what extent is he/she being treated as an <u>aged</u> person?

   (2) To what extent is he/she being treated as a <u>dying</u> person?

   (3) To what extent is he/she being treated as a <u>patient</u>?

   (4) What is his/her social visibility as compared with pre-nursing home life?

   (5) How permeable are the boundaries between this person and the larger community? In what directions?

(6) To what extent is the milieu specialized?

(7) To what extent is the milieu "pumped out" or enriched? Personal or de-personalized?

These questions are drawn from a list in The Psychological
Autopsy: A Study of the Terminal Phase of Life, Community
Mental Health Journal Monograph No. 4, by Avery D. Weisman
and Robert Kastenbaum and published by Behavioral Publications, Inc., 2852 Broadway, Morningside Heights, New York,
New York, 10025, 1968. The study was conducted at a
geriatric facility, Cushing Hospital, Framingham, Massachusetts.

2.   Prepare your own obituary for the newspaper. Why wait till
the last minute. You will want to include the following
information as closely as you can estimate it from this
vantage point.

(1) Your age at the time of death.

(2) Cause of death? If illness, length of illness.

(3) Survivors. Next of kin, marital status, etc.

(4) Vocational resume up until death including retirement
if relevant. Give names of employers and cities in
which you had worked up to time of death.

(5) Funeral arrangements, disposition of body if by
cremation or burial site. Will there be a service in
a church or synagogue? Where?

(6) Memorials suggested for any charitable purpose?

(7) Disposition of estate through will?

(OK, so you don't want to put it all in the newspaper.
Answer all seven anyway and keep confidential whatever
you wish. Perhaps you will think of other items of
interest and significance as you look back retro-
spectively on your life.)

3.   Attend a funeral as an observer. Ask yourself if it is
repressive-inspirational or oriented toward reality and
expression of grief. How would you describe the behavior
or attitude of the clergy, the mourners, and the
congregation?

CHAPTER 7

SIN AND WHAT TO DO ABOUT IT

Anything that is any fun is either fattening or immoral! That notion began when the Ten Commandments were first set in a negative framework. "Thou shalt <u>not</u> covet" or "Thou shalt <u>not</u> steal." Getting more for myself, satisfying my needs; you're saying that what is good for me is bad? No wonder Freud concluded that in order to have a civilization with its laws and strictures, you would have to pay the price of neurosis; you would have to repress and suppress your wishes, and you would suffer with unmet needs. (We shall return to this issue in the section on Morality and Mental Health.)

Religion has served as the basis and authority for morality, inculcating in its adherents a code of acceptable and unacceptable behavior and undergirding that code with a sense of righteousness. The violation of these standards is sin and is accompanied by shame in the normal person. A great deal of our current law is an elaboration or refinement of the Ten Commandments. Thus instead of the simple "Thou shalt not steal," we have armed robbery, bribery, theft, embezzlement, fraud, shoplifting, illegal possession of property, gambling, and a whole host of other methods of taking something without earning it. Each gradation of theft is carefully categorized so society will know exactly how much punishment to mete out for each level of offense. Theologians have assumed a universal moral capacity ever since Saint Paul wrote, "They (Gentiles) show that what the law requires is written on their hearts, while their conscience also bears witness..." (<u>Romans</u> 2:15a)

Since religion is the agency which has been responsible for creating moral standards, it is natural that it should also be responsible for creating some rehabilitative resource whereby a person who has fallen into disgrace could be restored to a state of grace, could once again become a member in good standing. Methods vary depending upon how seriously a religious group takes its moral standards. The action may be as drastic as "banning and shunning," public ostracism, or as mild as a person sitting in a pew Sunday morning privately confessing his sin to God (no one else in the congregation even knowing he is in trouble). Intermediate methods are priestly confessional, testimony time at mid-week prayer meeting,pastoral counseling, Holy Communion, etc. Any of these may be used as a remedy for sin, a way of getting back to a normal equilibrium. When such a method works well, the person also feels a sense of relief and restoration to self-worth.

Self-worth, you remember, was a theme that ran through several of Erikson's stages of childhood. Sin may reactivate the negative side of stages 2, 3, and 4: "shame and doubt," "guilt," and "inferiority." The reason for bringing up the issue of sin after the whole life cycle is completed is that it is an unscheduled crisis. One may be arrested at 7, 17, 37, 67. One may lie, blaspheme, get drunk, commit adultery, destroy a personal relationship, or even kill another person at a variety of ages. Whenever that happens, the person who is in touch with moral reality (thus excluding the mentally ill sociopath) feels a need to get out of the trouble. Hence the title of this chapter: "Sin and What To Do About It."

WHATEVER BECAME OF SIN?

"The disappearance of the word 'sin' involves a shift in the allocation of responsibility for evil. Perhaps some people are convinced of the validity of the Skinnerian thesis, and no longer consider themselves or anyone else to be answerable for any evil -- or for any good."

"Certainly the greatest impetus toward the new scientific attitude was Freud's discovery (about 1900) of the psychoanalytic method -- the technique of systematic exploration of unconscious psychological processes."

"Gradually the effects of 'the new psychology,' as it was called, began to be apparent and it did seem to many worthy people that morality was being invaded and eroded thereby. Much behavior that would be classed a priori as sinful had long since passed into the control of the law. What was considered criminal and so treated was understandably sinful. And now, increasingly, some crime was being viewed as symptomatic. Sins had become

crimes and now crimes were becoming illnesses;
in other words, whereas the police and judges
had taken over from the clergy, the doctors and
psychologists were now taking over from the
police and judges."2

The above book title and three quotes come not from a
pietistic evangelist but from the patriarch of the Menninger
psychiatric center in Topeka, Kansas, after more than fifty
years of pioneering work in the mental health field. He had
lived long enough to see the pendulum swing from moral judgmentalism to neutral permissiveness. In this chapter on sin
we need to take a realistic look at the role of morality, and
moral lapse, in the functioning of the personality.

Determinism has been espoused philosophically, theologically, psychologically, sociologically, and popularly, the
latter epitomized by comedian Flip Wilson with his quip,
"The Devil made me do it." Determinism lends itself to
rationalization and makes a very respectable justification for
disassociating oneself from a supposedly immoral act, for by-
passing the issue of responsibility, for the defense mechanism
of projection. Much depends upon the use to which this doctrine
is put, and I, for one, would be quite agreeable to accepting
a relative determinism. Case in point: If I am picked up by
a tornado and hurled through my neighbor's picture window, I
do not believe I am guilty in a moral sense; if I harbor a
hostility against my neighbor and pay a boy five dollars to
throw a stone through my neighbor's window, that's another
story. No doubt there are many shades of grey responsibility
in between. I am currently concerned about the _attitude_ one
takes toward his/her behavior; is it to be as responsible as
possible or to strive to be as _irresponsible_ as possible?
Let's get down to some specific cases.

CASE 1: FROM REPENTANCE TO SELF-JUSTIFICATION

A high school teacher was arrested outside a neighbor's
bathroom window for being a "Peeping Tom." His first impulse
was to explain that he had taken a short cut home from work and
was looking for his wallet, which he thought he might have
dropped while hurrying home for supper. Then, he told me, he
decided that he had had enough of this clandestine behavior,
this compulsive habit he had developed over the last two years.
He would admit he had done wrong, take his medicine, seek
therapy and marriage counseling, since he had a fine wife and
two cute boys whom he did not wish to lose. He was mystified
about his bizarre behavior because he seemed to have all his
"needs" met: great family, good job, community status, excellent health, many friends, the works. This was all told

to me on my first visit with him shortly after he was admitted
to the mental hospital for treatment as an alternative to going
to jail. In a couple weeks he had done a remarkable about face
concerning his responsibility for his unacceptable behavior.
He explained that he had learned a lot while in the hospital.
He now understood that there were many factors in his earlier
life which had <u>conditioned</u> him to be like he was today. He had
<u>come down</u> with a mental illness, and it was quite unconscionable
that he should have been arrested. After all, you do not arrest
someone for coming down with pneumonia or cancer; you don't haul
him before a judge and sentence him. He was now contemplating
suing not only the police for arresting him but also the newspaper which had violated his rights by publicizing his "disease."
I had the distinct impression that he was getting further from
rehabilitation in this latter state than he was in the earlier
repentant frame of mind.

CASE 2: "MY MOTHER MADE ME DO IT."[3]

Preliminary to some marriage counseling, I was seeing the
husband, who first presented himself with the stated purpose of
saving the marriage. There had been considerable fighting and
abuse on his part, which he readily admitted. It quickly became
apparent that he had been in counseling and psychotherapy on
several occasions and had signed up for the course, "A Little
Learning Is A Dangerous Thing," because he had picked up just
enough psychological jargon to defend himself. He smoothly
explained the "insight" he had gained thus. He had much
resentment against his stepmother (which was a long story that
held together very well). As a result of his early experiences
with his stepmother, he had always felt hostility toward women
even though he wished for intimacy; a clear case of ambivalence,
loving and hating his wife at the same time.

I calmly asked him, "On the last occasion when you beat your
wife, if she had called the sheriff, what would the charges have
been, if any?" He answered, "I don't think she ever would --
as a matter of fact it never occurred to me. But I guess she
would have a case; the charge would be assault and battery." I
pushed on. "And who would be tried and sent to the workhouse
for thirty days? You or your stepmother?" You may well wonder
at this odd remark; but because we had established a good
relationship, he fortunately did not perform assault and battery
on me. He was willing to explore the unworkable hypothesis on
which he was evaluating his behavior. Logically, you should
arrest the guilty party if there is to be any justice at all.
Even if he were not willing to accept responsibility for his
behavior, he knew the sheriff, the judge, jury, and society
would jolly well not throw his stepmother in jail because <u>he</u>

had beaten his wife. It just doesn't work that way in the real world even if some armchair philosopher says otherwise.

Actually, it was nothing I did or said which turned this "sinner" (notice how I still furtively put the word in quotes) around; there was some moral switch within himself which he had to turn on. In an earlier day we would have said that his "conscience" had finally gotten through to him with the message of responsibility.

CASE 3: THE TERRIBLE TEENAGERS

While working as a therapist in the educational department of a large state hospital (Ypsilanti, Michigan), I tried a free-wheeling experiment with a small group of boys who were almost completely out of control. They were all a combination of delinquency and mental illness, too anti-social for the detention centers and clinics in Detroit and other facilities throughout the state. Their language was profane and hostile, their sketches on textbook covers were pornographic and vulgar even to the non-prudish. Their thought patterns followed a very narrow and short rut indeed. One fifteen-year-old boy from Detroit was capable of fabricating a home made gun which would shoot accurately for 100 feet.

I was puzzled how to begin relating these ruffians to the society to which we were hopefully returning them. It did not appear that any of them would be socially responsible enough to hold a job for more than a day. If they were discharged before age sixteen, how could they be tolerated in the average school for even a short time? I decided to treat them as though they were responsible for what they said and did hoping to start a chain reaction of self-fulfilling prophecy. So far they had been treated as though they were not to be taken seriously; after all, every other word was abuse or profanity, hardly a grammatically sensible string of words among them.

It is well known that some persons will "act out" to get attention. A child might prefer being spanked for mischief to being ignored as though he/she did not count at all. We have seen in some mental hospital wards that the person who "talks crazy" and performs weird and destructive behavior gets the attention of a whole bevy of staff personnel, whereas the patient who makes no trouble may be ignored. Hospitals practicing behavior modification therapy, or operating a "token community," reward positive behavior and ignore or play down unacceptable behavior. I decided to take what each child said seriously and assume he meant exactly what he said and that his behavior was meaningful and purposeful. Such rough kids had usually been scolded, reacted to, punished, etc., but seldom taken seriously with genuine capacity and worth attributed to them.

The next time Elwood said, "God damn this wood" while building a bird house in the shop, I tried my approach. "I notice you are praying, Elwood; but I'm puzzled -- I thought you were trying to build a bird house up, but you are praying God to destroy it." Later, Lester was drawing a picture of two persons in intercourse on the inside of his textbook making quite sure that I saw it. (They were aware of my ordained status and often tried to shock me.) I commented, "I see you have a lot of interest in art, Lester; but your drawings look flat and not warmly lifelike. The human body is round. I'm sure Mrs. Potter, our art teacher, would be glad to help you improve your sketches." Another blurted out in disgust, "Fuck this reading book!" I inquired, "I don't understand. How can you have sexual intercourse with a reading book?" Never once did I say "Don't" or "Stop it" or "Behave yourself." That they had heard a thousand times, and no one had ever assumed these kids meant what they said. I was holding them responsible for every word they said and act they did and kept on asking how this was meeting their needs and helping them get what they wanted out of life. If they wanted not to get to go to the picnic, disruptive behavior made perfect sense, because this was exactly how not to go to the picnic. My goal was to help them accept responsibility for their decisions, their words, and their actions.

Within six weeks these "terrible teenagers" began challenging each other in class: "Elwood, don't talk nonsense," or "Say what you mean." It was quite a remarkable experience and made me reflect on the dynamics of morality and sin. So much of morality seems to be non-functional. It is a way for grown-ups to lord it over kids. "Just do it because I say so!" or "It's always been this way; just do it." Somehow they had never seen that whereas anti-social behavior might bring some short-term gains, it was not productive in the long run. That pertains to stealing, lying, and many other behaviors formerly included under the general umbrella of "sins." Sooner or later some "sin" is so costly or offensive to society that it is labelled a crime and the consequences are unpleasant and long lasting.

THE CLASSIC JUDEO-CHRISTIAN ANSWER

As a very early precursor to John Dewey, the biblical assumption is that before you can find an answer, you must first state the question or problem clearly. Repentance implies that the sinner knows the problem, that he/she has erred, done something that is socially or morally destructive, has violated a mandate of society about which there is common consensus among significant others. Without getting into the ethical niceties of which group's standards to use as criteria (Islamic, Hindu, Southern Baptist, Mennonite, Unitarian, Jewish, Episcopalian, or Communist), we would do well to use O. Hobart Mowrer's pragmatic definition of guilt: "If a person does something he does not want to have known, he is guilty." The repentant response to this state of mind is to experience guilt in a psychological sense, a sense in which the sinner feels alienated from his family or group of significant associates, feels the suffering of estrangement and loneliness. The penitent knows intrinsically that he/she has done wrong, is guilty.

Such moral isolates are encouraged to seek re-integration into their group through admitting their offense and praying for mercy, forgiveness, and reconciliation with both God and other persons, especially those offended against. This implies an intention to forsake the sinful and destructive behavior and return to an open, responsible, and honest relationship with the other members of the group or even society at large. Traditionally this has been called <u>confession</u>. The following rubric from the <u>Book</u> <u>of</u> <u>Common</u> <u>Prayer</u> introduces and invites this initiative on the part of the sinner:

> "<u>Then shall the Priest say to those who come</u>
> <u>to receive the Holy Communion.</u>
>
> "Ye who do truly and earnestly repent you
> of your sins, and are in love and charity with
> your neighbors, and intend to lead a life,
> following the commandments of God, and walking
> from henceforth in his holy ways; Draw near
> with faith, and take this holy Sacrament to your
> comfort; and make your humble confession to
> Almighty God, devoutly kneeling."[5]

Why make such a big fuss about repentance and confession? Why can't we just plain accept everyone since we are all human and "to err is human"? From God's point of view sin is sin.

> "You have heard that it was said to the
> men of old, 'You shall not kill; and whoever
> kills shall be liable to judgment.' But I
> say to you that every one who is angry with
> his brother shall be liable to judgment; who-
> ever insults his brother shall be liable to
> the council..."[6] (<u>Matthew</u> 5:21)

Theologically this may be true; but in our society, when
Secretary of Agriculture Butz made his off-hand racial reference
while relaxing with some persons on an airplane, he was not
sent to prison, but he certainly lost his job in a hurry.
Meanwhile, if one work crew member insults another, a simple
"I'm sorry" should suffice. There does not need to be a confession and apology over television or in the newspaper. Different persons have smaller or larger circles of "significant
others." In the social fabric, one needs to mend the garment
where it is torn and for as far as it is torn.

In the Roman Catholic Sacrament of Penance, the third part
is "satisfaction" or living satisfactorily and constructively
instead of sinfully and destructively. It is assumed that the
penitent has "aversion to sin" and is now eager to live a more
wholesome life out of gratitude for his forgiveness and rescue
from disgrace. Proverbs 26:11 states the opposite alternative
in an unappetizing way: "Like a dog that returns to his vomit
is a fool that repeats his folly." No room for "cheap grace"
here. Amendment, satisfaction, sanctification, whatever one
calls it, is the goal; it implies that the sinner is not only
forgiven but returned to a state of grace, restored to a worthy
calling (vocation) and heeding the conscience and moral guidelines so that he/she may lead a more useful life. Now he/she
can invest the energy in constructive service which was formerly
wasted in destructive selfishness. One liturgical form of
absolution following confession of sin exemplifies this dynamic:

> "The Almighty and merciful God grant unto you
> being penitent, pardon and remission of all
> your sins, time for amendment of life, and the
> grace and comfort of his Holy Spirit."
> (emphasis mine)[6]

What about the sin which seems so final because the one
sinned against is now dead and there is surely no way to make
amends? One reason for crying over spilled milk is that there
is no way one can wipe it all up and wring it out of the towel
back into the bottle. In a religion providing forgiveness
there is the assurance that one can be accepted nevertheless
because of the gracious attitude of the one sinned against.
The classic passage quotes the Lord as saying,

> ..."though your sins are like scarlet,
> they shall be as white as snow;
> though they are red like crimson,
> they shall become like wool." (Isaiah 1:18b)

So far we have spoken mostly of sacramental or formal
methods of dealing with sin in a therapeutic manner. We should

not overlook private, personal, meditative, worship-related, spontaneous handling of such distress which works for many persons. They may choose to discuss a problem casually with an uncle or friend, a fellow worker or even a stranger and get the help they need. Another may be in the midst of a prayer meeting or Bible study group and feel free to ask the members to share in his/her burden and find release and new direction. The mode depends upon the tradition of the individual and personal temperament as well as past experiences which have demonstrated that a given approach will likely be helpful.

What implications does this rehabilitative process have for our Spiral of Life? Quite clearly the person caught in a self-oriented sin is focusing on a group of one, not a very large fellowship. The hypocrisy, secrecy, and defense mechanisms used to hide this unacceptable behavior from significant others are constricting and isolating. The person would rather not be known for who he/she really is. In response to the question, "Who are you"? the sinner hopes the answer can be slanted to create a better image than the true identity. I hope you think I am an honest business man and that you will not discover the real "me" who is an embezzler, an alcoholic, an adulterer, a liar, or any other revelation of the dark side of the self. Self-regard shrivels, travel patterns are circumscribed to avoid running into certain embarrassments, associates are defensively chosen, and speech has to be guarded in certain circles (smaller and smaller circles). This is illustrated by the upper whirlpool in Figure 18.

In the upward thrusting spiral at the bottom of Figure 18, we see how the tightly bound and isolated individual can gradually be released to trust larger relationships, to share in a more open, more expansive sphere of influence. No longer does he/she have to fear that persons will find out who he/she is by some careless slip of the tongue. He stands up at the meeting and says, "My name is Jack and I'm an alcoholic." In the Speech Clinic we admitted we were stutterers and quit hoping others would not discover our "secret." Such a person is surprised to discover more acceptance than he/she had thought. Society finds honesty more attractive than hypocrisy. This does not mean that others are obligated to like stutterers, alcoholics (even recovering ones), ex-cons, etc.; but at least everyone knows where the person stands, and who that person really is. Before, in the state of hidden and shameful sinfulness, there was a certain mystery and untrustworthiness about the person. Now there are enlarging concentric circles of fellowship, relationship, and interaction. Socialization is enhanced as the person goes about seeking to amend his/her life and invest energy in constructive service instead of destructive and self-defeating sin.

163

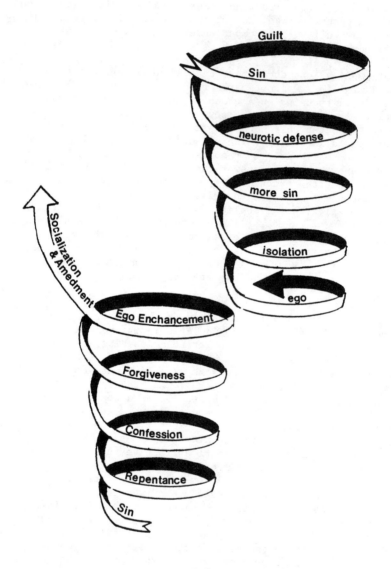

Fig. 18   Constriction or Enlargement of Moral Living Space

164

MORALITY AND MENTAL HEALTH

One of the Greeks said that the good man dreams about what the bad man does not have to dream about (because he does it, of course). A popular notion of the psychoanalytical explanation for neurosis was that a person got sick from trying to be too good -- repressing sexual desires and aggressive tendencies. This wishful thinking (not acted upon) led to frustration; the forbidden thoughts were repressed down into the subconscious something like putting the garbage into a dank cellar and then quickly shutting the trap door. Needless to say, it doesn't go away, it just ferments and gives off a lot of methane or other noxious gases. Repressed desires stew like that in the subconscious and either explode or seep out in unexpected ways, an anxiety attack, a phobia, a psychosomatic symptom like paralysis, or even a serious depression. The conscience (Super Ego) and excessive moral baggage was what weighed the person down. He/she needed to be freed from the over-severe voice of conscience.

O. Hobart Mowrer and others challenged this view of morality as a mischief maker.[7] Both in the role of academic psychologist and as a client in psychoanalysis, Mowrer began to feel that his personality needs were not being met. Something was missing in his treatment. It was not his "Id" (natural instinctive drives) that was being repressed, but his "Super Ego" (conscience). As he looked around among his fellow patients being treated for depression and other emotional disorders, he noticed that they too had been hiding significant parts of their lives. When I first heard him lecture on this theme, I was struck by the cogency of his argument. He diagrammed two curves on the board representing divergent constructs of socialization as shown in Figures 19 and 20. The so-called normal curve elucidates Freud's view that neurotic persons have been over-socialized and are trying to be too good, too moral -- suffering from excessive repression. Obviously the treatment of choice is to move the client toward the left -- ease up on the moral standards and "live a little." This theory operates under the assumption that neurotics have been too scrupulous in their observation of moral precepts.

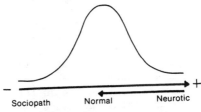

Fig. 19   The Freudian Schema of Socialization[8]

165

The reason Mowrer's criticism clicked with me is that I had wondered about the same thing as a result of attending many staff case conferences in mental hospitals and counseling clinics. The clients had put a great deal of store upon confidentiality, which, on the face of it, seems reasonable enough since we prize privacy so much in America. But the material revealed in interview or case record indicated a series of behaviors, which the client understandably wished to keep confidential because these acts were indeed shameful, some even criminal. They included child abuse, dishonesty, sexual perversions (by the clients' own standards), unfaithfulness about commitments marital and otherwise, theft, attitudes of hatred and revenge, secret alcoholism and drug addiction, cheating by falsifying documents, etc. These were actual misdeeds, not just wishful thinking.

Mowrer conjectured that the psycho-dynamic involved was precisely the old principle of retribution. They had not been "caught" so their misdeeds were not public nor punished; yet they somehow had a sense of moral justice which told them that they ought not to be getting off scot-free. They were punishing themselves with psychic unhappiness much like the accident prone patient "arranges" unconsciously to injure himself to meet a similar need. Here was the Book of Job re-visited. Under certain circumstances it would appear persons did, or could, suffer for their sins in a kind of self-induced retribution.

Lest you become incensed at this return of "moralism," like the person who claimed such understandings would put the counseling movement back fifty years, we should be clear that there can be many causes for mental illness or neurosis: genetic predisposition, glandular anomalies, or organic lesions like brain tumors, horrendous environmental circumstances which brutalize the human spirit like concentration camps or child abuse. For the moment we are discussing only those emotional and personality problems in which clearly accepted standards of morality have been violated, especially the standards to which the client himself assents or which represent the group to which he claims to belong or wishes to be considered a member.

Some children have never been reared in such a way as to develop frustration tolerance. They have always had their every desire and wish fulfilled. Then, when an adult responsibility faces them, such as marriage or child rearing or earning a livelihood through some job, they find the stresses too great and seek a short-cut through infidelity, child abuse, or embezzlement. They wish their misdeeds kept confidential because they cannot stand to face the consequences: the famous eat-your-cake-and-have-it-too syndrome. Fortunate is that child who was helped to face little disappointments when a little child, and a graduated series of hurdles and frustrations as he/she matured through later childhood and adolescence. Then going without sexual gratification while the spouse is absent a while will not seem so impossible a task; and going without a desired object until one has earned enough money to buy it will not seem unbearable in adulthood. Child psychologist Florence Goodenough first set me onto this understanding of frustration tolerance, which could also be called "living with the law."

In Figure 20 Mowrer agrees with Freud that the sociopath is at the extreme left, the truly unsocialized individual once referred to as the "moral imbecile." That person has never assimilated the ideals of society as his/her own, has never found any relationship worth having enough so as to worry about losing it through betrayal. Some worry that this percentage of our population is on the increase. (Please refer to "The Dilemma of the Will" in Chapter 2, also "Marriage as Religious Support" Chapter 5 for the Russian experience.)

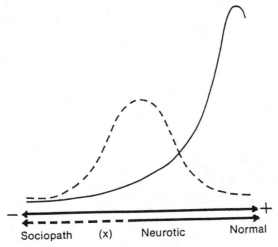

Fig. 20   Mowrer's Schema of Socialization[9]

The difference in Mowrer's schema (a J-shaped curve rather than a normal curve) is that normalcy is at the far right, i.e., the majority of persons go to work, obey the laws, pay their taxes, etc. Or, and this is important, some who do not are either arrested, have repented and revised their behavior, or in other ways have not remained in secrecy about their conduct. He maintained that what plagued the neurotic from a moral point of view was behavior that was both unacceptable and secret at the same time. Tragic consequences could follow from urging the client to move to the left, since that leads away from normalcy and toward sociopathy. This would account for some

clients who come apart at the seams when they have been "freed
up" in therapy, like the high school teacher arrested as a
"Peeping Tom" referred to as "Case 1: From Repentance to Self-
justification." On the other hand, "Case 2: My Mother Made Me
Do It" moved to the right in the course of therapy and accepted
increasing responsibility and was able to speak openly about his
problems in a group.

"Whatever became of sin?" It's still with us, and the solution is about the same as it has always been; only the players
and some of the lines have changed.

A CASE OF PENANCE THAT WORKED

The best way for me to illustrate the dynamics of this
chapter is to cite a case from beginning to end. (Anonymous, of
course, but the client, years ago, gave me permission to
describe his experience hoping it would "be helpful to the next
fellow.") The "beginning" for me was when the wife initiated
the contact.

Oct. 5   Sam's wife, age 43, had been an Episcopalian until
their minister had been defrocked for homosexuality;
she had not attended since. Her husband and son are
in a small business together, which is floundering because of
the husband's drinking and irresponsibility in the sales end of
the enterprise. Sam drank whiskey until he came down with T.B.
and was hospitalized in the VA Hospital. Now he drinks only
beer. To bring in some much needed money, he had become involved in political corruption serving a crooked ring as the
collector of bribes and pay-offs. After one of the elections
a political figure was murdered, and Sam's business card was
found at the site. Although innocent of the murder, the
association was still a scandal. Other rumors of running a
whore house, etc., were circulated about Sam, often not true,
but reflecting an unsavory reputation in the community.
Ironically, Sam knew he did wrong in the political corruption
but was resentful that he had not been paid more for his part
since other crooks were now wealthy. The session ended with an
invitation to the husband if he wished to come the following
Thursday. The wife, meanwhile, agreed to continue coming for
her own counseling needs.

(5:30 p.m. the same day the wife called in distress
indicating that Sam had told his daughter-in-law that
life was not worth living and was now sound asleep in
the bedroom. He had said no one would miss him if he did away
with himself. I urged her to waken him and talk about it and
call me back, which she did. He indicated he wished to see me.)

Oct. 9   Sam began by telling about his job, the crooked poli-
          tics, and the close scrape with the murder scandal.
Then he divulged that whereas he had been very true to
his wife and does not "cheat on her," he admitted that there had
been a couple lapses in infidelity. He despises psychiatrists
(having seen five in the service and afterwards) and asked if I
were one. I clarified my role as pastoral counselor. His present complaint is that in the last six months he has been "going
to pieces." "I am getting edgy, nervous, sweat, can't write
checks or call on customers, perspired just coming to see you."
After a brief reference to his wife's comment that he is "too
sociable" in his drinking, we agreed to meet again.

Oct. 13   Told in more detail about his collecting and handing
          over bribes and graft money to underlings of high
          state officials, some as high as $500 a month. He
had continued this after the scandal even though he had promised
his wife he would quit. When I commented on his sliding over his
infidelity casually last time, he opened up extensively on a
long series of lying and hypocrisy and how he was not only two-
faced but wore many masks in the community. Finally, this lying
became a whole way of life built into all his relationships, with
his son in the business, with customers, fellow members in the
local American Legion Post. His wife thought he drank only
beer; but he had devised a cunning scheme to keep a stable amount
of alcohol in his system. He secretly drank vodka (odorless
to his wife and son and customers), bottles of which were
hidden around home and at the small business. Then one beer
or two was enough to give him a "glow"; and no one assumes a person is an alcoholic if he drinks one beer with lunch. He wept
as he reported that that afternoon he had driven down to the
river and sat about three hours wondering if he should drown
himself. He wanted to see me again.

Oct. 13   Sam's wife told a long story of her husband's going
          from one job to another. Great weeping about the
          problems her husband had caused her and how she takes
one highball an evening to ease the tensions of the day. She has
had to provide what financial stability there has been in the
home and she does not like this role of having to be "the head
of the house."

Oct. 16   Sam continued confessing his political and marital
          wrong-doing. I sensed that there was still lack of
          genuine repentance because he often focused on the
faults of others, wished mostly for symptom relief. It is
premature to pronounce the absolution over a penitent whose
major confession is that "my wife thinks I drink too much," "my
son doesn't understand me," and "I've had a pretty tough life."
This would need to become part of our agenda before progress

169

could be made; yet I do not want to stand in judgment over him like a self-righteous parson.

Oct. 19   During this session Sam began to accept responsibility for <u>his</u> part in his problem and the deep remorse in his tears were not difficult to diagnose. He felt a revulsion for his past life style unmitigated by rationalizations. I asked if he would like to be restored to his church. After all, I was a stranger whom he had only recently met, and from whom he had not been alienated to start with. In his local parish, he had sometimes sought relief through reception of the Eucharist, but it had never helped, and he had gone away disappointed. We discussed how he had been ambivalent about his behavior. How he had first passed over his infidelity lightly and with no feeling, the story he had told five psychiatrists in well rehearsed case study fashion. How he had admitted it was wrong to be in graft, but wished he had gotten a bigger payoff (hardly over 60% on the repentance scale). I proposed that he could make use of the church's ministry of private confession if he felt ready for that; but not to do it until he felt deeply genuine about it this time. He asked if I would help set up such an appointment as he had not been in the church for a long time and felt strange about it.

(I was also glad to visit with the Episcopal priest about the forthcoming sacramental confession since it could be run through as just another liturgical duty. Sure enough, the priest said that no more than 1 or 2 percent of his parishioners ever made use of sacramental private confession. He explained the denominational rubric as "all may, some should, none must." He agreed to pay serious attention to Sam when he came, and would try to be supportive of him in the future.)

Oct. 26   Sam picked me up at 3:00 p.m. and we talked about ten minutes before entering the church. He spoke of "being afraid, scared stiff and nervous." He had shared some of his remorse with his wife and she knew that he was coming for this ministry of reconciliation today. I urged him to hold nothing back but make this a total experience of sharing with the priest, to trust himself to honesty. He told the priest that he would like for me to sit in the back of the church as his moral support. The priest sat in a chair inside the altar rail, and Sam kneeled for the lengthy and deeply remorseful confession. He sobbed and wept loudly during the process, which I could hear, but the statements were between the two of them and God. I sat in the back profoundly moved and prayed for Sam in his agony of struggle and release. After the benediction he shook the rector's hand warmly, thanked him and said he would be back Sunday to receive Holy Communion.

Sam told me on the way to the car how grateful he was for this release, "like a great burden has been lifted from my shoulders. I appreciated our talks together but without this it would not have been complete. Why didn't I do this fifteen years ago Today I have a new start in life."

(Sam and his wife found a new fellowship in the church, but, as you can well imagine, it was not finished. We had followed the Sacrament of Penance through the first two steps of repentance and confession and the priest had declared the words of forgiveness in the absolution. There remained yet the third step of amendment of life. To make a long story short, Sam and I went on to open Alcoholics Anonymous meeting and he willingly accepted that program of further rehabilitation. By now he was already past step 5. It was December 4th before he got rolling in AA, but there was steady progress from then on. Over the years he has sponsored numerous fellow alcoholics into the program and has created several new chapters in neighboring communities. He and his son became not only reconciled but very effective partners in the business, which now thrived. Sam's wife continued to grow in her own way and became active in Al-Anon. We kept in touch for several years. Sam now had a better understanding of sin and also what to do about it.)

NOTES

1. Menninger, Karl, Whatever Became of Sin?, New York: Hawthorn Books, Inc., 1973.

2. Ibid., pp. 17, 39, and 45.

3. This case is cited in my book, Guilt: Where Religion and Psychology Meet, Chapter 4, "Patient and Penitent," Englewood Cliffs, New Jersey: Prentice-Hall, Inc., 1963, pp. 53-54.

5. _____, The Book of Common Prayer and Administration of the Sacraments and Other Rites and Ceremonies of the Church, New York: The Church Pension Fund, 1945, p. 75.

6. Service Book and Hymnal, Minneapolis: Augsburg Publishing House, 1958, p. 16.

7. Mowrer, O. Hobart, The Crisis in Psychiatry and Religion, Princeton, New Jersey: D. Van Nostrand Company, Inc., 1961. See also his The New Group Therapy, D. Van Nostrand, 1964; "Abnormal Reactions or Actions?" a chapter in Introduction to Psychology: A Self-Selection Textbook, Editor Jack

171

Vernon, Dubuque, Iowa: Wm. C. Brown Company, Publisher, 1966; and "Changing Conceptions of Neurosis and the Small-Groups Movement," Education, Volume 97, Number 1, Fall, 1976, pp. 24-62. A survey of the decade of debate that resulted from Mowrer's criticism of the Freudian interpretation of the role of morality in mental illness was written by W. Robert Sorensen, From Sigmund Freud to O. Hobart Mowrer: The Emergence of Integrity Group Therapy. An Evaluation from the Perspective of Pastoral Counseling, Ph.D. Dissertation, University of Iowa, 1977.

8. I heard Mowrer explain these two diagrams (Figures 19 and 20) several times during 1961 and 1962.

9. See Mowrer, "Abnormal Reactions or Actions?", supra, p. 32.

A CASE OF YOUR OWN AND SOME QUESTIONS

1. Assume that you are the College Chaplain or a member of the Board of Directors of a small, church-related college, which is known for its strict moral standards. There may be no beer in dormitory rooms and a recent room check resulted in several dozen students being fined for violating that rule. Last spring the President of the college refused permission for the production of a modern drama which he considered too risque. Now, this fall, the state's largest newspaper carries the headline, "College Head Granted Leave; Arrested in 'Hooker' Case." It turns out that he had solicited a policewoman decoy for the "act of sex with pay."

    (a) As a member of the Board of Directors how would you recommend that this matter be handled?

    (b) As the College Chaplain how would you proceed?

    (c) As a member of the drama class how would you react?

    (d) Should the President be fined, jailed, fired, disciplined (how?), defrocked (he was an ordained pastor), excused, forgiven, ignored, _____?

    (e) Should the man's social status and profession enter into the discussion or should all be treated "equally," president, professor, secretary, janitor, student, etc.?

2. Would a "moral inventory" be as useful for you as for an Alcoholics Anonymous member?

3. What facts about yourself do you not wish to have known?

4. What would be the social or economic consequence if these matters were known?

5. What price are you currently paying for your "secrets"?

6. Would you benefit from more "openness" and honesty in your life?

7. Discuss the proposition: Hypocrisy is safer than honesty.

8. Define: shame, guilt, sin, crime, rebellion, poor etiquette, immorality, and mistake.

9. On what grounds or basis is the following appropriate: punishment, discipline, education, forgiveness, repentance, rehabilitation, and counseling?

10. Do you perceive of morality as primarily positive or negative? Discuss how you arrived at this view.

CHAPTER 8

ILLNESS AND HEALTH: CURSING AND BLESSING

The linkage between religion and health goes back in time immemorial. Consider just a few of the divinities from classical Greek and Roman times, and you will note the legacy they have left in our language:

Hygeia	the former title of the American Medical Association's lay magazine now called Today's Health
Panacea	literally - "cure all"
Uterina	was blamed for difficult labor in childbirth
Mania	the goddess of insanity
Asclepius	the father of Hygeia and Panacea and the god of healing for whom many temples and health spas were named (His serpent-entwined staff is today the symbol of the medical profession and reminds us of the serpent of brass which Moses erected upon a pole for healing his people.)

Healing connected with shrines, places made holy by association with the extraordinary experiences of special people, are resorted to by the sick and crippled. For example, the Grotto where Saint Bernadette Soubirou had her special encounter with the Blessed Virgin Mary draws millions of sick pilgrims to Lourdes in the southwest of France. In Saint Joseph's Oratory of Mount Royal, Montreal, Canada, may be seen in the votive chapel, crutches and braces left behind by grateful believers.

It is reminiscent of the Temple of Asclepius where grateful, healed persons would leave a memento of the improved body part in the form of a carved or moulded ankle, breast, knee or ear. At Saint Joseph's Oratory, penitents ascend the ninety-nine steps on their knees and in a state of prayer. Some are wheeled in or are carried on stretchers to the holy place. Another 179 steps bring one finally to the main church.

> "Most of the manifestations of divinity recorded in Holy Writ were staged on heights, to wit, Mount Sinai, Mount Thabor, Mount Calvary and the Mount of the Beatitudes. What more suitable a symbol could be found of the heights of holiness to which we must all aspire, than the glorified summit of a mountain?"[1]

Every age has its religious healers, usually with a large following. Mary Baker Eddy created an entire denomination, Christian Science, with healing central. Amy Sempel McPherson (Divine Science) claimed 80% cures. Oral Roberts' television popularity over healing has finally resulted in a university with both dental and medical colleges in Tulsa, Oklahoma. The charismatic movement includes healing as one of the "gifts of the Holy Spirit." The concern of a wide variety of religious movements with illness and health is very pervasive indeed.

JOB AND HIS "FRIENDS"

The classic discussion of the meaning of illness in the Book of Job revolves around the doctrine of retribution. Plainly stated, it means that the righteous are blessed with good health and prosperity, whereas, the wicked are cursed with illness and adversity. It was agreed between God and Satan that Job should be a test case of whether a person might be found who would believe in and serve God out of a pure motive without hoping to gain a blessing as payment for righteousness. He is not much comforted when his so-called friends suggest that he must be pretty wicked to account for the loss of his home, children, and even his health, all in rapid succession. Though hard pressed, he cannot find sufficient sin to confess to justify his predicament.

Professor George Paterson found, in his study of how parents handled the long-term distress of having a cerebral palsied child, that parents might rather even have the explanation that their suffering was caused by sin (hence a punishment) than that this very significant part of their life would have no meaning at all.[2] A purely scientific explanation for illness might report some cold statistics, too much of this or too little of

176

that in the body, too many germs and too little immunity, etc.
The patient presses for meaning. "Yes, Doctor, I know that is
what is wrong with me, that is how my body is malfunctioning;
but I want to know why. Why am I sick; what is the meaning of
my illness?" Since religion presumes to provide meaning, purpose, heritage, destiny for life as a whole, it is not surprising
that persons also expect to find the meaning of illness in religious terms. And for some, everything is either black or
white, right or wrong, a curse or a blessing. They are like
Job's friends with a simple answer to a complex question.

Paterson found that other meanings could also be attributed
to suffering, such as finding in it a means to grow in grace and
maturity of character, a kind of testing and spiritual
strengthening which carried within it another kind of blessing.
Viktor Frankl maintained that to be truly human required that
a person find or create meaning even when none seemed to be ob-
vious.³ Religious persons may seek to find such answers in
prayer and meditation. We have heard dying patients say that
the last months of their lives have been especially meaningful,
and a closeness of fellowship has been found with spouse or
family they had never experienced before. Even though their
illness had gotten worse, they had been blessed in the end.

In the previous chapter we saw one way of possibly suffering for our sins by which we could rightfully be expected to
experience guilt -- mental suffering. Studies in psychosomatic
illness have alerted us to the possibility of damaging our
bodies by compulsive over work, by repressed anger, and by
unhealthy habits such as alcoholism, or smoking cigarettes.
Hence, peptic ulcers, lung cancer, hypertension, and cirrhosis
of the liver are diseases which may be examples of the old
doctrine of retribution fufilled in the life of a person who
has brought these unfortunate consequences upon himself or
herself. We should be careful about jumping to conclusions
since each person's disease has to be thoroughly studied from
a medical point of view. A certain syndrome may develop for
different reasons in two different patients; and the same
behavior in two people may not result in exactly the same consequence. Also, some person may have a genetic predisposition
toward an ailment or an innate weakness of the body to which
no guilt should be attached. But for many persons, the moral
side of their life, their life style, must change for them to
make a good recovery. Treatment of the psyche (mind, soul,
or personality) may be as crucial as treatment of the soma
(body). One needs both the stomach surgery for the ulcer and
a new attitude to replace the anger-revenge relationship or
whatever anxiety was bugging one.

ASU: SUFFERING AND SICKNESS

Like sin, sickness or accident is not limited to certain points on the life cycle. It can strike in infancy and be a congenital birth defect; it can bring down a high school athlete or middle aged farmer; or it may save its ravages for old age. Whenever it strikes, it puts the personality to a test. It is a hurdle to be crossed with whatever resources the person can muster. In our scientific age of medical marvels, it is assumed that symptoms are to be conquered. We have been rightfully proud of gigantic strides in progress. Even smallpox has just recently been declared extinct according to world health records. Polio is no longer a threat; and the same is true of whooping cough, scarlet fever, tuberculosis, etc. Also, there is the growing conviction that no one need suffer distress. A slight headache brings out the aspirin bottle, and it is possible that the vast majority of the populace is on one kind of pill or another. The United States is a highly medicated population as befits a country with the highest (?) standard of living in the world.

Have we set too much store in progress, and are our expectations unrealistic? I would like to propose a strange analogy and urge a project for measuring suffering (whether it is practical or not). We find the B.T.U. a helpful measure of heat -- British Thermal Unit. An engineer can tell quite accurately how much heat your furnace is putting out. What about a measurement of suffering? The A.S.U. could stand for the American Suffering Unit. This would be a standard unit of suffering or pain (mental or physical) regardless of cause (just like the B.T.U. measures so much heat whether it is generated by coal, gas, or electricity).

Let us take suffering from traffic accidents for example. Although it is true that we have enormous numbers of persons suffering from traffic injuries, some with lifelong disabilities and pain, it was true that there were accidents with Roman chariots, and every now and again someone was kicked in the head by a horse. As we improved automobiles and highways, people drove faster and accidents became more dramatic. Fairly often we hear of planes going down with far more passengers than Charles Lindbergh could carry in "The Spirit of Saint Louis." Our city has an excellent water treatment plan for purifying water, but when the improved herbicides, pesticides, and fertilizers run off the farms into the Iowa River, the treated water is almost unpotable. At the same time as we have invented big air conditioners to improve our air, cities have developed such dense smog that the aged and persons with respiratory conditions are told not to go outside and breathe the sickly air. Do we lose on one hand just about as much as we gain on the other? Does the overall, basic amount of suffering remain roughly the same for a lifetime of an individual today as in days gone by?

There are indications that chronic diseases and maladies have been on the increase in the same era that the acute and infectious diseases have been markedly reduced. Our nursing homes are full of semi-conscious and suffering persons whose lives of considerable suffering can be extended for years by good medical care. The number of kinds of medicines has skyrocketed, some very potent. When we established a sophisticated toxicology center at my university, one of the purposes was to study the bad side effects of good medicine as well as "improved" commercial chemicals of all kinds. I was asked to offer the invocation at the dedication. Part of that prayer went as follows:

> "O Lord of life and mankind, we are grateful for every new revelation of the workings of nature around us and for every insight into our own selves -- our intricate bodies and complex minds. Preserve us from the idolatry of worshipping the ancient goddess, Panacea, whose solutions to life's sickness were so easy and superficial. When we build for service with lofty ambition and noble intention, preserve us from the human pride that results in a Tower of Babel with all of its confusion and self-destruction. For all about us we see wonderful scientific miracles and promising inventions being used by man against himself...."

Let us assume, just for the sake of argument, that there will always be a certain amount of suffering of one kind or another. How should an individual view his/her suffering or sickness -- penalty for sin, the price of progress, fate, the result of ignorance, without meaning, or what else? The mature person needs to be able to include such painful realities within an over-arching and unifying philosophy of life, a sufficient theology. If you do not like my A.S.U., come up with your own guesstimate for determining if we are making progress or "progress."

TYPE A AND TYPE B PERSONALITY

In 1976, Professor Hans Selye revised and re-issued his book, The Stress of Life, and claimed that the assumptions of the first edition printed twenty years earlier still held good.[4] His "General Adaptation Syndrome" stirred great interest as an explanation of how stress and threat to the organisms's welfare or homeostasis can result in tissue damage and illness.

The General Adaptation Syndrome is a composite of three stages: (1) An "Alarm Reaction" is the result of a threatening stress, and the alarm alerts the organism to take some defensive measure such as fight or flight. The danger or stress which triggers the alarm signal might be the invasion of a noxious chemical, extreme heat, or any perceived threat. It is conceivable that this threat could be social (loss of job, status, marriage, etc.) or emotional as well as physical. (2) "Stage of Resistance." "Adaptation is acquired due to optimum development of the most appropriate specific channel of defense."[5] The defensive reaction might take the form of inflammation, secretion of hormones, and other preparations to deal with the stress. (3) "Stage of Exhaustion" finally sets in because the body can keep up this defensive posture only so long. "...if irritation continues over a very long time, the directly-affected cells eventually break down from 'fatigue,' wear and tear, or, if you wish, from exhaustion of all local stores of adaptation energy."[6]

The practical application of Selye's stress theory is that if one so lives as to be in constant danger: unnecessary exposure to stresses of cigarettes and alcohol, retaliation by persons whom one has harmed, anxieties of dog-eat-dog competition, fear of failure through misplaced goals or being an "over-achiever," loss of friendship because of bearing false witness; to be in such danger is not good for one's health. Damage to one's health for these reasons, with its attendant suffering, might often be preventable. And by common understanding the above life styles would be "works of the flesh" and certainly not "fruits of the spirit." (Galatians 5:19-23)

A specific application of life style and personality type to heart disease was made by two cardiologists, Meyer Friedman and Ray H. Rosenman in their book, Type A Behavior and Your Heart.[7] Their researches revealed the following characteristics of coronary-prone individuals: they were compulsive in regard to time and statistics, felt inordinate pressure of competition, success, etc. Unfortunately just such a person is likely to be promoted in business, rewarded socially, and, if a clergyperson, admired for "dedication and consecration." The eulogies at the funeral of such a self-destruct personality are laudatory, and no one would have the ill grace to point to the suicidal tendencies in the person who had been warned about smoking and the "need to slow down" by his/her physician. Such self-destructiveness can masquerade under the righteous labels of "service," "stewardship of one's talents," "ambition," the "Protestant work ethic," and "the kind of drive that made our country great."

180

Even as I write these lines I feel slightly fearful that I might be providing some slothful person with a "cop-out" for irresponsibility. That rationalizer would plead, "I'm taking very good care of my heart and health generally by relaxing all the time; after all my body is a 'temple of the living God.' (II Corinthians 6:16a) You see, I am a Type B Personality." The opposite of A is not indolence, but rather, work minus the anxiety, punctuality without compulsion, a balance of work and play, a practical and functional use of budgets, time schedules, and statistics. A full day's work should result in fatigue, which in turn is assuaged by sufficient sleep; and a full week's work should find adequate recuperation in the weekend's rest and recreation. Planning for tomorrow is quite different from being anxious for the morrow as in the passage from the Sermon on the Mount:

> "Therefore do not be anxious about tomorrow,
> for tomorrow will be anxious for itself.
> Let the day's own trouble be sufficient for
> the day."
>
> (Matthew 6:34)

The Type A Personality can turn a perfectly good and useful vocation into a curse by bringing the above mentioned negative and rigid attitudes to bear upon his/her work. This life style can also make one's spouse uptight because such a person is often as judgmental about others as about the self, fussing about details and "standards," progress and promotion.

All that has been said thus far should not imply that a sound mind will always result in a sound body (the Roman's slogan: Mens Sana in Corpore Sano notwithstanding). A person who is not accident prone may still have an auto accident; a person who does not smoke may still get cancer; and a person who is not neurotically compulsive may still come down with cardiovascular disease.

If you were to attempt to write a psycho-history of a person's life cycle, illness and health would be important factors to report. Is there a pattern of illness, a theme of suffering? If your subject is frequently ill, what is the attitude toward the illness: self pity, martyrdom, exhibitionism and bragging about symptoms, realistic search for therapy and rehabilitation, fatalism, courage, or some other response that is characteristic of this individual?

Paterson illustrates the constructive contribution of[8] religious resources for coping with the crisis of illness. In Figure 21, "Spiritual Resources for the Crisis of Illness," he

181

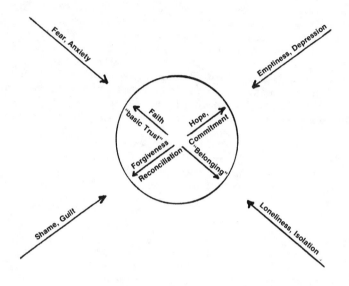

Fear, Anxiety

Emptiness, Depression

Faith "basic Trust"

Hope, Commitment

Forgiveness Reconciliation

"Belonging"

Shame, Guilt

Loneliness, Isolation

Fig. 21   Spiritual Resources for the Crisis of Illness

indicates that certain positive and redemptive attitudes can serve as antidotes or counter-balances to the negative and destructive potential of the stress of illness.   Thus, Faith and "Basic Trust" can neutralize or diminish the power of Fear and Anxiety.   Likewise, Loneliness and Isolation are deficiencies which can be off-set by congregational members extending fellowship and providing the weakened, ill person with a sense of "Belonging."   The negative forces push inward and serve to constrict the individual's self-regard and living space, whereas the positive forces within the circle tend to be Ego-enhancing and enlarging the sphere of significant existence.

ANOINTING, PASTORAL CARE, AND VISITATION

> "Is any among you sick? Let him call for the elders of the church, and let them pray over him, anointing him with oil in the name of the Lord; and the prayer of faith will save

the sick man, and the Lord will raise him up;
and if he has committed sins, he will be forgiven. Therefore confess your sins to one
another, and pray for one another, that you
may be healed." (James 5:14-16a)

Regardless of the supposed cause of illness, those who are
cursed by it desire a blessing instead. The blessing may be
complete healing, postponement of dying, partial healing, or at
least support and comfort amidst their suffering. The above
passage from the Epistle of James is part of the tradition which
finally developed into the so-called Last Rites of the Roman
Catholic Church. Currently this Extreme Unction (anointing at
the extreme end of life) has been modified to put stress on
prayer for healing. In one way this revives the ancient symbolism of anointing with oil, which was simultaneously spiritual
and medicinal. In Israel Kings were anointed as a sign of God's
approval, but in David's shepherd psalm, we are reminded that
the bruised or wounded sheep were treated with the soothing oil.
(Psalm 23:5b) Episcopalians, Mennonites, Brethren, and others
may request anointing at time of illness. In any case, the
prayer part of the admonition of James is common.

As indicated in the previous discussion about Job and his
afflictions, illness has an element of mystery. Disease can be
a powerful enemy, made more so by its seemingly capricious and
invisible character. One can feel a general weakness that is
hard to describe to the doctor; nausea, pain, and other symptoms
can roam about within the body, and one feels helpless and
frustrated. This does not call for a "rite of passage," to use
the anthropologist's term. It does not call for a ceremony
like Confirmation or Marriage, which is designed to assist the
person in making a transition from one stage of life to the
next. Rather, what is called for is a "rite of intensification,"
a support during a period of stress or weakness. The healed
child is still a child, and the healed adolescent is still an
adolescent. The goal is to help the patient maintain the
status quo or return to the status of health.

Some sick persons are not granted healing, nor even a clear
and definitive explanation of their illnesses, since the current
state of medical knowledge cannot provide an answer. Such may
resort to "Basic Trust," to faith in their Creator; may find
comfort in meditation and the following kinds of Scripture
passages:

"The eternal God is your dwelling place,
and underneath are the everlasting arms."
(Deuteronomy 33:27)

"I lift up my eyes to the hills,
    From whence does my help come?
My help comes from the Lord,
    who made heaven and earth."
                    (Psalms 121:1)

"If we live, we live to the Lord, and if we die,
we die to the Lord; so then, whether we live or
whether we die, we are the Lord's."
                    (Romans 14:8)

"For my thoughts are not your thoughts,
    neither are your ways my ways, says the Lord.
For as the heavens are higher than the earth,
    so are my ways higher than your ways
    and my thoughts than your thoughts."
                    (Isaiah 55:8-9)

A cancer patient, who was dying, had lost practically all of his
hair during the chemotherapy treatments. His favorite passage
of Scripture was from the fifth chapter of Luke (12:6-7) "Are
not five sparrows sold for two pennies? And not one of them is
forgotten before God. Why, even the hairs of your head are all
numbered. Fear not; you are of more value than many sparrows."
He found comfort that by the grace of God he would never be
abandoned no matter how worthless his body became. As far as
this patient was concerned, Jesus could just as well have been
talking about cancer cells when he said, two verses earlier,
"I tell you, my friends, do not fear those who kill the body,
and after that have nothing more that they can do." (verse 4)

    Note that the five passages referred to above are supportive
of the sick whether they are healed or not. They represent an
acceptance with a commitment. Some dying persons of devout
attitude have quoted the words of Jesus from the Cross: "Father,
into they hands I commit my spirit!" (Luke 23:46b) Such
religious orientation has set aside questions of causation, is
no longer looking for logical explanations or even solutions.
It partakes of the "now" to which Clements referred as the
experience of the mature aged, those who have attained "Ego
Integrity." (See above, Chapter 6, section on "Time and
Meaning.")

    Another religious tradition in keeping with the "rite of
intensification" is that of pastoral care and visitation. Precisely when the sick person begins to feel unworthy of the
attention and good regard of his/her neighbors because of de-
teriorating body and lessened capacity for useful production,
then others of the community should step up their associations
and counteract alienation with increased fellowship. Clergy

have visited the sick regularly as symbolic of the concern of the whole congregation. Lay visitors may take on this task voluntarily or be assigned by a committee of social concern. Next of kin as well as the extended family come to the hospital or sick bed at home to express their concern and support. That is the ideal, of course. In cases of longstanding hostility and rejection, even extreme suffering may not be able to warm the hearts of those who have known this "isolate" (or he/she may have opted for utter privacy). When one such lonely person died in a very large hospital, the nurse left the TV on with its blaring mid-day soap opera, "so he wouldn't have to die alone."

Chaplains are now available in all institutions (general medical-surgical hospitals, mental hospitals, prisons, etc.) of such size that the patients are drawn from a large area. Thus if the patient has been removed from customary religious resources of altar, pulpit, pew, congregation, and home town clergy, such a person could still have the benefit of ministry in this special time of need -- prayers, sacraments, other forms of worship or pastoral care and counseling.

The role of religious, spiritual, and emotional factors in illness and health is now widely recognized. Where not primarily causative of illness, negative emotions can at least exacerbate the problem. Confessional admission of these destructive attitudes and feelings (hate, fear, guilt, despair, self-pity, revenge, pride, etc.) is a good beginning. With the help of a pastoral counselor or other therapists the person may be emboldened to try out a new response to life, a new life style using constructive attitudes and behaviors (love, service, interest in and concern for others, altruism, hope, forgiveness, acceptance of reality, faith, etc.). This transformation takes different forms in different personalities: dramatic conversion experience, many months of painful counseling and gradual insight together with tentative testing out of new methods of coping, group therapy support in the struggle for a new life, etc. Above all, it must be authentic and integral to the person wrestling with the problem. It does not help in the long run for me to tack "my solution" onto another person like a bandaid. That would not be an authentic experience for the "client." It would be what Allport called "extrinsic." (See Chapter 1, the section on "Intrinsic and Extrinsic Religion.") Some would do anything for "peace of mind" even to the extent of violating their integrity. Such "cheap grace" is not therapeutic. It is important that the person seeking recovery find or create a new, positive life style with wholesome attitudes, activities, associations, and commitments; the kind that legitimately enchance one's self-worth and fill life with some meaning, spontaneity, and joy. Otherwise, the healing is temporary and the person goes from one symptom or disorder to another.

"When the unclean spirit has gone out of a man,
he passes through waterless places seeking rest;
and finding none he says, 'I will return to my
house from which I came.' And when he comes
he finds it swept and put in order. Then he
goes and brings seven other spirits more evil
than himself, and they enter and dwell there;
and the last state of that man becomes worse
than the first." (Luke 11:24-26)

POSTSCRIPT ON INFORMAL AND SPONTANEOUS RELIGIOUS RESOURCES NOT SCHEDULED BY THE LIFE CYCLE

Because we have followed a design of the stages of life
with their unique stresses, initiation rites, and steady progression, we may not have stressed enough the individualized,
regular, and somewhat less formal types of religious resources
which countless people use daily or weekly. Private prayer,
Bible study groups, prayer fellowships, occasional revival
meetings, periods of meditation (scheduled or spontaneous), intimate conversation with a trusted friend about an important
life issue, routine weekly worship with a congregation during
periods when life presents no difficulty, and many other religious experiences. There are also great festivals which evoke
a lot of positive enthusiasm from the entire community: an
Islamic pilgrimage to Mecca, the Jewish season of Hanukkah with
its lights, Christmas with its celebrations, to say nothing of
birthdays and other anniversaries. These provide seasonal
rejuvenation and serve as good preventive medicine in the mental
health sphere on top of their theological significance or
doctrinal function.

We should remind ourselves of the psychology of individual
differences. Some persons seem to thrive on structure; others
rely on being moved by the Spirit in an unscheduled way. "The
wind blows where it wills, and you hear the sound of it, but you
do not know whence it comes or whither it goes; so it is with
every one who is born of the Spirit." (John 3:8) One person
needs more celebration and zip than another, who wants peace
and little noise. If we have not spent as much time as you
might desire on all the varieties of religious experience, it
is not because they have been considered of little importance,
but just that this study has chosen a particular format and
point of view.

TWO BRIEF CASES

1. REFLECTIONS ON A PASTORAL CARE ENCOUNTER[9]

Susie L. (fictitious name) was a 20-year-old unmarried
woman who gave birth two months premature to a baby boy by
C-section. He lived approximately 48 hours and was baptized
on Monday evening, the night before he died. The chaplain who
had baptized the baby Steven Robert (also fictitious), was to
be out of town the day Susie wanted the Memorial Service.
Consequently, a second chaplain entered the scenario the day
before the Memorial Service and followed Susie during the re-
mainder of her hospitalization which was nine days. This is
written by the second chaplain.

During our first visit Susie came across as a shy, pleasant
person who was still in much pain due to the recent ordeal,
which included a stubborn infection. She knew she wanted a
Memorial Service for her son the following day since such was
the only time her family could be present. Although she wanted
the service to be short and to include scripture readings, Susie
did not have any other suggestions. She noted that she believed
in God, but had not been to church in a long time when asked
about her faith journey. I returned a few hours later to share
some scripture references (Psalm 23 and Romans 8:35-39) and an
anthem ("Joy is Like the Rain") for her response. She found
them satisfactory with the song bringing tears to her eyes.

Her energy level was a bit higher the next day, though she
still did not feel up to par. Several IVs remained in her arms.
Susie was brought to the Chapel in a wheelchair; her parents,
grandmother, brother, sister, sister-in-law, girlfriend, and
current boyfriend (but not father of her child) were present.
The service concentrated on the celebration of life, the pain
of death, and God's presence regardless of what we face due
to divine acceptance, love, and grace. Following the service
Susie had her boyfriend wheel her to where I was standing and
said, "Thank you very much -- that was very meaningful. I
appreciate it very much."

When I saw Susie the day after next she asked for a copy
of what I had shared in the service, and said that she re-
gretted not having tape recorded the service. I indicated
I would provide her with a written copy as well as a recorded
one, which greatly pleased her. She thanked me again for the
service saying, "You don't know how much it means to me."

Susie was more alert during this visit; she had more
energy. She volunteered verbally more about her story. During
this visit -- in addition to the next three -- Susie worked on

untangling her feelings regarding her pregnancy. She also tried
to put it into perspective in relation to her life as a whole.
With few visitors she had plenty of time for thinking and reflecting. Susie demonstrated much courage which was in keeping
with her style of facing circumstances directly.

Several times I shared material for my story to help illustrate a theme or dynamic we were discussing. In short, a
relationship of trust and intimacy began and grew quickly in
a week's time. During our last visit Susie said she had never
before had someone come by on a steady basis just to talk with
her. I sense she was moved by someone having genuine interest
in her journey.

What can be said regarding the pastoral care dimension of
Susie's hospitalization? First, she and her child were accepted
as children of God by God's spokepersons. Susie was informed
that such unconditional affirmation was a result of God's grace.
Further, judgmental comments regarding children out of wedlock
were withheld. Second, she found some closure for her ordeal
with the Memorial Service -- an official ending.

Third, Susie was able to confess some aspects of her story
without receiving a demand to change. This was new for her,
which helps to explain her comment about trust being difficult.
Fourth, Susie was able to relate several segments of her life
in order to gain more insight into who she is. And, finally,
she utilized pastoral care for reflecting where she might be
going in the future; how the past would impact her upcoming
journey; and how God might be involved in the future.

Memorial Service

for

Steven Robert

Opening Prayer
We call upon you, God, in order that we might be in your
presence. We have gathered to remember Steven Robert -- to
affirm the gift of life as well as to recognize the pain of
death. We know the value of faith, God, but sometimes it is
difficult to trust when there is so much going on with our lives
like death and illness. It is our hope that this service may
be meaningful for you as well as for us. We pray in Christ's
name. Amen.

Scripture Readings
Old Testament - Psalm 23 (RSV)
"The Lord is my shepherd,I shall not want;
  he makes me lie down in green pastures.
He leads me beside still waters;
  he restores my soul.
He leads me in paths of righteousness
  for his name's sake.

Even though I walk through the valley of
  the shadow of death,
  I fear no evil;
for thou art with me;
  thy rod and thy staff,
  they comfort me.

Thou preparest a table before me
  in the presence of my enemies;
thou anointest my head with oil,
  my cup overflows.

Surely goodness and mercy shall follow me
  all the days of my life;
and I shall dwell in the house of the Lord
  forever."

New Testament - Romans 8:35-39 (TEV)
"Who, then, can separate us from the love of Christ? Can
trouble do it, or hardship, or persecution, or danger, or hunger,
or poverty, or death? As the scripture says, 'For your sake we
are in danger of death the whole day long. We are treated like
sheep that are going to be slaughtered.' No, in all these things
we have complete victory through him who loved us! For I am
certain that nothing can separate us from his love: neither
death nor life; neither angels nor the other heavenly rulers
or powers; neither the present nor the future; neither the world
above nor the world below -- there is nothing in all creation
that will ever be able to separate us from the love of God
which is ours through Christ Jesus our Lord."

Anthem
"Joy Is Like the Rain"
  --The Medical Mission Sisters

Meditation
"Joy is like the rain." Sometimes the rain comes as a
welcomed blessing; sometimes as a dreaded burden. Why it
doesn't come when we need it and does come when we don't need
it is often a mystery to us.

Life is like the rain. Sometimes the events in life are a cause for us to celebrate; sometimes they cause us to mourn. The why behind such events may be unknown to us -- such can be a lonely and perplexing feeling.

Earlier this week there was cause to celebrate as Susie gave birth to a baby boy. The beginning of a new life is often an exciting experience -- it is not unlike the hope and strength we can derive from spring as it breaks through after a long and tiring winter.

Later this week there was cause to grieve and mourn due to the death of Steven. Understandably, this generated feeling of disappointment -- maybe there were also feelings of anger, bewilderment, uncertainty, frustration, and confusion. It is OK to have such feelings; it is OK to express such feelings. Often tears are a helpful manner for such expressions. If this weren't enough, Susie also found herself struggling with a stubborn infection which still lingers.

Where has God been this week? Susie, when you and your family and your friends were rejoicing -- however brief -- God was rejoicing with you; when you were grieving God was grieving with you. When Steven Robert was baptized into the church community, God was present blessing that event. This evening God is here with us. God loved Steven just as God loves each of us. Paul, in his letter to the Romans, tells us that not even death can separate us from the love of God."

Closing Prayer and Benediction
    Thank you, God, for loving us -- for being with us no matter what we face. Thank you for family and friends to share our moments of happiness along with our moments of sorrow. Thank you for the healing -- physical, spiritual, emotional -- that has already occurred for Susie; may it continue at a fast pace. Thank you for showing you faithfulness to us through Jesus Christ our Lord. And now may the love of God the Creator, the grace of our Lord Jesus Christ the Redeemer, and the fellowship of the Holy Spirit the Sustainer be with us all now and forever more. Amen.

2. THE FOURTH COMMANDMENT DISTORTED 180 DEGREES

    "Honor your father and your mother, that
    your days may be long in the land which
    the Lord your God gives you." (Exodus 20:12)

    A person once said about a favor done for his superior, "It was the very least I could do (then under his breath to a

companion) that's why I did it." I recall an unhealthy example
of legalistically fulfilling the above commandment but resenting
it subconsciously during the entire twenty-five years of
"service."

A young woman had married a man of whom her mother never did
approve. Early in the marriage the mother intruded in such a
way that it clearly accelerated the separation of the young
couple from each other. The daughter told me as much fifteen
years after the divorce. What had happened was that the
daughter had never really separated herself from her parents
and never felt free to join herself to her husband. The
divorcee told me as much and was almost able to admit the
insight that she was angry with her mother for having never "let
her go."

Sometimes a person cannot afford to acknowledge certain
problems because it would be opening up a can of worms. It seems
safer to bury the mess in the subconscious and "grin and bear
it." Secondly, the individual may get positive rewards for
martyrlike behavior. This was certainly the case with the
woman in question (by now middle aged). How faithful she was in
caring for her invalid mother! She was a clerk in a large insurance company. Her life was a ritual of service to her
mother. She must come home from work immediately because her
mother was lonely. She could not sing in a church choir because
her mother would be lonely. Her recreation was practically
limited to weekly grocery shopping and brushing her teeth.
Members in the church praised her for her steadfast devotion
with pious remarks such as "I don't see how you can do it;"
"How fortunate your mother is to have such a devoted daughter;"
and "You're so Christ-like and forgetful of self."

Meanwhile, this frustrated and subconsciously angry woman
was not righteous at all, but guilty on two counts: first, her
hatred for her mother, secondly, her hypocrisy for pretending
otherwise. She did not need to hate her mother for not "letting
her go." The Scripture quoted at her marriage gave full
permission for her to "cleave" to her spouse and "leave" father
and mother. She had not been responsible in regard to the new
"one flesh" relationship to which she should have committed
herself. The Commandment on honoring father and mother does
not demand total slavery nor destruction of self. Her willingness to overdo her dedication to the mother was a compensation
to counterbalance the submerged anger which she could not handle
in any other way. But, as Freud pointed out, repressed negative
emotions don't just go away; they come out in social, mental,
or physical symptoms. In her case it was arthritis as she
became increasingly stiff. Perhaps (if she were lucky enough)
she would become so invalided that she would no longer be able

191

to "serve" her mother and then it would not be her fault.
Naturally, this interpretation should be taken tentatively
without the full medical case records of the woman at hand,
but her history fits so well with Selye's "General Adaptation
Syndrome" that it is provocative of discussion as we consider
the theme of this chapter: Illness and Health: Cursing and
Blessing.

NOTES

1. From a booklet describing the Oratory published by Saint
    Joseph's Oratory of Mount Royal, Montreal, Canada (text by
    Henry Bernard, C.S.C.), 1959, p. 5.

2. Paterson, George W., Helping Your Handicapped Child,
    Minneapolis: Augsburg Publishing House, 1975.

3. Frankl, Victor E., Man's Search for Meaning, New York:
    Washington Square Press, Inc., 1963.

4. Selye, Hans, The Stress of Life (revised edition), New York:
    McGraw-Hill Book Co., 1976. See also his very technical
    bibliographic review of the literature on this topic,
    Stress in Health and Disease, Reading, Mass.: Butterworths
    Inc., 1976, or his popular treatment of the topic, Stress
    Without Distress, New York: J. B. Lippincott, 1974.

5. Ibid., p. 163.

6. Ibid., p. 165.

7. Friedman, Meyer, and Ray H. Rosenman, Type A Behavior and
    Your Heart, New York: Alfred A. Knopf, 1974. See also
    George W. Paterson, The Cardiac Patient, Minneapolis:
    Augsburg Publishing House, 1978, in which he demonstrates
    the religious significance of "Living with Heart Disease"
    in Chapter 6.

8. Ibid., p. 110.

9. This report was written by Bruce D. Williams.

REFLECTIONS AND DISCUSSION

1. Define in your own words the terms "a curse" and "a
    blessing." Give an example of each.

2. Cite one example in your own life of how you could substitute something conducive to a healthy life style for something that is currently conducive to illness.

3. What preventive medicine measures are most urgently needed in our society concerning: (a) physical health, (b) mental health, (c) spiritual health?

4. What would be some criteria that would justify going to a shrine for healing? Do you think of any contraindications? How would you relate such an approach to a modern scientific medical approach to illness? Are they compatible or mutually exclusive?

5. Have you known of a case where the retribution concept of illness seemed to be operative? Was such an interpretation helpful in that case, i.e., did it motivate the subject to some constructive solution? What are the risks or disadvantages of the retribution theory of sickness being a punishment for sin?

6. Would the author's "American Suffering Unit" approach lead to undue pessimism and discourage research in science and medicine? Would the illusion of "progress" be useful even if it were not true -- like the pot of gold at the end of the rainbow? Would you like to pit the "power of positive thinking" against such an approach?

7. What is the difference between the kind of stress that leads to headaches, ulcers, and hypertension as opposed to the kind of stress one encounters in tennis, jogging, and physical fitness exercises? Would the ideal be to experience no stress, ever? What is the opposite of neurotic stress? What is the opposite of healthy stress? Can too much worry about whether one is experiencing too much stress be a destructive dynamic in itself? How?

8. There are two axes or sets of opposites in Paterson's diagram (Figure 21). Can you give specific examples from your own life or that of another person you know to illustrate these forces?

9. Give your own critique of how the chaplain ministered to Susie. For example, what was your reaction to his use of the baby's name on several occasions; was it good "catharsis" or too "heavy" for the mother at this time? What should have been done with the body of the baby who died? What premarital counseling problems do you think might emerge if she marries the new boyfriend? How should such problems be dealt with?

193

10. Might the author have read too much into the weeping of the teenage mother during the baptism? Sigmund Freud is supposed to have said, "Sometimes a cigar is just a cigar." Does too much psychologizing make you feel uncomfortable? Feel free to criticize the approach of this book; it's a free country.

PART II

YOU IN A WORLD VIEW

"From the construct theory standpoint, a man's
personality is his total view of himself, his
life and his world. How he reacts to his
world is totally dependent upon his view of
that world.... His interpretation may not
always be a very good fit on all events, but
he is seen as constantly trying to live consistently in terms of his view of the world.
In these terms, a man's personality and his
construct system are synonymous."[1]

How is personality viewed by various religious and world
view perspectives? It makes a great deal of difference to my
self-perception if others perceive me as basically good or
pervasively evil, strong or weak, essentially free to choose
between alternatives or locked into a predestined determinism
by forces beyond my control, whether I am an essential part of
nature or so special that I am set over against the rest of
nature, whether I belong to a group that believes my life is of
inestimable worth and that I have a meaningful destiny to
fulfill, or I belong to an existentialist faith group committed
to the proposition that life is absurd and meaningless.

Not all world views or philosophies of life seem obviously
religious; yet they may fulfill some of the functions we have
usually associated with religion, providing meaning, an interpretation of personal and social existence and fostering a set
of values and guidelines for behavior. Primitive, animistic
tribesmen have a theology that not only explains how and why
the world is as it is, but also what individual persons are like
and how they are to live compatibly with the rest of nature.
One only needs to visit the People's Republic of China to see
that the little red book containing the quotations of Chairman

Mao fulfilled very much the same function as a Christian catechism in speaking of meaning, values, and destiny.

For the majority of persons their view of the world is largely shaped by the world view of the culture group to which they belong. This group or society is shaped in part by the beliefs and traditions handed down by the religious heritage, the wisdom literature, the myths and stories, the accumulated experiences of the ancestors. Among these understandings are notions about what it means to be a person, the role of the person in relation to other persons, the capacity, limitations, and options available to the person -- in short, a theory of personality. Fransella, cited above, refers to a "construct system"; such a perspective could also be called a world view, a philosophy of life, a theology, a rationale for one's existence. Everyone has one, and seems to need one whether he/she is aware of it or not. It is the function of Part II to examine several world views and try to understand how personality is defined and explained by each one.

We will begin with the world view of primitive animism. There is more animism in our every day lives than we realize. Since the West has been so heavily influenced by Judeo-Christian thought and tradition, it is illuminating to trace many of the popular concepts of personality to biblical sources. In many ways our western civilization is based on the Greek rather than the Hebrew way of thinking. Our current scientific-technological society relies heavily on reason, logic, and objective analysis. Often feelings are sacrificed for efficiency; sentiment is not as cost effective as mathematics when it comes to production and the gross national product. Where does the human personality fit into the gross national product? We are said to be living in a secular age. Secular substitutes have been created to fulfill certain functions which were formerly taken care of by traditional religion. How does such "civil religion" work to meet the developmental and adjustment needs of personality -- the kinds of needs we dealt with in Part I and the issues addressed by Erikson in his life cycle? Finally, we will try to bring together a synthesis of the many facets of personality into a wholistic system.

It is difficult to project oneself into a culture or world view quite different from one's own; but try it. Ask yourself how you would function differently, view yourself differently, have a higher or lower self-regard if you were to live in that other time or place. Such a tour can make you a more ecumenical person and, at the same time, help you to become more aware of what your own philosophy of life is doing for (or to) you.

196

"Psychologically speaking, we should point to the close analogy that exists between a religious orientation and all other high-level schemata that influence the course of becoming. Every man, whether he is religiously inclined or not, has his own ultimate presuppositions. He finds he cannot live his life without them, and for him they are true. Such presuppositions, whether they be called ideologies, philosophies, notions, or merely hunches about life, exert creative pressure upon all conduct that is subsidiary to them (which is to say, upon nearly all of a man's conduct)."[2]

NOTES

1. Fransella, Fay, Personal Change and Reconstruction, London: Academic Press, 1972, p. 54.

2. Allport, Gordon W., Becoming: Basic Considerations for a Psychology of Personality, New Haven: Yale University Press, 1955, pp. 95-96.

CHAPTER 9

PRIMITIVE AND PRESENT SYMBOLISM

"What we find as soon as we place ourselves in
the perspective of religious man of the archaic
societies is that <u>the</u> <u>world</u> <u>exists</u> <u>because</u> <u>it</u>
<u>was</u> <u>created</u> <u>by</u> <u>the</u> <u>gods</u>, and that the existence
of the world itself 'means' something, that the
world is neither mute nor opaque, that it is not
an inert thing without purpose or significance.
... Probably, in a very distant past, all of
man's organs and physiological experiences, as
well as his acts, had a religious meaning.
This is understandable, for all human behavior
was established by the gods or culture heroes
<u>in</u> <u>illo</u> <u>tempore</u>; they instituted not only the
various kinds of work and the various ways of
obtaining and eating food, of making love, of
expressing thought and feeling, and so on, but
even acts apparently of no importance."[1]

In our era of concern for ecology, it is instructive to
note that primitive persons have a feeling of close kinship with
nature; thus to damage nature would be tantamount to damaging
oneself. The practical applicability of these ancient ideas
amazes us today. Let us consider some categories of concern
and meaning.

ANIMISM: THEN AND NOW, HERE AND THERE

Animism is the term (derived from the Latin word meaning
breath of life, spirit, or soul) which describes a belief that
spirit is infused into everything; that rocks, trees, and
waterfalls, have a spiritual aspect just as do animals and
human beings. There are also disembodied spirits or beings who

can have a direct participation in daily life much like visible, flesh-and-blood, living persons. It is the pervasiveness of this spiritual reality or power which provides animism with its vital force and significance for primitive societies. Obviously this intangible or spiritual aspect of existence must be taken into account on a par with the usual experiences perceived by the senses of touch, sight, taste, etc.

OUR DEBT TO ANTHROPOLOGISTS

Cultural anthropologists have studied cultural remains as well as contemporary primitive societies to determine how they perceive their world and themselves within it.[2] Four aspects of life are commemorated or dealt with in primitive animism: propagation, nutrition, totemism, and death.

Propagation of the race is the very basis of the existence of society and of continuing ongoing life in the universe. Hence the powers of generation and fertility, not only in man but in nature, are commemorated and given social support and come under social control. Accounts of sexual behavior sometimes seem to be license at harvest festivals or fertility rites, but are not necessarily merely indulgence; they express in the primitive mind a reverent attitude toward these powers. Sex is thus "sanctified" and accepted as an essential process including socially approved patterns of family life.

Nutrition, the satisfaction of the instinct of hunger, is also a powerful process. Primitive man celebrated nutrition by ceremonies preceding hunting or fishing expeditions or the harvesting of food. Again we see religious meaning and social controls merged in the incorporation of a strong instinctual drive into a workable social process. In more highly developed religion this function continues to have religious significance in terms of feeling of dependence, the notion of "providence," and simple rituals of grace at meals. In the primitive mind animal sacrifice and other ceremonies involving food function as a propitiation of spirits or elements of the universe because man is taking something from the universe in the process of eating. This could be viewed as a hostile act, and he needs to do something to make up for devouring any part of nature, whether it be animal or vegetable.

Totemism is another common function that we find in primitive religion. This is man's selective interest in nature. Man is interested in the qualities and special characteristics of certain animals because he admires them and desires these capacities as his own possession. He may wish to be as strong as a lion, as agile as a fox, or as free as an eagle. It is clear that eating such a creature goes far beyond providing nutrition; it has a magical quality. Religious ceremony may be needed to appease the particular species which is being devoured in order that that kind of animal will not withhold itself from him, either as a source of food or as a source of some characteristic he admires and desires to incorporate into his own personality.

> "Totemism appears thus as a blessing bestowed
> by religion on primitive man's efforts in dealing
> with his useful surroundings, upon his 'struggle
> for existence.' At the same time it develops his
> reverence for those animals and plants on which
> he depends, to which he feels in a way grateful,
> and yet the destruction of which is a necessity
> to him. And all this springs from the belief of
> man's affinity with those forces of nature upon
> which he mainly depends. Thus we find a moral
> value and a biological significance in totemism,
> in a system of beliefs, practices, and social
> arrangements which at first sight appears but
> a childish, irrelevant, and degrading fancy
> of the savage."[3]

Death is the fourth element with which religion must deal. In the primitive tribe death dealt a shattering blow to the group, breaking the circle of security. Primitive man could not live alone in the jungle, but needed the support and strength of the group. The weakening of the group by the loss of a member through death was a threat to each member's own existence. Every person counted for food-gathering, for protection against the elements, and protection against neighboring tribes. Death is a great crisis because it focuses all of life's goals and values at the very point of losing them.

Two contradictory attitudes arise: an intensification of love for the dead person -- an attraction, and at the same time a strong negative feeling of loathing or being repelled by the corpse. Correspondingly, both are represented in primitive man's burial ceremonies. In one tribe the mourners sit in a row with the dead person resting on their knees, and as they stroke the body they feel very close to him. Yet, at the same time, they feel repelled and a certain amount of revulsion at the lifeless corpse. Likewise, there are contradictory impulses of wanting to preserve the corpse and wanting to annihilate the body; embalming and setting apart food for the departed spirit, as well as sometimes leaving it for vultures to consume, setting it adrift in a canoe or burning the remains. Thus there is ample tangible opportunity to express a variety of feelings toward the experience of death.

Influence of Spirit over Man and Nature is well illustrated in the Waura tribe of South America, who live along the Xingu River, a tributary of the Amazon.[4] Not only will the shaman or medicine man go into a trance and rush to the river's edge to bring back the "shadow" of a dying person, but the same spirit-over-matter exercise will be enacted to bring back fish into the river after a long period of scarcity. The latter ceremony requires the carving of a model of a fish, which is attached to a rope on the end of a long stick. The movement and whirring of this object draws the fish back upstream. The calling back of the "shadow" of the fish is so similar to the concept of attracting back to the near lifeless body of a person the soul or life of the patient, that the identification of man with nature appears quite simple and direct. Man is really not that different from other creatures and forces of nature. The primitive or animist belief provides a "unifying philosophy of life" -- to use Allport's phrase.

A returned missionary tells about the personality-nature relationship among the Bantu tribesmen of the Congo.[5] Even though these people do not have a cause-and-effect theory of events as we know it from a scientific point of view, they have a theory that makes sense to them. For example, if a tree falls on a person's leg and breaks it, that is not because the chopper of the tree was careless about where he was standing, but because this person had violated the tree or forest in some way. Perhaps he had not performed a certain ceremony before chopping it down, if it were a totem tree symbolic of the tribe; or the tree's spirit may have been cooperating with some other person in the tribe who wished him harm, such as a witch or sorcerer. In other words, it was no accident, as we would think of it, but the event had a specific and personal meaning. Hence, the animist's religious interpretation of the relationship between personality and nature includes the world of spirits. This principle is especially prominent in explaining illness and healing.

Mana is a force that primitive man believes exists in a way like gravity. It may exist in trees, animals, stones, spears, as well as in persons; yet it may also be incorporated into one's personality. For example, a spear has power in itself as well as by virtue of the one who throws it; and the mana of the spear increases with each victim killed, for the victim's mana has become merged with the spear. So also, if I eat the heart of a lion, I may receive the courage and ferocity of the lion. The Algonquin Indians believed that if one ate the heart of a slain victim, the victor would incorporate the "manitou" or power of that victim into himself.

Celestial bodies have always held a certain fascination for man. There is something mysterious and attractive about the moon and the stars as they change their positions and peek out from behind clouds in unexpected ways. The sun has long been associated with life and growing things. Primitive man often attributed masculinity to the sun and feminity to the moon, thus giving them personal characteristics like his own. There are certain similarities between rhythm of celestial bodies, the cycle of nature, and human patterns. The most obvious is the twenty-eight-day menstrual cycle of the woman and the period of time required for the moon to renew herself. That is why the moon appears in connection with fertility rites. But not only men and women, but all of nature is on a cycle of the seasons regulated by the sun, especially in the northern and southern hemispheres where the length of days varies and the growing season is governed thereby.

Sacred time is a further elaboration of the influence of the sun and the moon. Certain times are propitious for hunting, other times for travel or battle. There may be a "good time" to be born, a time when the elements of nature are just right. In the Bible the term kairos is used to indicate that something has "come to pass in the fullness of time," at a significant time, at an "appointed time," a time fulfilling prophecy, etc. This is more filled with meaning than the simple marking off of minutes into seconds of equal length or the accumulation of minutes into hours, which is covered by the term chronos (from which we derive the word chronology and chronometer). Primitive man viewed the time dimension of his existence as significant and full of religious or spiritual meaning.

Sacred places can have both symbolic and practical significance for primitive or animistic man. People do not choose a sacred place; they do not make something sacred; they discover it. For example, a bull may be let loose; and where the tribesmen later find it, there is the proper place to build the temple or village. It is not just any place; it is the right place attested to by omens and signs. When stones are set in a circle, or walls built around a place of worship or sacred grove, there may very well be two functions fulfilled at once. First, it does serve the practical purpose of keeping out wild beasts or enemy tribes. Secondly, there is a symbolic dynamic at work in the very fact that amidst all the uncertainties of nature with its storms and dangers, there is within this sacred circle a place of security. Within this place certain things will happen with ritual-like predictability. There is some sense of control over what happens within the safety and protection of this enclosed area. In this little cosmos or world there is order.

The Chinese practiced geomancy (the latter part of the
word comes from the root, mania), meaning divination in relation
to the earth. Certain persons would be consulted to find out
the "right place" to bury a family member, perhaps at the most
propitious place to be able to relate to the spirits beyond and
the persons of significance still living on earth in bodily form.
In China today one can still see tombstones and monuments
scattered helter skelter in the midst of fields. It is not easy
for the Maoists to convince the peasants in rural areas that
these obstructions to modern agriculture can be moved into more
compact cemeteries. Some such folkways linger long after
official rejection.

MODERN ANIMISTS AMONG US

Traces of animism may be found among us in many forms even
in Twentieth Century America. One of my father's Norwegian
immigrant parishioners in central Minnesota was a case in point.
One day when he called at their farm home, he found this woman
churning butter in the back yard with the Bible supporting one of
the four legs of the butter churn. After he got over his shock
at this disrespectful use of the Bible, he inquired why she had
not used a stick or board to keep the churn level. She explained, "As long as I have the churn on the Bible, the Trolls
(forest elves) in the woods cannot keep the cream from turning
into butter."

One of my Danish parishioners in Boston believed that if a
candle went out on the Altar during a worship service, someone
in the congregation would die that year. Once, while I was
preaching, two candles which had been leaning towards each other,
combined to flame up in a hazardous way. One of the deacons
went up and quietly extinguished it. After the service, an
elderly man asked me pensively, "I wonder who it will be?" The
deacon reassured him that in this case that folk-belief did not
apply since the candle had been put out and did not go out by
itself. The old man was somewhat relieved, but I was not, since
I had an average of ten funerals a year. Very likely someone
would die that year, the year the candle went out on the Altar.
And as the old man would leave the next funeral service and
shake hands with me at the door, he would very likely shake his
head slowly and say, "You remember the candle. To think that
it would be Hans, and he so much younger than I."

Another believed that if a bird flew against a window and
broke its neck and died, someone living in that house would
die, almost as though it were a life for a life. The day I
called on a terminally ill woman, this very thing had happened.
A bird had broken its neck trying to fly through a picture
window. And she did die that year.

There is often some connection between the ancient belief and the actual events. Indeed, if you place the butter churn on the Bible and churn very sincerely and vigorously, the chances are very good that you will get butter. It is also true that if a candle goes out on the Altar, there is a good chance that someone will be baptized, confirmed, or married that year too. But these are not matters for reason, statistics, or scientific inquiry. The butter churn, old man, and the ill woman were not interested in that line of discourse.

Recently I stayed in a brand new Hilton hotel. If members of a convention of physicists or statisticians had wanted to stay on the 13th floor on principle, namely, that they were not to be intimidated by any supersititions about the number THIRTEEN, they could not have done so. The numbers on the elevator indicator skip safely from 12 to 14. Baseball pitchers may wear a certain cap for good luck, carry a rabbit's foot, or touch their left ear on each windup. Some of our compulsive mannerisms may well represent a latent, subconscious animism. It is more pervasive in our society than most of us realize. You can add to the list from your own psyche or, safer still, from the notions of your friends and relatives. Numerous are the devotees of astrology, scientology, numerology, hari krishna, snake handling, and mystery cults, which are heavily seasoned with animism. Nor are these religious beliefs limited to the uneducated. A biology major from an excellent liberal arts college told me soberly that if a person ate organic food, that person would never get sick. But we must turn our attention to the psychological dynamics underlying animism: symbolism.

SYMBOLISM

The historical continuity of some common symbols seems easy enough to trace. Fire warmed the ancient family in their cave, kept the tiger away from the entrance to their home, and finally served them well in the cooking of food. We also see fire used in sacrifices and burnt offerings upon altars. Moses had a significant religious experience in the presence of the burning bush as he heard God's voice say, "...put off your shoes from your feet, for the place on which you are standing is holy ground." (Exodus 3:5b) Later the Holy Spirit descended upon the disciples in the form of "tongues of fire." And still candlelight dinners, a cozy fireplace, and the fireworks on the 4th of July add something special to life.

Consider water as another basic element in our environment which has been infused with meaning beyond its physical characteristics of H_2O. Again we begin with the practical and life-giving answer to the instinct of thirst since the body is made up of such a high percentage of water. Then there is water for cooking and bathing. Rain is needed for crops and fruit trees to thrive. There is also the ominous aspect of water: flood and drowning, as in <u>Psalm</u> 42:7.

> "Deep calls to deep,
>   at the thunder of thy cataracts;
> all thy waves and thy billows
>   have gone over me."

Noah's flood was for sin; and people still drown in their sins and have a sinking feeling. In tabernacle and temple, water also stood for purification. Saint Paul speaks of baptism as a washing of regeneration, a washing away of sin. Even before we were born, we floated in amniotic fluid.

What does it take to make a symbol? It is the combining of some tangible object with a commonly agreed upon meaning. Thus, a short and a long stick mean nothing in and of themselves; but if one is attached to the other in a certain way it becomes a symbol of Christ, the crucifixion, forgiveness, Christianity as a religion, etc. A few strips of red cloth and white cloth in one hand and a bunch of cut-out stars in the other hand do not mean much in and of themselves; but put the stripes in an alternating pattern and put exactly fifty of the stars on a blue field in the upper left-hand corner, and you symbolize the United States of America, the American way of life, democracy, patriotism, and much more. This colorful pattern would not be a symbol if I were the only person on earth who thought it meant anything special. By symbolization we usually mean that a consensus has been reached by some group as to the meaning of this or that object. It becomes a form of communication, a means of solidifying a group, a short-hand method of condensing much meaning into a brief compass.

JUNG'S IMPORTANT CONTRIBUTION TO THE PSYCHO-DYNAMICS OF SYMBOLISM[7]

> "In addition to our immediate consciousness, which is of a thoroughly personal nature and which we believe to be the only empirical psyche (even if we tack on the personal unconscious **as** an appendix), there exists a second psychic system of a collective, universal, and impersonal nature which is identical in all individuals. This collective unconscious does not develop individually but is inherited. It consists of pre-existent forms, the archetypes, which can only become conscious secondarily and which give definite form to certain psychic contents."[8]

206

Carl Gustav Jung was convinced from his clinical experience and other research that just as personal experiences from child- hood are never lost but remain in the personal unconscious (if not available to conscious memory), so the collective experi- ences of the human race also have not been lost. In other words, you enjoy your cozy fireplace, but there is still a faint trace of the meaning of fire from the ancient caveman's experience which lingers to influence you even though you may be totally unaware of it. As a pschoanalyst, he believed he could trace these ancient symbols (archetypes) in the dreams and free asso- ciations of his patients as well as in folk lore and mythology. A dream may use the indirect and symbolic communication of drowning in water; and, according to Jung, that language can be interpreted through an understanding of the primordial and uni- versal archetype of water. Thus we are linked not only with other human beings of our generation but also with our ancestors back into the dim recesses of animism, the experiences and meanings of antiquity.

Circles and squares were both significant for Jung in sym- bolic terms. The circle is found in nature, the earth, the moon, the orbits in which celestial bodies make their pilgrimage. The sexual connotations of round openings is obvious, as well as the mouth of a cave and the mouth of a person. No wonder we see so many circles in ancient symbolism. The square represents the number 4: the four seasons, the four directions (north, east, south, west) as well as the ends of two axes (as in up, down, to and fro). Multiples of four also fit into this symbolism as in the points of the compass or the Wheel of the Law in Buddhism and the lotus flower symbolizing Brahma, the Creator,in Figure 22.

Jung believed that four was so basic a symbol that he was not surprised to find "quaternity" in many places which would have eluded others. The mandala fascinated him. In oriental art he found schematic illustrations which combined concentric circles, the seasons of the year, attributes of gods and goddesses, etc., which had the motif of circle and four. (See Chapter 11 for further references to the number four, the four elements described by the Greeks.)

The significant point of all of this discussion for the study of the pyschology of religion is the assumption on the part of Jung that accepting our linkage with the near and far distant past is wholesome. We should accept our heritage even when it includes ancient animism. To deny it is to cut our- selves off from our roots, to float on the tides of history without any moorings. We need not be ashamed of primitive roots just because we now live in a scientific-technological age.

The Wheel of the Law is a symbol of
Buddhism. The spokes represent the
Eightfold Path.

Lotus flower symbolizes god Brahma
the Creator. Attached to the earth below the water, it nevertheless floats
unperturbed above the waves.

Fig. 22   Two Symbols of Circle and Four

Viktor Frankl would second the motion, agreeing that today one
of our problems is lack of meaning; Jung would say, the kind of
meaning every age has needed and found useful.

     True symbols are not made up like a painting or street sign
in a deliberate way. They grow from vital experiences related to
basic life issues and elemental realities like the seasons and
weather, birth and death, sin and danger, security and protection, emotional trauma and peace of mind that come s from
resolution of the problems of existence. Such symbols evolve
through the ages and are potent precisely because of what they
have come to stand for. They imply a philosophy of life and a
world view that has significance for personality development
and adjustment.

SYMBOLS AND THE THEMATIC APPERCEPTION TEST

The TAT (Thematic Apperception Test) is a projective instrument designed to ferret out from a subject impressions,
associations, and feelings to which the individual may not be
able to give conscious voice in normal conversation and declara-
tive sentences. The method is quite simple. A shadowy
silhouette-type picture is shown to the person, e.g., a young
person standing against a window holding a violin. The one
tested must describe this situation in his/her own words. One
says the boy is happy that his father gave him this wonderful
instrument because he has great confidence in his son's musical
ability. Another says the boy is going to commit suicide by
jumping out of the window because he was not admitted to a famous
music school, a life long dream. Where do the tested subjects
get their information? Not from the picture, which is neutral
showing neither smile nor scowl. They get their impression
from within their own psyche, their own personal experience.
Another picture shows two shadowy figures facing each other: one
sees anger, another love in the relationship; and so forth.

Religious symbols may operate as such a projective test.
Show the Star of David to a devout,orthodox Jew and he/she
will sense not only worshipful connotations but awareness of a
long history of religious tradition. A bigoted WASP seeing the
same symbol intensifies his/her prejudicial anger at a group
with all kinds of negative associations.

Religious stories and myths are symbolic because each
listener projects a personal meaning onto the heroes thus
described. If the story of the Prodigal Son is read to a congregation, some will identify with the father, some with the
estranged son, and others with the hard working son who stayed
home and tended to business. Some religions even have gods
and goddesses for various occupations: Neptune, Mars, and Ceres
with whom sailors, soldiers, and growers of cereals could
identify. It would be interesting to know what ten of your
friends thought was the meaning of various stained glass windows
in a church as you all stood looking at them. It is doubtful
you would get a consensus. If you included the feelings and
emotional overtones associated with these symbolic windows, the
difference would become more varied. Each would project onto the
window more than the image contained. Naturally this diversity
increases in proportion to the abstraction of the symbol.

Words and phrases can also be symbolic and carry much
freight. What do you think of, what do you feel, in connection
with the following:

The Pope	Synagogue	Hell
God the Father	Christmas	Speaking in Tongues
Heaven	Mosque	Seder
Salvation	Blessed Virgin	Ramadan
Satan	Abraham	Beatitudes

If some of these terms are unfamiliar to you, they do not carry
much weight; others arouse warm memories from childhood and
ethnic traditions which go back for centuries.

Symbols have power to motivate, to focus attention, to
control behavior, to inhibit, etc. They help to shape personality, and, at the same time, the person may be selective in
how a given symbol is assimilated into the individual's experience and personality. Let us examine one symbol in detail to
see how it can operate.

THE SWASTIKA: AN EXAMPLE OF ANIMIST SYMBOLISM[9]

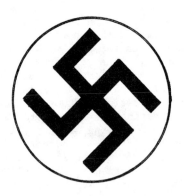

Fig. 23   The Swastika

"The swastika as a graphic symbol is found
in almost every ancient and primitive cult
throughout the world. It appears in Christian

catacombs and pre-Columbian temples. It
was used by the Hindus, the Chinese, the Celts,
and the Germanic peoples.[10] Its origin and development reveal what Urban identifies as the
process of symbolization -- from copy to
analogy, from analogy to symbol.[11] Zelia Nuttall, in The Fundamental Principles of Old and
New World Civilizations, provides a comprehensive study of the origin, development, and
meaning of the swastika.[12] Nuttall demonstrates
that the swastika was originally a composite
copy of the shape of the constellation Ursa
Major as it moved from sunset to sunrise,
through the four seasons of the year around the
star Polaris. The swastika began to appear
throughout the world around 4,000 b.c. at a
time when Ursa Major was "circumpolar." The
primitive period of swastika development ends
somewhere between 500 b.c. and 1200 a.d.; during
this time the Pole Star ceased being "con-
spicuous" and "immovable." The movement of
Ursa Major around the Pole Star conveyed the
idea of motion and progression. In the Mexican
and Egyptian Calendar the swastika became a
sign for one year or cycle. The center of the
swastika, the immovable Pole Star, was used to
ascertain direction by night; by analogy it
became associated with feelings of trust, dependence, and gratitude toward the one changeless entity in nature. Each society invested
the swastika with its own specific values and
derived from it a way of interpreting the
particular forces of nature which determined
its destiny. In agrarian societies it was
associated with the dry and rainy seasons.
Its center, rooted in the changeless Pole Star,
gave reason to hope that the one who controlled
the seasons would send rain to enliven the dead
soil. By analogy, it became a symbol of the
creator whose power extended over four seasons
and four corners of the world.

Primitive Christian use of the swastika
was natural. Not only did it denote the Father-
Creator's control over nature, but it had an
inherent ability to represent basic tenets of
the Christian faith. Christ is the new creation
in whom, according to Colossians, the whole
world holds together[13]; further, Christ

commanded his disciples to preach to the four
corners of the world.[14]

The most obvious connection of the primitive church with the swastika lies in its
formal relation to the shape of the cross.
The following passages from the Nestorian
Tablet, dated 781 a.d., were written by a
priest of the Syrian Christian Church to
eulogize the propagation of the Christian religion in China. These words demonstrate the
association of swastika ideas with the cross:

> Our eternal, true lord God.... He
> appointed the cross as the means of
> determining the four cardinal points,
> he moved the original spirit and pro-
> duced the two principles of nature;
> the sombre void was changed and
> heaven and earth were opened out; the
> sun and moon revolved and day and
> night commenced; having perfected all
> inferior objects, he then made the
> first man....the illustrious and
> honorable Messiah, veiling his true
> dignity, appearing in the world as
> man...a bright star announced the
> felicitous event (of his birth)...
> he fixed the extent of the eight
> boundaries.... As a seal (his dis-
> ciples) hold the cross, whose in-
> fluence is reflected in every di-
> rection uniting all without dis-
> tinction. As they strike the word
> the fame of their benevolence is
> diffused abroad; worshipping towards
> the east they hasten on their way to
> life and glory...[15]

For the Christian Church of the Middle Ages
the swastika most generally symbolized the movement and power of the sun, and of the Son; although, it was still seen as a symbol of the
movement of the Christian message into the four
cardinal directions.[16] Nuttall conjectures that
the swastika lost much of its force following
the Middle Ages because the primary object which
gave it birth and shape had ceased to exist. The
swastika shape was no longer clearly visible in
the stars. The replacement of the sun for the

pole star and its constellation as the symbol
of movement and power is evidence of this change.
It was natural that the dominant light of day
would replace the dominant light of night when
that night light ceased being permanent.[17] The
death of the swastika as a living symbol was
completed as reference to the four cardinal
directions become part of the cross symbol. By
the time of Hitler the swastika had degenerated
into a decorative form of the cross.[18] With
the adoption of the swastika by the Nazi Party
as its official emblem, the swastika received
new power as a symbol.

The swastika banner was designed by Hitler
himself, who write in Mein Kampf:

I myself after countless attempts had
laid down a final form: a flag with a
background of red cloth, having a white
circle, and in its center, a black
swastika....
    As National Socialists we see our
program in our flag. In the red we see
the social idea of movement, in the
white the nationalistic idea, and in
the swastika the fight for the victory
of Aryan man and at the same time for
the victory of the idea of creative
work, which in itself was and always
will be anti-Semitic.[19]

In Hitler's description of his banner dim re-
minders of earlier meanings of the symbol are
evident. The idea of movement is linked to the
field which contains the swastika. With imagination the idea of Aryan supremacy and its
creative work can be associated with the task
of the Creator to govern the four corners of
the world. Just as the swastika received new
meaning for Hitler's Germany, it also received
new meaning for the allied nations fighting
against fascism. As a result of this new encounter with the symbol, its symbolic meaning,
as Goodenough suggests, has been so signifi-
cantly changed that its power as a religious
symbol for this century has been lost; it has
for all practical purposes become a sign of
totalitarianism and anti-religion."[20]

CONCLUSION

Carl Gustav Jung would not have been surprised at the popularity of Alex Haley's book, Roots. Following the widely watched television version of that book, many individuals were prompted to inquire into their own antecedants, their own heritage. He maintained that among his psychotherapy clients an essential ingredient of their recovery was their coming to grips with basic, primordial issues of life often revealed in their dreams as primitive and animistic symbols. He would have agreed with Isaiah 51:1b, "...look to the rock from which you were hewn, and the quarry from which you were digged." Persons who disdain their lowly primitive heritage run the risk of being cast adrift, rootless, like the lotus blossom severed from its source of life.

Our intellectual dealing with reality is like the top of an iceberg; there is much more to it than that. Below the surface is the personal unconscious, and below that the collective unconscious of history. According to Jung, it is all part of the same iceberg, and we disregard it at our peril.

NOTES

1. Eliade, Mircea, The Sacred and the Profane, New York: Harper & Row, Publishers (Torchbook Edition), 1961, pp. 165, 167, and 168.

2. Important contributors to this field are Ruth Benedict, Clyde Kluckhohn, Margaret Mead, and Eliade (cited above). Beside the standard anthropology textbooks, The American Museum of Natural History's series of source books in paper provides a wide assortment of readings under such titles as Personalities and Culture, edited by Robert Hunt and Myth and Cosmos; Gods and Rituals; and Magic, Witchcraft, and Curing, all edited by John Middleton. This series was published in 1967 by The Natural History Press, Garden City, New York.

   For insights into specific aspects of primitive concern discussed in this section, I am also indebted to Bronislaw Malinowski's Magic, Science and Religion, Glencoe, Illinois: The Free Press, 1948. ("Life, Death, and Destiny in Early Faith and Cult," pp. 36-53).

3. Malinowski, op cit., p. 47.

4. Schultz, Harald, "The Waura: Brazilian Indians of the Hidden Xingu," National Geographic Magazine, Volume 129, No. 1, January, 1966, pp. 142-143.

5. The Rev. Rudolph Martens was one of my graduate students.

6. Eliade, Mircea, _Patterns in Comparative Religion_ (Trans-
    lated by Rosemary Sheed), Cleveland: The World Publishing
    Company, 1963, Chapter 4.

7. Reference has already been made to Jung's _Memories, Dreams,
    and Reflections_ in Chapter 3. A few other Jungian sources
    related to the topic of this chapter are: _Man and His
    Symbols_, Garden City, New York: Doubleday, 1964; _The
    Archetypes and the Collective Unconscious_, (translated by
    R. F. C. Hull, New York: Pantheon Books, 1959; _The Undis-
    covered Self_, (translated by R. F. C. Hall), Boston: Little,
    Brown and Company, 1958; _Psychology and Religion_, New Haven:
    Yale University Press, 1938; _Modern Man in Search of a
    Soul_, New York: Harcourt, Brace and Company, 1933.

8. Jung, _The Archetypes and the Collective Unconscious_, p. 43.

9. Benuska, Daniel Alan, _Religious Symbolism: A Study of the
    Contemporary Significance of Ten Christian Symbols_. Un-
    published M.A. Thesis, University of Iowa, August, 1969.
    These excerpts are drawn from pages 15-18 in Chapter 2,
    "The Nature of the Symbol."

10. Cirlot, J. E., "Swastika," _A Dictionary of Symbols_ (trans-
    lated by Jack Sage), New York: Philosophical Library,
    1962, p. 307.

11. Urban, Wilbur Marshall, _Language and Reality_, New York: The
    MacMillan Company, 1939, pp. 401-403, 446.

12. Nuttall, Zelia, _The Fundamental Principles of Old and New
    World Civilizations_ (Vol. II in _Archeological and
    Ethnological Papers_ of the Peabody Museum), Cambridge:
    Peabody Museum of American Archaeology and Ethnology,
    1901, pp. 15-19.

13. _Holy Bible_, Revised Standard Version, _Col._ 1:17.

14. _Ibid._, _Matt._ 28:19.

15. _Nestorian Tablet_, cited by Nuttall, _op. cit._, p. 304.

16. Cirlot, _loc. cit._

17. Nuttall, _op. cit._, p. 461.

18. Goodenough, Erwin R., _The Problems of Method and Symbols
    from Jewish Cult_ (Vol. IV of _Jewish Symbols in the_

Greco-Roman Period), New York: Bollingen Foundation Inc.,
c. 1954, pp. 34 and 35.

19. Hitler, Adolph, _Mein_ _Kempf_, cited in _Readings_ _on_ _Fascism_
and _National_ Socialism, selected by the Department of
Philosophy, University of Colorado, Denver: Alan Swallow,
n.d., pp. 86 and 87.

20. Goodenough, _op_. _cit_., p. 35.

EXAMINATION AND APPLICATION

1. Can you think of some superstition or fantasy which you hold
privately and would be a bit embarrassed to admit? How has
it affected your behavior or decisions?

2. Is the return-to-Mother-Earth movement with its organic food
enthusiasts and ecological emphasis tinged with a touch of
animism? Have you heard a young person say that "getting
it all together" makes one feel better? Does this relate
to binding the conscious and personal subconscious closer
to the collective unconscious?

3. What difference might it make to a person to feel that one's
personality is in close and inter-dependent relationship
with nature instead of believing oneself to be set over
against nature in a manipulative or controlling stance?

4. If "Clothes make the man," how does this compare with the
animist who believes that his spear gets stronger as it
draws upon the "mana" from another source?

5. What are the symbolic implications of clothing and fashion
(policeman's uniform, blue jeans, shoes, clerical garb,
nurse's uniform, etc.)? What is being communicated concerning values, status, beliefs, interpersonal relations,
and functions? In what way do these factors influence
personality -- experientially and functionally?

6. Name three symbols which make a positive impact on you,
three that make a negative impact on you. Can you suggest
why?

7. Do you value those aspects of religion which are intellectual or cognitive more than those which are emotional or
affective? Can you give a few examples? Did this chapter
take sides in this matter?

8. Do you deal with danger by reason or through the dynamics of animism? Cite examples from the past two months. Along this same line, how does "totemism" operate in your life, your community?

9. What examples of "mandala" (symbols of circle or 4) can you point out in your environment?

10. What is your favorite religious or cultural hero? Can you think of any way in which you use such a one as a role model?

11. If you subscribe to both scientific-technological interpretations of nature and an influence of Spirit (or mind over matter) in the world, how do you reconcile these or hold both at once? Need they be mutually contradictory?

12. How has this chapter related to your "unifying philosophy of life?"

13. Is it safe to end this chapter with 13?

CHAPTER 10

BIBLICAL VIEW OF HUMAN NATURE

When we consider the wide range of cultural settings and historical periods represented between the covers of the Bible, we appreciate the difficulty of finding one single theory of personality. Attitudes toward marriage and the family changed considerably from the Patriarch's polygamy to Saint Paul's esteem for celibacy. The personality of the wandering nomad had to endure different stresses from those of the citizen in busy Jerusalem under Roman government. We cannot deal with all the nuances but will select certain important themes, classical characters or illustrations which are typical of a biblical view of personality.

PERSONS WITH PROBLEMS AND POTENTIAL

The biblical method of presenting human nature is not so much theoretical as personal, frequently in the form of a case history. Faith is illustrated by the case of Abraham, a man who left familiar surroundings and followed God's leading in the belief that his destiny would be revealed to him in due course. So also, King David is the model of the repentant sinner, and Doubting Thomas is the example of another struggle in personal commitment. The teachings of Jesus bear the same stamp: The Woman at the Well, the Good Samaritan, the Rich Young Ruler, etc.,all portray one or another facet of personality conflict, issue, or growth. Some illustrate ideal types to be followed; others demonstrate immaturity and character defect.

The individual is seen in relationship to others through the convenant, as part of a tribe, the chosen people of Israel, as a part of corporate worship in tabernacle, temple, or church, in fellowship with other believers. One could characterize this psychology of personality as one of inter-personalism. This is one of the reasons that so many of the biblical case histories are ethical in nature, dealing with interpersonal responsibility -- sin, forgiveness, love, and helpfulness. But first, we should clarify some distinctions between the biblical view of human nature and the animist perspective of the last chapter.

God, as the _universal_ Person, is central. God is referred to with a personal pronoun, "He," not "It." God is not described as "Divine Intelligence" or "First Principle." It is for this reason that human beings can understand God in a limited way by revelation, prayer, etc. Yet there is great care taken that created persons not think more highly of themselves than they ought to think. No one should attempt to make a statue or likeness of God (as Greeks and Romans freely did), nor should any person presume to be God's equal in any way (Garden of Eden tragedy, Tower of Babel confusion).

> "For as the heavens are higher than the earth,
> so are my ways higher than your ways and my
> thoughts than your thoughts."
> (_Isaiah_ 55:9)

Distinct from the animist concept is the clear distinction between the nature of persons and the nature of rocks, trees, and animals. The creation story in _Genesis_ sets Adam and Eve apart because God said, "Let us make man in our image, after our likeness; and let them have dominion over the fish of the sea, and over the birds of the air, and over the cattle, and over all the earth....male and female he created them." (_Genesis_ 1:26-27) Witchcraft and sorcery were not to be practiced. Also, instead of a multiplicity of gods and spirits to whom one might owe obedience, there is in the Bible the clear teaching of monotheism.

> "I am the Lord your God ...
> You shall have no other gods before me ...
> for I the Lord your God am a jealous God."
> (_Exodus_ 20:2,3,5)

This raises interesting questions to which I provide no answer. How does the impact of divinity upon a person differ when it is dispersed among many gods from when it is concentrated in One Person? Does it increase the intensity or focus attention? Is polytheism or monotheism easier for a mentally retarded person to relate to? What advantages or disadvantages lie in the anthropomorphic descriptions of God? Is there a gradual de-emphasis on the anthropomorphic down through the centuries during which the Bible was recorded? Obviously there are questions that go beyond the purview of this book into the field of scriptural studies, but I hope we have indicated the directions in which biblical view of mankind is moving away from many animist presuppositions.

God is seen as personal. God loves, judges, speaks to, and forgives persons. In the background there is always the question: How can an individual come into relationship, or be restored to a relationship if alienated, with The Person who is God? That is what is assumed to give the individual worth and meaning in life, to be in wholesome relationship with the God who not only created him/her and all that exists but who continues to care for each individual. God is continually calling people to realize their true identity; namely, that they are children of God who should live as such. But the peril of each individual is that he/she is tempted to reject this call, to set the self up against God, to assert a rebellious self-sufficiency. Such a one needs to be humbled under the mighty hand of God, to repent, to be reborn or converted to a right relationship with God. That is salvation, one's proper destiny. The problem is that persons are ambivalent by nature; and we need to deal with that in further detail.

IMAGE OF GOD

The positive side of man's personality is given in his creation according to the Imago Dei, the creative and good side of the universe characterized by God's own nature. When this aspect or leading of personality is being exercised, then blessings, righteousness, love, and productivity follow. In Erikson's epigenetic diagram (page 273 in Childhood and Society) it would seem that the upper alternative at each stage represents this wholesome side: basic trust, autonomy, initiative, industry, identity, intimacy, generativity, and ego integrity. Paul speaks of the this godly life in this way: "...the fruit of the Spirit is love, joy, peace, patience, kindness, goodness, faithfulness, gentleness, self-control..." (Galatians 5:22-23).

God looked upon his creation and saw that it was good. The psalmist states that man is "little less than God." (Psalm 8:5) Human beings have great potential and opportunities to live in joy and fulfillment. That is the positive side.

THE OLD ADAM OR ORIGINAL SIN

The negative side of human nature, according to the Bible, is the tendency of longstanding to misuse the self, to be disobedient to God's commandments, to be foolish, to want to put oneself in the center of things thus displacing God. The temptation in the Garden of Eden was sneakily put by the serpent: "...you will be like God..." (Genesis 3:5) The lower animals do not have the capacity to sin like human beings have.

221

They are governed by instinct and generally quit eating when they
are full. Adam and his kind are smart enough to put two and two
together, to see the relationship between hunger, eating, and
pleasure. At that level of reasoning, the temptation can arise:
"I know I have eaten enough to satisfy my physical needs because
I am now no longer hungry; but I will continue to eat for the
pleasurable taste." The serpent enters the scene with the
temptation of gluttony. Other sins to choose from are drunkenness, sexual perversion, stealing, and a whole host of behaviors
that make good sense to "The Old Adam" in us.

The negative, self-destructive, and anti-social alternatives on Erikson's epigenetic diagram (see again page 273 in
Childhood and Society) are mistrust, shame and doubt, guilt,
inferiority, role confusion, isolation, stagnation, and despair.
Paul speaks of these sinful ways thus: "Now the works of the
flesh are plain: immorality, impurity, licentiousness, idolatry,
sorcery, enmity, strife, jealousy, anger, selfishness, dissen-
sions, party spirit, envy, drunkenness, carousing, and the like."
(Galatians 5:19-21a) The biblical view of personality is not
surprised to find persons violating the Ten Commandments because
there is this downward pull toward selfishness.

Theologians and psychologists alike are divided into two
camps; some schools of thought seeing humanity as basically good
and only touched from the outside with smudges of sinfulness,
as often as not caused by bad environmental influences; and
other schools of thought declaring that mankind is basically
sinful, and if left to one's own natural tendencies will follow
the laws of the jungle "red in tooth and claw," grasp for
"territoriality," and seek selfish gain at the expense of
neighbor. The implications of these two distinct anthropologies
have marked significance for counseling and psychotherapy, which
take us beyond the discussion of this chapter; but let us consider the Freudian attitude toward the Id and the latent forces
of aggression on the one hand and the hopeful and optimistic
view of Carl Rogers that if only the external pressures and
judgmentalism of others could be set aside in the accepting
atmosphere of the counseling room, the client will be able to
use his/her own inner strengths and insights creatively in the
problem solving process.

In the section on "The Dilemma of the Will" in Chapter 2,
we quoted Paul's words about his moral dilemma. A few verses
later in the same chapter he elaborates further his sense of
tension between the positive and negative side of his personality.

> "So I find it to be a law that when I want to
> do right, evil lies close at hand. For I de-
> light in the law of God, in my inmost self,

but I see in my members another law at war
with the law of my mind and making me captive
to the law of sin which dwells in my members.
Wretched man that I am! Who will deliver me
from this body of death?" (Romans 7:21-24)

The tension between good and evil is not only "out there in the
world," it is in his own nature between the Image of God and
the Old Adam. Derwyn Owen clearly distinguishes how this view
of man's moral nature differs from other interpretations.

"Thus, the Biblical aetiology, given in the
Old Testament story of creation and the Fall,
is radically different from the characteristic Orphic aetiology of the "religious" anthropology. In the Old Testament, there is
no tendency to regard matter as evil; it is
created by God and is good. There is no tendency to regard man as a composite being, con-
sisting of a divine, immortal soul that comes
down from the eternal, heavenly realm and a
mean, perishing body that belongs to an inferior level of reality. On the contrary,
man is made of the dust of the ground, with
the breath of life breathed into it but,
more important, with the image of his Creator
stamped on his nature. Nor is there any tendency to locate the source of evil in the body
and its appetites. The origin of evil in
human life is located in the tendency, possible
only for a being made in the image of God, to
act and to think of himself as though he were
God; to assume, in the words of C. S. Lewis,
the status of a noun when he is really only an
adjective. This means that the whole of human
life is really only an adjective. This means
that the whole of human life is thrown off its
true axis; all elements in man's nature, the
spiritual and rational as well as the physical
and material, become in a subtle way perverted.
It means that men do not become what they were
meant to be, sons of God enjoying the glorious
liberty of the children of God (Romans 8:21);
they become, instead, sons of perdition en- [1]
slaved in the terrible bondage of corruption.

PSYCHOSOMATIC UNITY OF THE PERSON

In Judaism the person was not divided into two parts: spiritual and material. Rather the individual was a whole person, a unity, an integral entity. Only in the last few decades have we made any serious efforts to reunite the person whom we have separated into two spheres by the Greek dichotomy which created the body-mind split or spirit-matter cleavage.

The Hebrew word we translate as "spirit" is _ruach_, which literally means "wind" (Latin - _spiritus_). The ancients perceived wind as vital and full of life. Some believed that when wind blew over horses on a hillside they became pregnant and filled with new life. Naturally, wind was synonymous with and the source of life since when a creature ceased to breathe, the life had gone out of it. To this day we say that a person who has died at the hospital has expired (_ex-spiritus_). On the contrary a person filled with wind, i.e., filled with life, vitality, and spirit, is _inspired_.

Likewise, the term Paul used for spirit, _pneuma_, is found in our contemporary vocabulary: "pneumonia," a disease of the wind or breathing, pneumatic drills run by air pressure, etc. In the creation story of Genesis it was quite natural that

> "God formed man of the dust of the ground and
> _breathed_ into his nostrils the breath of life;
> and man became a living being." (_Genesis_ 2:7)

Thus life is associated with one of the natural elements, air in motion. Spirit is not necessarily set apart from, or over against, nature.

Let us consider the concept of "body" in biblical usage. Some Hebrew and Greek terms for body or "flesh" elude our grasp when we read the English translations. The Hebrew term _basar_ stands for all of a person's life, not only the body. Therefore, bodily terms could represent the condition of the whole person: "bowels of compassion," "no health in my bones because of my sin," "A tranquil mind gives life to the flesh, but passion makes the bones rot," "Eat thou not the bread of him that hath an evil eye." Or consider this classic psychosomatic description of axiety:

> I am poured out like water, and all my bones
> are out of joint; my heart is like wax, it is
> melted within my breast; my strength is dried
> up like a potsherd, and my tongue cleaves to
> my jaws; thou dost lay me in the dust of death.
> (_Psalm_ 22:14-15)

In short, one could use a mental state to describe a bodily condition or a physical symptom to describe a spiritual reality. Such is the holistic view of human personality portrayed in the Bible. Man does not _have_ a body, he _is_ a body.

From this vantage point it is not strange to symbolize the covenant (promise of many descendants from generation unto generation) with the mark of circumcision of the penis. Quite contrary to frequent pietistic references to the sinfulness of the body or physical appetites in later time (after the body-mind problem arose), the Bible does not assume that the body or any part thereof is evil in itself because God says that his creation was "good."

In the New Testament two Greek terms for body are used. Soma means simply body as a whole unit as in the following passage of Saint Paul:

> "Do you not know that your body is the temple
> of the Holy Spirit within you, which you have
> from God? You are not your own; you were
> bought with a price. So glorify God in your
> body." (I Corinthians 6:19-20)

Obviously body is not the opposite of spirit in this case.

Sarx can be translated as "flesh" in two senses of lustful appetites, the frailties of human nature, sins of passion, etc., not because of their physical involvement, which may be relatively incidental, but because of their immoral intentions or anti-social consequences. Thus Saint Paul can speak of the "works of the flesh" as contrasted to the "fruits of the spirit."

> "Now the works of the flesh are plain: im-
> morality, impurity, licentiousness, idolatry,
> sorcery, enmity, strife, jealousy, anger,
> selfishness, dissension, party spirit, envy,
> drunkenness, carousing, and the like.... But
> the fruit of the Spirit is life, joy, peace,
> patience, kindness, goodness, faithfulness,
> gentleness, self-control; against such there
> is no law." (Galatians 5:19-23)

Note the works of the flesh are not necessarily physical but reflect sinful ways of relating to others or of misusing the body to injure oneself (e.g., drunkenness), also attitudes (e.g., jealousy and anger).

ATTITUDES TOWARD ILLNESS

The doctrine of retribution assumes that illness is the natural and just punishment for sin. Job's counselors insist that his boils and other misfortunes must be due to some sin which he is unwilling to confess and for which he is not repentant. Contemporary psychosomatic medicine is raising this possible interpretation for some physical and mental disorders. Repressed anger, hidden guilt, morbid fear, anxiety over self-seeking status aggrandizement, etc.,can lead to or aggravate peptic ulcers, high blood pressure, and certain chronic diseases in which long-term stress is a factor. Insofar as this can be demonstrated in individual cases, we would have to say that there can still be some validity in the doctrine of retribution. Naturally, it has to be applied cautiously so as not to make it apply to every condition of illness.

There was also the interpretation that evil spirits could cause illness:

> "(A man met Jesus) who had demons; for a long time he had worn no clothes, and he lived not in a house but among the tombs...many times it had seized him; he was kept under guard, and bound with chains and fetters, but he broke the bonds and was driven by the demon into the desert. Jesus then asked him, "What is your name?" And he said, "Legion"; for many demons had entered him." (Luke 8:26-37)

Usually such conditions are similar to what we would call mental illness and psychotic episodes. Note again the term "spirit"; this time an _evil_ spirit.

In the Epistle of _James_ (5:14-16) we again see the spiritual meaning attributed to illness. It should be treated with social concern: "Is any among you sick? Let him call for the elders of the church, and let them pray over him, anointing him with oil in the name of the Lord." Prayer and faith are considered strong medicine in this case. Secondly, "confess your sins to one another, and pray for one another, that you may be healed." This is the basic foundation for the Catholic Sacrament of the Sick formerly called Extreme Unction. (See Chapter 9)

Another meaning of illness is its use in character testing and personality development. Saint Paul (II Corinthians 12:1-10) considered his "thorn in the flesh," an unspecified infirmity, to be sent by God to keep him humble since he might be tempted to consider himself better than others in the church because of his special revelations such as being taken up into the seventh heaven and having experienced unspeakable visions. If this latter condition prevails, obviously a sick person should try to discern what he is intended to <u>learn</u> from his sickness. If it helps him to "grow in grace," the illness could well be a blessing in disguise.

Jesus implies in the following verse that misfortune may also be truly accidental and not related to sin or spiritual matters at all.

> "or those eighteen upon whom the tower in
> Siloam fell and killed them, do you think
> that they were worse offenders than all the
> others who dwelt in Jerusalem?" (<u>Luke</u> 13:4)

The laws of nature, such as gravity, are part of God's created order. Also "(God) makes his sun rise on the evil and on the good, and sends rain on the just and on the unjust." (<u>Matthew</u> 5:45b) Thus we have a variety of meanings ascribed to illness, suffering, and adversity.

FAITH, MYSTERY, AND THE UNKNOWN

Returning to the concept of Original Sin being the mistaken ambition of the creature to assume the omnipotence and omniscience of the Creator, we see one of the functions of faith. It means that one does not have to know everything -- and should be able to rest content with that limitation. There is nothing against normal use of one's mind to exercise the vocation of having "dominion over" other creatures of a lesser order as cited in <u>Genesis</u>; it is the arrogance and pride involved in over-extending oneself. Note what happened to the people of Sinar who made this mistake.

> "Come, let us build ourselves a city, and a
> tower with its top in the heavens, and let
> us make a name for ourselves, lest we be
> scattered abroad upon the face of the whole
> earth. And the Lord came down to see the
> city and the tower, which the sons of men
> had built. And the Lord said, 'Behold, they
> are one people, and they have one language;
> and this is only the beginning of what they
> will do; and nothing that they propose to do
> will now be impossible for them. Come, let
> us go down, and there confuse their language,
> that they may not understand one another's
> speech.' So the Lord scattered them abroad
> from there over the face of all the earth,

and they left off building the city.
Therefore its name was called Babel, because there the Lord confused the language
of all the earth; and from there the Lord
scattered them abroad over the face of all
the earth." (Genesis 11:4-9)

Currently this is a pressing bio-ethical problem when it
comes to experimentation on human beings, test tube babies,
cloning, DNA, human engineering, etc. What is the limit beyond
which it is not safe for us to go in our inquisitiveness and desire for progress and achievement? How tall is the Tower of
Babel?

As Moses met God on the mountain, the Lord said to him,

"Behold, there is a place by me where you
shall stand upon the rock; and while my
glory passes by I will put you in a cleft
of the rock, and I will cover you with my
hand until I have passed by; then I will
take away my hand, and you shall see my
back; but my face shall not be seen."
(Exodus 33:21-23)

As much as a person, even a holy person like Moses, might want
to know all there is to know about God, it is not possible; it
is a mystery. Saint Paul intimates the same finite limitation.

"For now we see in a mirror dimly, but then
face to face. Now I know in part; then I
shall understand fully, even as I have been
fully understood." (I Corinthians 13:12)

Jesus explained to an educated Pharisee, Nicodemus, that he could
not hope to understand spiritual matters fully.

"The wind blows where it wills, and you hear
the sound of it, but you do not know whence
it comes or whither it goes; so it is with
everyone who is born of the Spirit." (John
3:8)

How does this relate to the ASU in Chapter 8? An eminent
heart surgeon told me he would rather operate on a simple,
believing Mennonite farm wife than a sophisticated graduate
student who thought that enough expert knowledge would guarantee
control of nature. The former would be trusting and relaxed,
a much better candidate for surgery. The latter would be
anxious and burdened by a sense of responsibility -- maybe he/she

228

should have read more medical journal articles and studied the technique thoroughly before submitting to heart surgery. What do you think?

Have our very heroic efforts to control nature and be in charge of everything actually brought about our ecological crisis? It is a heavy burden to feel that you have to make everything in the universe happen on time in the right way. Perhaps it is useful to have a category called "mystery," which is humbly acknowledged. This could be the function which faith, mystery, allegory, worship, inspiration, and revelation play from a religious perspective. One does not have to be omnipotent, omnipresent, omniscient, or omni-anything-else. In fact that is the very thing the Bible warns against trying.

TWO CASE RECORDS FROM THE BIBLE

1. King David sins, is apprehended by the prophet, repents, confesses, and is forgiven. Tradition attributed Psalm 51 to him as he worked through his problem devotionally in heartfelt prayer.

> "In the spring of the year, the time when kings go forth to battle, David sent Jo'ab, and his servants with him, and all Israel; and they ravaged the Ammonites, and besieged Rabbah. But David remained at Jerusalem.
>
> It happened, late one afternoon when David arose from his couch and was walking upon the roof of the king's house, that he saw from the roof a woman bathing; and the woman was very beautiful. And David sent and inquired about the woman. And one said, 'Is not this Bathshe'ba, the daughter of Eli'am, the wife of Uri'ah the Hittite?' So David sent messengers, and took her; and she came to him, and he lay with her. (Now she was purifying herself from her uncleanness.) Then she returned to her house. And the woman conceived; and she sent and told David, 'I am with child.'
>
> So David sent word to Jo'ab, 'Send me Uri'ah the Hittite.' And Jo'ab sent Uri'ah to David. When Uri'ah came to him, David asked how Jo'ab was doing, and how the people fared, and how the war prospered. Then David said to Uri'ah, 'Go down to your house, and wash your feet.' And Uri'ah went out of the king's

house, and there followed him a present from
the king. But Uri´ah slept at the door of
the king's house with all the servants of
his lord, and did not go down to his house.
When they told David, 'Uri´ah did not go
down to his house,' David said to Uri´ah,
'Have you not come from a journey? Why did
you not got down to your house?' Uri´ah
said to David, 'The ark and Israel and Judah
dwell in booths; and my lord Jo´ab and the
servants of my lord are camping in the open
field; shall I then go to my house, to eat
and to drink, and to lie with my wife? As
you live, as your soul lives, I will not
do this thing.' Then David said to Uri´ah,
'Remain here today also, and tomorrow I will
let you depart.' So Uri´ah remained in
Jerusalem that day, and the next. And David
invited him, and he ate in his presence and
drank, so that he made him drunk; and in the
evening he went out to lie on his couch with
the servants of his lord, but he did not go
down to his house.

In the morning David wrote a letter to Jo´ab,
and sent it by the hand of Uri´ah. In the
letter he wrote, 'Set Uri´ah in the forefront
of the hardest fighting, and then draw back
from him, that he may be struck down, and die.'
And as Jo´ab was besieging the city, he assigned Uri´ah to the place where he knew there
were valiant men. And the men of the city came
out and fought with Jo´ab; and some of the servants of David among the people fell. Uriah
the Hittite was slain also. Then Jo´ab sent
and told David all the news about the fighting;
and he instructed the messenger, 'When you have
finished telling all the news about the fighting to the kin, then, if the king's anger rises,
and if he says to you, 'Why did you go so near
the city to fight? Did you not know that they
would shoot from the wall? Who killed Abim´-
elech the son of Jerub´besheth? Did not a
woman cast an upper millstone upon him from
the wall, so that he died at Thebez? Why did
you go so near the wall?' then you shall say,
'Your servant Uri´ah the Hittite is dead also.'

So the messenger went, and came and told David
all that Jo´ab had sent him to tell. The

messenger said to David, 'The men gained an advantage over us, and came out against us in the field; but we drove them back to the entrance of the gate. Then the archers shot at your servants from the wall; some of the king's servants are dead; and your servant, Uri´ah, the Hittite is dead also.' David said to the messenger, 'Thus shall you say to Jo´ab, 'Do not let this matter trouble you, for the sword devours now one and now another; strengthen your attack upon the city, and overthrow it.' And encourage him.'

When the wife of Uri´ah heard that Uri´ah her husband was dead, she made lamentation for her husband. And when the mourning was over, David sent and brought her to his house, and she became his wife, and bore him a son. But the thing that David had done displeased the LORD.

And the LORD sent Nathan to David. He came to him, and said to him, 'There were two men in a certain city, the one rich and the other poor. The rich man had very many flocks and herds; but the poor man had nothing but one little ewe lamb, which he had bought. And he brought it up, and it grew up with him and with his children; it used to eat of his morsel, and drink from his cup, and lie in his bosom, and it was like a daughter to him. Now there came a traveler to the rich man, and he was unwilling to take one of his own flock or herd to prepare for the wayfarer who had come to him, but he took the poor man's lamb, and prepared it for the man who had come to him.' Then David's anger was greatly kindled against the man; and he said to Nathan, 'As the LORD lives, the man who has done this deserves to die; and he shall restore the lamb fourfold, because he did this thing, and because he had no pity.'

Nathan said to David, 'You are the man. Thus says the LORD, the God of Israel, 'I anointed you king over Israel, and I delivered you out of the hand of Saul; and I gave you your master's house, and your master's wives into your bosom, and gave you the house of Israel and of Judah; and if this were too little, I would add to you as much more. Why have you

231

despised the word of the LORD, to do what is evil in his sight? You have smitten Uri´ah the Hittite with the sword, and have taken his wife to be your wife, and have slain him with the sword of the Ammonites. Now therefore the sword shall never depart from your house, because you have despised me, and have taken the wife of Uri´ah the Hittite to be your wife.' Thus says the LORD, 'Behold, I will raise up evil against you out of your own house; and I will take your wives before your eyes, and give them to your neighbor, and he shall lie with your wives in the sight of the sun. For you did it secretly; but I will do this thing before all Israel, and before the sun.'' David said to Nathan, 'I have sinned against the LORD.' And Nathan said to David, 'The LORD also has put away your sin; you shall not die. Nevertheless, because by this deed you have utterly scorned the LORD, the child that is born to you shall die.' Then Nathan went to his house." (II Samuel 11:1-12:15)

"Have mercy on me, O God,
    according to thy steadfast love;
  according to thy abundant mercy
    blot out my transgressions.
Wash me thoroughly from my iniquity,
  and cleanse me from my sin!

For I know my transgressions,
  and my sin is ever before me.
Against thee, thee only, have I
    sinned,
  and done that which is evil in
    thy sight,
so that thou art justified in thy
    sentence
  and blameless in thy judgment.
Behold, I was brought forth in iniquity,
  and in sin did my mother conceive me.

Behold, thou desirest truth in the
    inward being,
  therefore teach me wisdom in
    my secret heart.
Purge me with hyssop, and I shall
    be clean;
  wash me, and I shall be whiter
    than snow.

Fill me with joy and gladness;
   let the bones which thou hast
     broken rejoice.
Hide thy face from my sins,
   and blot out all my iniquities.

Create in me a clean heart, O God,
   and put a new and right spirit
     within me.
Cast me not away from thy presence,
   and take not thy holy Spirit from
     me.
Restore to me the joy of thy salvation,
   and uphold me with a willing
     spirit."   (Psalm 51:1-12)

2.   The Prodigal Son illustrates the concept of grace, unmerited and totally accepting love. This has been a great comfort to persons who had worried that their defects of body or character would make it impossible for God to accept them. This theme has been repeated in numerous hymns, sermons, and devotional literature.

"There was a man who had two sons; and the younger of them said to his father, 'Father, give me the share of property that falls to me,' And he divided his living between them. Not many days later, the younger son gathered all he had and took his journey into a far country, and there he squandered his property in loose living. And when he had spent everything, a great famine arose in that country, and he began to be in want. So he went and joined himself to one of the citizens of that country, who sent him into the fields to feed swine. And he would gladly have fed on the pods that the swine ate; and no one gave him anything. But when he came to himself he said, 'How many of my father's hired servants have bread enough and to spare, but I perish here with hunger! I will arise and go to my father, and I will say to him, 'Father, I have sinned against heaven and before you; I am no longer worthy to be called your son; treat me as one of your hired servants.' And he arose and came to his father. But while he was yet at a distance, his father saw him and had compassion, and ran and embraced him and kissed him. And the son said to him, 'Father, I have sinned against heaven and before you;

233

I am no longer worthy to be called your son.'
But his father said to his servants, 'Bring
quickly the best robe and put it on him; and
put a ring on his hand, and shoes on his feet;
and bring the fatted calf and kill it, and let
us eat and make merry; for this my son was
dead, and is alive again; he was lost, and is
found.' And they began to make merry.

Now his elder son was in the field; and as he
came and drew near to the house, he heard
music and dancing. And he called one of the
servants and asked what this meant. And he
said to him, 'Your brother has come, and your
father has killed the fatted calf, because he
has received him safe and sound.' But he was
angry and refused to go in. His father came
out and entreated him but he answered his
father, 'Lo, these many years I have served
you, and I never disobeyed your command; yet
you never gave me a kid, that I might make
merry with my friends. But when this son of
yours came, who has devoured your living with
harlots, you killed for him the fatted calf!'
And he said to him, 'Son, you are always
with me, and all that is mine is yours. It
was fitting to make merry and be glad, for
this your brother was dead, and is alive; he
was lost, and is found.'" (Luke 15:11-32)

CONCLUSION

Theological libraries are filled with thousands of books
just interpreting passages of the Bible. Our discussion has
pointed out only a few instances in which the Bible has exhibited attitudes toward the nature of personality, a perspective on human nature. Our purpose has been to consider what
kind of impact this perspective might have on the individual in
terms of self-regard, adjustment to the kinds of problems that
bother people, one's destiny, etc.

I am fully aware that a great variety of doctrines has
emerged from the Bible around which different denominations have
been gathered in faith commitment. My purpose in citing these
passages has not been to create theological doctrines but to
stimulate the reader to look at them from the perspective of
the psychology of religion, the impact of this kind of religion
on personality in the spiral of life process. I hope this has
at least opened up a field of inquiry for your own further investigation.

NOTE

1. Owen, Derwyn R. G., _Body and Soul: A Study on the Christian View of Man_, Philadelphia: The Westminster Press, 1956, pp. 169-170.

THEOLOGICAL AND OTHER ISSUES FOR DISCUSSION

1. Match the following biblical passages with a corresponding school of psychology or psychologist (more than one may match, and some may have no match at all):

(a) Train up a child in the way he should go, and when he is old he will not depart from it.

1. Logotherapy

2. Mowrer

3. Psychoanalysis

(b) He who spares the rod hates his son, but he who loves him is diligent to discipline him.

4. Glaser

5. Integrity therapy

6. Behaviorism

(c) I came that they may have life, and have it abundantly.

7. Carl Rogers

8. Skinner

(d) ...the truth will make you free.

9. Client-centered counseling

(e) Judge not, that you be not judged.

10. Freud

11. Maslow

(f) Nothing is covered up that will not be revealed, or hidden that will not be known.

12. Operant conditioning

13. Jung

14. Erikson

(g) For we hold that a man is justified by faith apart from the works of the law.

15. Allport

(h) Therefore confess your sins to one another, and pray for one another, that you may be healed.

The scripture passages are: (a) Proberbs 22:6, (b) Proverbs 13:24, (c) John 10:10b, (d) John 8:32b, (e) Matthew 7:1, (f) Luke 12:2, (g) Romans 3:28, (h) James 5:16a.

2. What doctrines or teachings about human nature found in the Bible, which were not touched upon in this chapter, do you find helpful or especially interesting? Why?

3. What biblical teachings would you find compatible with Hans Selye's stress theory as expressed in the General Adaptation Syndrome? How would they apply in specific?

4. What are the implications for personality development or adjustment of such biblical words as faith, sin, forgiveness, salvation, commandments, grace, hope, love, guilt, eternal life, damnation, and hardness of heart?

5. What symbolic associations do you have with the following terms: prophet, priest, disciple, martyr, savior, God the Father, Last Supper, Jesus, Holy Spirit, Judas, The Virgin Mary, Herod, Solomon, and Moses?

6. Can you think of how some biblical teaching might influence a person in the last stage, "Ego integrity vs. Despair"? How?

CHAPTER 11

CLASSICAL GREEK THOUGHT .

In many ways our western civilization is based on the Greek, rather than the Hebrew, way of thinking. Our current scientific-technological society relies heavily on reason, logic, and objective analysis. Often feelings and emotions are sacrificed for efficiency; sentiment is not as cost effective as mathematics when it comes to production and the gross national product. It was hard thinking, not sentiment, that made it possible to walk on the moon.

Even the Hebrew and Greek languages reveal different attitudes or ways of looking at reality. Biblical Hebrew did not concern itself with past and future tense, but had a way of indicating whether something was (or would be) fulfilled or accomplished. It had verb forms indicating more or less intensity connected with a given action -- concerned more with meaning and intention than measurement. Greek syntax, a very accurate language indeed, provides more verb tense forms than English. A friend in the classics department commented that the Greeks seemed to have a "disposition toward precision." Whether clear thinking created their logical language, their precise language helped them think more clearly, or whether there is a continuous interaction between speaking and syntax, thinking and grammar in a circle of reinforcement is a problem for others to solve. We can best see what contribution the Greeks made to a psychology of personality by taking a brief look at some of their chief spokesmen.

THE THREE GIANTS OF GREECE

Socrates left no writings of his own, but one phrase characterized him: "Know thyself." He believed that virtue was based on knowledge; wickedness was based on ignorance.

237

Hence no wise man would choose deliberately to do evil. A great deal of emphasis is placed upon rational capacity. Objectivity, provided by reason, is necessary to be able to distinguish between opinion and knowledge. The Socratic method of teaching persisted in questioning and challenging students so they would be able to sift out whim and fancy from objective reality, knowledge. Another famous dictum: "a life without inquiry is not worth living." His concern for the demands of individual conscience and his willingness to be "that gadfly which God has attached to the state" was also his undoing. Condemned to die, he drank the hemlock as a model of calm self-control.

Plato thought it important to go beyond sense perceptions to penetrate to the intelligible world of ideas and forms. This calls for the capacity to think in terms of mathematics and abstractions. Such an approach relies on the deductive method, logic, reason, and argumentation from general principles. He assumed that human nature is composed of three primary "faculties" or functions: emotion, volition, and intellect (not all that different from Freud's Id, Super Ego, and Ego). Using the deductive method, one begins with certain principles and then tries to account for individual behavior and personal traits according to that preconceived formula. It is a bit like placing a waffle iron lid upon some batter and forcing the semi-liquid stuff to conform to the grid of the iron. It raises the old question as to whether certain principles exist in the abstract apart from human experience; e.g., beauty, truth, justice, etc. But that leads us in the direction of philosophy rather than the psychology of personality.

Dualism, which is one of Plato's contributions, has had a pervasive and profound effect on our thinking about personality. If you see your wife eating lunch with a strange man, you are to feel reassured when it is explained that the relationship is simply "Platonic" -- meaning that only their ideas and not their bodies are involved. This cleavage between mind and body, between spirit and matter, is quite different from the Judeo-Christian notion discussed in the last chapter. The Bible, assuming a wholistic unity of the person, indicates that the whole person dies and the whole person is resurrected again (hence the reference to the "resurrection of the body" in the Apostles' Creed). Plato, on the other hand, maintained that the soul is immortal, i.e., it does not die but escapes from the body like a confined person escaping from prison. Being in a cave is also a bit like the soul being in a body; there is a cramping and limiting effect, and the light is not very good. It is as though being encased in the body is a handicap to the soul.

It is that dualistic aspect of Platonism that re-emerges in Christian pietism, Puritanism, and Victorian demeaning of the

238

body: the body is inferior to the soul; the body prevents the soul from functioning properly in spiritual freedom. One should be cautious about generalizing, but dualism can be spotted here and there in hymns, sermons, and conversation of persons who do not remotely suspect that they are more Platonic than biblical in their understanding of the nature of personality. As indicated in Chapter 8, we must continually work to put the whole person back together into a unity again, as in the field of psycho-somatic medicine.

Aristotle, a student in Plato's Academy, developed an interest in what we would call scientific research, and earned his place as "The Father of Psychology." Perhaps it was the influence of his physician father; at any rate, he began observing and classifying animals. It is said that he was acquainted with five hundred species and had dissected fifty in detail. He analyzed living things and began with the raw data. Then he inductively drew interpretations from the connections, similarities, differences, and functions which he observed. For example, plants and animals both are capable of growing; animals and human beings both have senses like hearing and seeing, which plants lack; and human beings share with animals the capacity of remembering (related to senses); but human persons alone are able to think. It is this process of beginning with specific data and building up to more complex interpretations that we refer to as the scientific method. Aristotle clearly was an innovator in this regard.

Perspective changes when you shift from abstract ideas and mathematical concepts to organic and biological processes involving the senses. Living organisms change, whereas theorems do not. Aristotle saw the dynamic functions of the organism as pressing on toward some end or goal. This is clearly so with the appetites and instincts; they are purposive. Living things have the capacity for self-direction within themselves. This vitalism is different from both the static realm of ideas and the primitive notion of governance from outside spirits and animistic forces. Aristotle wrestled with the problem of trying to understand how the senses operate to achieve their purpose. Are all of these senses coordinated by a common sense? He saw the complexity of the human personality.

Aristotle was also interested in applying psychological interpretation to events about him. For example, he explained the cathartic function of theater, an interpretation we could well accept today after Freud. Watson explains it thus:

"Catharsis is brought about by transferring to the tragic hero our own sufferings. In him we see ourselves, and, in his fate, our

doom. But since this is not the actual
situation, since his particular fate is not
ours, we shift our fear into fear for him.
This emotional use of the play allows us to
release our apprehensions and to deflect
our psychic burden to another's shoulders.
Self-pity gives way to compassion, and we
are the better for the experience."

We should note that Thomas Aquinas, famous pace setter
theologian and philosopher of the Church (1225-1274) found
Aristotle so helpful in interpreting the meaning of personhood
that he used The Philosopher extensively in his teachings. He
made an exhaustive commentary and response to De Anima.

THE FOUR TEMPERAMENTS

Humoral psychology goes back to the ancient Greeks, who
believed that one's temperament depended upon how the fluids
(humors) of the body were mixed (temperare, Latin, meaning
to mix). They would mean it literally when saying that a person
who exhibited an unpleasant disposition was "in a bad humor";
he suffered from too much yellow bile and hence was "choleric."
If a person were depressed, it meant that he had too much black
bile in his system and was therefore "melancholic." Although
the Greek's basic four fluids have now been multiplied into
numerous endocrine secretions and a highly complex physiological
psychology, it is still interesting to see how their system
worked.

The Greeks believed that there were four cosmic elements
in the universe: air, earth, fire, and water. Naturally, since
living things exist in the universe, they must be made up of
varying proportions of these elements (not the more than one
hundred elements listed in The Periodic Table of a modern
chemistry textbook). Note how these four elements fit nicely
into the Jungian quaternity. Each element has certain characteristics warm or cold, dry or moist. Allport's chart, Fig.
24, shows how Hippocrates and Galen, the famous physicians,
translated these into body fluids and personality temperaments. [4]

The lazy person with little initiative looks sleepy and
drools a lot (phlegm), obviously contains more water (saliva)
than the average person. The hothead is burning up with eager-
ness to get the job done, is angry at anything which impedes
the project he is pursuing with such vigor. He has a sharp set
to the jaw something like Dick Tracy, the sharp detective. The
melancholic person has a furrowed brow because he always sees
the dark side of every issue and worries a lot. When he

Cosmic Elements	Their Properties	Corresponding Humors	Corresponding Temperaments
Empedocles, cir. 450 B.C.		Hippocrates, cir. 400 B.C. Galen, cir. A.D. 150	
Air	warm and moist	blood	sanguine
Earth	cold and dry	black bile	melancholic
Fire	warm and dry	yellow bile	choleric
Water	cold and moist	phlegm	phlegmatic

Fig. 24   The Four Elements and Four Temperaments

meditates it is usually on trouble, sin, failure and overwhelming odds against him. He or she is a deep thinker. Finally,
the sanguine person is hopeful, naive, open hearted, warm
hearted, full of warm blood, which is what sanguine means.
There you have the four temperaments in a nutshell. Now look
at the sketches Allport presented and guess which character is
melancholic, choleric, phlegmatic or sanguine. You are correct:
1, 2, 3, 4, in that order.[5] (See Fig. 25)

Ole Hallesby, for forty years, a professor at the Independent Theological Seminary (as opposed to the state church's
theological faculty at the University of Oslo) has written seven
books of a devotional and warmly pietistic nature, which have
gone through 165 printings. He seemed to have a knack for speaking to the human condition. In 1940 he wrote a book about temperament and religion, which lay dormant for 22 years before
being translated into English.[6] It is not surprising that a
pietist should be intrigued by moods and feelings, described in
terms of temperament.

Using the classic four Greek temperaments, Hallesby described the strengths and weaknesses of each character. Each one
comes to life, and we feel he is describing one or another of
our friends or even ourselves. I am indebted to his treatment
of the subject for the following discussion. We will trace his
line of reasoning concerning two of the four temperaments. (I
use the pronoun, "he," as Hallesby did in his book to indicate
male or female, any person. Much of this material is paraphrase.)

241

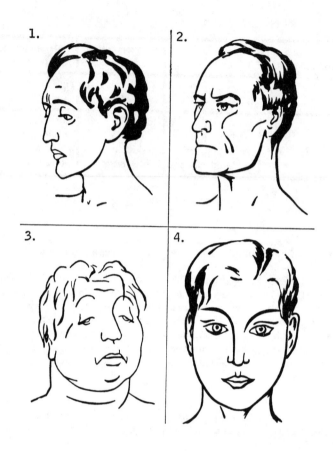

Fig. 25

Physiognomic Representations of the Four Temperaments

The melancholic person is likely to brood and think deeply about something, while the sanguine person tends to be superficial and shallow in his experience and in his way of viewing things. Concerning pleasantness and unpleasantness, the melancholic and the choleric would be listed on the unpleasant side, and the sanguine and the phlegmatic on the pleasant side. On a continuum from excitability to calmness, the choleric and the sanguine would be toward the excitability end, while the melancholic and the phlegmatic would be toward the calmness end.

There are many ways in which these four temperaments can be categorized and mixed together. For example, whereas the melancholic would be the calm person who tends to be withdrawing, the phlegmatic would be the calm person who tends to be more outgoing. Both the sanguine and the choleric would be active, but with this difference: the former would be more of an active optimist, and the latter would be active but with an irascible, cutting edge to his personality.

In Hallesby's description of the four temperaments, he lists the melancholic as being the suffering temperament, in contrast with the sanguine which enjoys life. The sanguine individual absorbs and enjoys everything that happens. The melancholic is so preoccupied with some particular impression -- preferably one that is painful -- that he can enjoy little or nothing of all that is bright and encouraging around him. His mental outlook is narrow and dark. He associates everything with his own self. And to contribute further to his own unhappiness, he has a strong predisposition to judge and evaluate everything. The melancholic type compares everything he experiences with an image he carries in his mind, weighing and measuring everything in relation to his own standards. Usually everything fails to measure up to those standards, and his is a pretty dark world because everything is a little off-key, clouded over with this gloomy outlook.

The experiences of the melancholic always fall short of an ideal. He is disappointed because he sets himself up for disappointment. His search for perfection becomes this burden in life because he never attains his goals. Consequently he takes very little interest in the present; he bemoans the past and how things did not work out well. He is fearful about the future: perhaps things will continue not working out. His dreams of the future perfection and his sad retrospect both turn out to be very unpleasant for him.

There are certain strengths and certain weaknesses in connection with this kind of temperament. A strength is that he does have a rich, sensitive life. His nature does allow him to spend a long enough time to explore, investigate, and compare things so that -- in contrast to the superficial sanguine person -- he can see things from all sides. He tends to be thorough. Even though he is always going to come up short, he does become deeply involved with whatever interests him. He has an awareness of his own limitations, even though it is in a sad way.

The melancholic person will be dependable because he will not be flighty like the sanguine person who is so optimistic and cheerful that he flutters along on the surface in a very undependable fashion. Unlike the sanguine person, whose attention is easily distracted from the subject at hand, the melancholic person will stick with one project or idea for a sufficient amount of time. Others will not derive much happiness out of a dependable association with the melanchotic person, but at least they can always count on him to be there with his same sad outlook.

What suggestions could be given to such a person? Hallesby says that perhaps the melancholic temperament ought to have a kind of treatment to offset the disadvantages or liabilities and to capitalize on the advantages. Such a person should make a deliberate effort to serve others unselfishly in order to counteract his tendency toward withdrawal, introspection, and meditation. He needs to turn his thoughts away from himself. The more he can be occupied with others in loving service, the more easily he will forget himself. Another prescription for him might be that he should struggle against useless brooding. He must be able to see the sinfulness of it and to realize that it leads him to dream away his actual life while his real problems and responsibilities are left untouched.

Hallesby suggests that by specific training and discipline, the melancholic person can make himself carry through his daily duties, large or small, moving from task to task. He needs to become task-oriented. He should not let himself be frightened by the ordinary routine of things -- the fact that some things go well, and some things do not. He needs to be able to move on to the next project, from one effort to the next, not allowing himself to stay too long with one thought, one task, or one attitude.

Finally, the melancholic person should take up the struggle against the strong tendency to criticize, and against the self-conceit that accompanies it; i.e., by constantly comparing a high standard of how things ought to be in contrast with how things really are. When he looks into the world he is always going to be disappointed if he maintains this high standard, because things will not measure up. The author fell into this trap one day while going to class. He pointed out to one of the students with whom he was walking that erosion was developing under the steps of the Old Capitol building on the University of Iowa campus. The landscaping was not providing the water to drain properly into the drain. If a person goes around like this looking for little defects under trees and behind bushes, it is not difficult to find many things that could be improved upon.

Any melancholic person thus chastened in discipline, Hallesby said, becomes a valuable member of the group. He will never be hearty and infectious like the sanguine person. But, on the other hand, he is thorough, deep, and genuine. In conversation he never takes a leading part; but when he does say anything, it is not only well considered but also it is expressed with originality and deep thought. Having this temperament, a person can possess both strengths and weaknesses.

The choleric person can serve as one more example of Hallesby's religious diagnosis of the temperaments. The choleric temperament involves the person who has the hot fluid -- the hot temper -- in his body. The choleric person has a great deal of self confidence. He is an activist. He is outgoing. No other person is as well qualified with firm character, self-confidence, and the ability to move ahead and organize things.

And the activity of the choleric person is of the will-directed sort. It is teleological -- purposeful. It aims toward a goal. Such a person usually wants to get on with the job, to accomplish the task, to finish the project. He organizes and rushes ahead. Even though his plan may lack thoroughness, at least he does have a conscious, premeditated plan. The problem is that he may tend to run roughshod over other people, because the choleric person is insensitive to the needs of others. But he is very practical in that he does rush ahead to get the job done.

In contrast to the choleric person, the melancholic person may just brood about some need but not be able to marshall his resources to do anything about it. The melancholic wastes time and energy, pondering the different methods of reaching the goal. The choleric person sees what is to be done right here and now. The practical bent of his mind results from the fact that he does not live his life in an imaginary world. He lives energetically in a world of reality. He is an opportunist. (Here again is the element that the end justifies the means.) He utilizes the present moment for his own plans.

A weakness of the choleric person is that he is hard. His emotions tend not to be very warm in the sense of interpersonal relationships. He is hot-tempered concerning getting a project done. He is impatient with anything that stands in his way, and he is not warm-hearted in the social sense. Unlike the melancholic person who says, sympathetically, "Well, I know what suffering is; I have it every day," the choleric person is unable to sympathize with other people who have trouble. The choleric is more inclined to say, "If a person has trouble, why does he not do something about it?" The choleric person lacks compassion. He seems harsh. However, the fact that he gets

245

something done, which may in the long run benefit other people, would be a mitigating circumstance in his personality.

What should he do about his personality? Hallesby suggests that the choleric person is made of stern stuff and the methods to modify him will have to be pretty strong measures. He is a hard nut to crack. He is violent, aggressive, heedless of counsel and advice from others. His tendency would be to fight against advice and stand up for his own rights rather than absorb the opinion of others. With conscious effort he must find the means to subdue this violent temper. There is no more certain remedy than forcing him to apologize every time his temper runs away with him. To apologize is more humiliating to the choleric person than to anyone else. But for just this reason, it is an effective means of holding his fiery, reckless nature in check.

Finally, the choleric must take up the battle against his impulse to split groups and form new parties. The choleric person has the temptation of pride and self-confidence, and the willingness to criticize other people and to rush ahead with the solution. Craving activity, he hurries ahead with a project rather than taking the long,slow process of working the problem out. The choleric is quickly exasperated by what other people are doing. If he cannot reform them in a hurry, he will just split off from this group and organize a new body.

It would be very interesting to study the origin of the numerous religious bodies which have been organized in the United States. Could it be that a large number of them have been organized by people with a choleric temperament, who rush into action, set up a new constitution, organize a new charter, and suddenly present to the public a new group? Such people say, "Move on with the activity. Let's not wait to work out some compromise which will take ten to fifteen years going through several committees. Let's get on with the action. If people can't catch up with us, that's just tough!"

All of a sudden there exists a new group. And this group remains safely intact until another choleric person is also impulsively eager to get on with the action. Divide and rule is the method of such a person. And generally all this is easily accomplished. Hallesby says, for example, that there are nearly always enough sanguine people in the group who are eager to work against leaders. But the shrewd choleric makes use of them in his disruptive work. The sanguine persons are excellent agitators, but they need the choleric person to come along and crystallize their naive attitudes into new organizational structure which will go on to some new tasks. It is only when the choleric learns to humble himself under the mighty hand of God that he can win a victory over this conflict, says Hallesby.

246

This has been a practical application of two of the four temperaments. The other temperaments should be discussed with the same kind of approach. Do they have certain assets? certain liabilities? What would such a person have to do in order to mature and become a more effective personality? Rather than try to exchange one temperament completely for another, supposedly better one, an individual should try to maximize whatever temperament seems to be indigenous to that person's nature.

It is especially good to point out the strengths. So often people are overwhelmed by the disadvantages of their personalities and they give up, saying, "Well, I have all these problems, inadequacies, and negative factors in my personality which make me not work out well in society. It's just too depressing." If the strengths and assets can be pointed out, the person will receive some encouragement in realizing that he has some healthy aspects in his personality. Even the melancholic person could be led to make a real contribution if he is helped to see that he could use his characteristics in certain ways. This does not mean that the melancholic person has to stop being this type of person entirely; but perhaps he can minimize the disadvantages of his personality trait and maximize the contribution that he could make. So also with the choleric person.

Most groups need several types of people in the group in order to function. They need leaders and followers, those who keep spirits high and those who criticize. Can a religious group have all these types; or do they have to divide and have one denomination of sanguine people, another of melancholic, another of choleric, and still another of phlegmatic? Religious groups often claim to be all-embracing. But it may be an interesting diagnostic question to ask any group whether or not their membership really is open to all four types of temperament.

TYPOLOGY: HELPFUL and/or HARMFUL

As soon as we place a person in a category, we rely upon stereotype and lose sight of the uniqueness of the individual. We are tempted to say, "You know how that type operates; they're all like that." This can apply to temperament, but also to race, ethnic group, religious denomination, occupation, social class, and numerous characteristics. (See Figure 10 in Chapter 2)

For some purposes it is useful to get persons of one type together. Extracurricular events in school are organized around common interests. Those interested in the chess club meet in Room 106; and those interested in boxing report to the gymnasium. It is useful not to get these two groups mixed up. There is also the chorus, school newspaper, and student government to choose

247

from. Vocational guidance counselors use aptitude tests and
interest profiles to help students sort themselves into certain
occupational categories. Such a client ought not to be upset
over labels, but rather seek out which labels suit him/her best.

When Dr. Coffey was in charge of the testing and placement
of employees at Dayton Department Store in Minneapolis, Minn.,
he perceived his task as fitting the person to a job which
suited his/her temperament or personality type. For example,
an introvert would not thrive as a clerk at the glove counter,
which was just inside the front door through which thousands
of customers poured all day long. That person might thrive in
the marking room at the back of the sixth floor where there was
very little traffic, social challenge, or confrontation. The
extravert would enjoy all the excitement and chance for human
contact, which a first floor sales counter would provide. If
the shy person wants to become more outgoing, well and good; let
such a one sign up for a Carnegie "How To Win Friends and Influence People" course; but let us not foist it upon an unwilling
victim as though everyone has to become a jolly back slapper.
We need an ecumenical attitude concerning temperament just as we
do toward faith and life style. To require everyone to fit one
mold can distort and stifle personality.

Prejudice thrives on typology. I recall a page full of
photographs from a textbook on the sociology of race used by
the Nazis in the 1930s. It showed pictures of the healthy,
symmetrical, handsome Aryan race, Ubermensch, Superman. And
then it showed pictures of withered, misshapen, horrid looking
hags and derelicts who were supposed to be typical of the
Semitic race. Propaganda during wartime requires a typology
wherein everyone in our group is good, sincere, patriotic; and
everyone in the enemy's camp is vicious, treacherous, and
beastly. It would be unthinkable to have a war in which our
side pillaged, raped, and massacred, and the enemy spent their
time attending worship services, milking cows, and harvesting
crops to feed the hungry of the world.

How does typology serve to characterize denominations? I
have attended churches where their happiest hymn sounded like a
funeral dirge. Other groups clap their hands, shout, and burst
forth in charismatic speaking in tongues. Another group is
considered intellectual and serious minded. How would you
characterize or type the following religious groups? Match
them.

248

___ Roman Catholic	(a) Stoical
___ Lutheran	(b) Rational
___ Jewish	(c) Joyful
___ Unitarian	(d) Sorrowful
___ Southern Baptist	(e) Extraverted
___ Methodist	(f) Ethical
___ Salvation Army	(g) Social
___ Greek Orthodox	(h) Introverted
___ Islam	(i) Meditative
___ Baha'i	(j) Personal
___ Quaker	(k) Spiritual

Do not ask me to grade this quiz. I would not touch it with a ten foot pole. Obviously, not everyone in any one of these groups would be exactly like other members of that same group. You could find greater differences between members of the same group than between the averages of some groups which seemed far apart. Typology has its limits.

Since World War II there has been much talk about the ecumenical movement and merger of religious bodies, yet there have simultaneously arisen many new movements and some cleavages of denominations. Perhaps it is difficult to maintain the loyalty of many diverse temperaments to one pattern or style of religious life. Those who do not feel their needs are being met will join a different group or, if need be, create a new group altogether.

For good or ill, the Greeks gave us the desire and the methodology for categorizing. They provided the philosophical framework for ascribing order and rationale to the world in which we live. They stressed reason over intuition. Many among us could not return comfortably to animism once the Greeks had introduced us to the salvation and security of reason.

NOTES

1. See Chapter 3, "Aristotle: The Founding of Psychology" in Robert I. Watson, The Great Psychologists from Aristotle to

Freud, (2nd Edition), Philadelphia: J. B. Lippincott
Company, 1968, pp. 38-73.

Aristotle's De Anima, in which he deals with the nature and
functions of the soul, has been translanted by J. A. Smith
and published in Volume 3 of The Works of Aristotle (W. D.
Ross, editor), London: Oxford University Press, 1931.

2. Watson, op. cit., p. 62.

3. For a full discussion of this topic see all of Chapter 3 in
Allport's Pattern and Growth in Personality, pp. 36-54.

4. Ibid., p. 37.

5. Ibid., p. 41.

6. Hallesby, Ole, Temperamentene i kristelig lys, Oslo, Norway:
Lutherstiftelsen. It was published by Augsburg Publishing
House of Minneapolis in 1962 under the title, Temperament
and the Christian Faith (106 pages) (a more accurate
translation of the title would be Temperament in a Christian
Light.)

7. Ibid., pp. 37-59.

8. Ibid., pp. 60-78.

THINGS TO THINK ABOUT

1. Can one, or should one try to, change one's temperament?

2. Concerning your own temperament (assuming it is one of the
four) what do you consider the strengths and weaknesses
involved? Do you focus more on the one or the other?

3. Did you see anything in these four temperaments that reminded you of "healthy-minded" religion or the "sick soul"
type which William James described in his Varieties of
Religious Experience (Refer to Chapter 3, section "Crisis,
Conversion, and Mystical Experience").

4. If you were a bishop and looking for a pastor to serve in
the following way, which temperament would you want for
each position?

    _____(a) Organizing a new mission in a rapidly ex-
panding suburban development.

_____(b) To get a building program off the ground, which has been needed but not accomplished under the leadership of the last four clergy-persons.

_____(c) A ministry to students on the edge of the campus of Harvard University.

_____(d) A parish of blue collar factory workers in the Pittsburgh steel mills.

_____(e) A century old country church of 500 members in the corn fields of Iowa.

_____(f) As Camp Director for the new youth and retreat center on Clear Blue Lake.

_____(g) To replace yourself as bishop since you will be 75 in October and retiring.

5. What relationship do you see between integrity and temperament?

6. Do you have difficulty with persons of certain temperaments? Which kind? And why, do you suppose?

7. Do you (or someone you know) play different roles, exhibit different kinds of temperament in different situations? At a party, family reunion, on the job, at worship, during your vacation?

8. In the "Peanuts" cartoon strip, what temperament is Charlie Brown, Lucy, and Linus?

9. Do you consider yourself Platonic or Aristotelian in the way you approach life, religion, yourself? Explain.

10. Is dualism in religion a desirable perspective? Why?

11. What are some practical consequences of dualism in: Health? Ethics? Worship? Government? Education?

12. What do you mean by pietism, orthodoxy, liberalism, and fundamentalism? Are they in any way related to temperament?

CHAPTER 12

BEHAVIORAL SCIENTISTS ANALYZE PERSONALITY

Many people have resisted scientific interpretations because they sensed that something precious was being lost in the
process. For example, when Copernicus explained that the earth
was not the center of the universe, but just another planet revolving around the sun, it was a real blow to human pride. Likewise, when Darwin explained in his Origin of Species just how
far down the animal kingdom human origins went, there was another
outcry. This was degrading in the minds of those who saw it as
an attack on the doctrine that man was created in the Image of
God. Anyone who sees the Bible as a textbook on everything,
including astronomy, geology, and biology usually assumes that
science is at war with religion. There are others who maintain
that these two levels of discourse can exist compatibly much
like the artist and chemist studying the rose in the introduction
to this book.

The third affront to human pride was developed in the mind
of Sigmund Freud, for he made an even more personal assault on
human dignity. He as much as said that persons are not as fully
in charge of their own destiny as they had assumed. Dark and
sinister forces lurk in their unconscious to influence their
lives in ways of which they are not even aware. To the turn-of-
the-century carriage driver it must have sounded analogous to
saying that he was not really in charge of driving the team of
horses but that an invisible leprechaun astride one horse's neck
was actually steering the horses. Psychoanalysis was vigorously
opposed by moralists and logicians alike who wished to preserve
the role of responsibility and the powers of reason as essential
parts of human nature.

There are many schools of thought among twentieth century
psychologists, and we have touched upon several so far in our
study. For the purposes of this chapter we are interested in

how three quite different schools of thought view personality. They are psychoanalysis (Freud), behaviorism (Skinner), and the humanistic psychology or person-centered approach of Rogers.

We live in an age heavily influenced by behavioral science and social science. We are bombarded by advertising designed by psychological researchers and motivational specialists. We interact in groups engineered by social psychologists and social planners. Human engineering from urban renewal to medical research is permeated with scientific justification. One day a staff of hospital chaplains was discussing the new wave of "professional performance appraisal" proposals, forms, and methodology. The first reaction was that an outside "consultant" would have to be engaged to provide the necessary objectivity. It was not even possible for the University of Iowa to prepare the new personnel program for its several thousand merit employees (See Figure 16, "Classification of some workers by class, grade, and salary"). An outside consulting firm with special scientific research capabilities was brought in. If Aristotle could only see us now.

PSYCHOANALYSIS[1]

Sigmund Freud (1856-1939) had some bad experiences with religion as he was growing up, among them anti-Semitism, which excluded the possibility of a career in academic medicine at the University of Vienna. Instead, he opened up a private practice in neurology on Easter morning. Mental illness fell under the discipline of neurology (neurosis meaning literally a swelling of the nerve). He was a creative investigator, who did not close his mind to the new interest in hypnosis with its potential for alleviating hysterical conversion symptoms in patients who were not helped by physical or chemical treatments.

In the scientific twentieth century more credence is given to the statements of a person with the credentials of an M.D. degree than to a poet or philosopher. It is for this reason that Freud could get by with leaping to fairly far fetched conclusions without sufficient evidence. He saw himself as a modern day Moses who would lead people out of the bondage of superstition and the illusions of religion; but he discussed the original Moses in ways that other scholars would not condone. He also may have stretched his argument when he jumped from the struggle for supremacy among the young males to be the chief bull of a herd in the animal kingdom to supposed replication of the same conflict in the human family. But we should not judge him too harshly; he was dealing with the Darwinianism and anthropological researches current eighty years ago. Nor was he the first to write about sexuality, sibling rivalry (Cain and Abel), incest (the Greek tragedy, <u>Oedipus</u> <u>Rex</u> was written by Sophocles about 430 B.C.), and the unconscious (Shakespeare's <u>Hamlet</u> and others). His three basic writings dealing with religion are <u>The</u> <u>Future</u> <u>of</u> <u>an</u> <u>Illusion</u>, <u>Moses</u> <u>and</u> <u>Monotheism</u>, and <u>Totem</u> <u>and</u> <u>Taboo</u>.

Freud's genius lay in his capacity to build a coherent psychological system or philosophy of life from his clinical observations and wide readings. The fact that his "Ego" is no more demonstrable in the neurology laboratory than the "soul" should not deter us from recognizing the heuristic appeal of his theory about the nature of personality. He spent a lifetime applying his theory in a unique form of psychotherapy, a profound kind of counseling which dealt with the unconscious as well as the conscious contents of the mind. In this sense his perspective was wholistic, concerned also about the past experiences as well as the present malady and dis-ease of his clients. He was concerned about intra-psychic experience and the impact of the external world of society upon personality development and functioning. His provocative theorizing has profoundly influenced literature, education, and the mores of our contemporary society.

Freud saw personality as a tripartite unity with each of the three parts representing important psychic functions. The <u>Id</u> ("it") is the source of vital energy, instincts, and the kind of animalistic drives we have within us as a result of our body needs. These are the forces of sexuality, hunger and thirst, aggressiveness, and other drives of an impersonal and amoral nature. It is the <u>Super-ego</u> (colloquially referred to as "conscience") that incorporates the moral standards of society, that internalizes the demands of society, and passes judgment on our instinctual drives, and grants or withholds permission for their expression and fulfillment. A veto means repression of that drive, and the individual has to handle that frustration one way or another (more of that later). The Ego ("I" or self) is the executive branch of this enterprise. The Ego must choose between the demands of society (as mediated through the Super-ego) and the demands of the Id. This sounds simple and straight forward like a well organized factory with raw material, a manager, and quality control. The product is human behavior. But we must turn our attention to the matter of consciousness, which seriously complicates the picture.

There are three levels of consciousness. At the <u>conscious</u> level I can ask you what you see across the street, and you can reply, quick as a wink, "My neighbor's house." You are also conscious of your itching athlete's foot or the cold taste of ice cream in your mouth. If I ask you the name of your third grade school teacher, you have to work at it; it is not in your

conscious mind at this present moment. You can, however, recall
it from your preconscious and become aware of if. The third
level is deeper and inaccessible. Let us suppose that you have
such traumatic associations with that vicious third grade teacher
who beat you, humiliated you before the class, and was otherwise
too repulsive for words, that you repressed her name totally.
You have buried her in your unconscious. She is beyond recall.
Freud would not agree that she is "Out of sight, out of mind."
She has been repressed into the deepest recesses of the mind much
like potatoes buried in the root cellar in a corner of your
basement are still in your house even though out of sight.

Repressed thoughts and experiences are not innocuous just
because they are tucked away so far out of reach of consciousness. They are still full of power and active according to their
own psychic laws. If not granted conscious expression, they will
sometimes find expression in dreams, symbolic phobias, fantasies,
indirect expression through symbolic behavior (like proposing
legislation to eliminate the third grade state wide), developing
physical symptoms (like a severe headache on the eve of the
fiftieth reunion of your third year class -- providing you had
not succeeded in getting hopelessly lost trying to find your
home town with its infamous third grade classroom), etc.

Other mechanisms of defense beside repression are:
rationalization (I didn't want to go out with that cheerleader,
Alice Hielingdoerfer, anyway, because she comes from a bad family
of German Catholics); projection (It's my boss' fault I'm so-
called late for work because he sets the starting time too
early); sublimation (Why shouldn't I use mostly yellows and
browns in my paintings -- even though my analyst says it represents unresolved attitudes toward my early toilet training?);
delusion of grandeur (Please let me in at the head of the lunch
line since my name is Napoleon and I am responsible for all
these troops). What do all these and other mechanisms of defense
accomplish? They protect the Ego from discomfort or injury.
Going over the above list, rationalization protects me from the
devastation I am about to feel by being turned down; projection
protects me from the criticism of irresponsibility; sublimation
serves as a safety valve for old frustrations; and delusion of
grandeur protects me from the horrible feeling of being a nobody.
In all these matters Freud maintained the individual was fooling
himself or herself unintentionally and unconsciously. In this
way strange behavior began to make sense. People even act in
ways diametrically opposed to their stated beliefs because they
are not aware of their underlying hidden dynamics.

Psychoanalysis was Freud's effort to bring repressed
psychic material into consciousness so that the client would
have a chance to deal with reality. Once these debilitating

materials were brought out into the light of day, the person was free to discard them without repression through conscious choice. But in order to do this the client needed <u>insight</u> into his/her own psychodynamics. The therapist helped the patient gain insight by showing the connections between factors formerly unknown to the person. Since much repressed material was originally morally suspect or condemned by society (lust, hate, envy -- basically the Seven Deadly Sins), the one thing the patient needed was an atmosphere so non-judgmental that he/she knew it would be safe to become aware of, and to share, these "bad" thoughts or experiences. Originally, classically trained analysts sat behind their clients so that even a smirk of disapproval upon their countenance would not militate against a <u>free association</u> of ideas. The client lay on a couch as relaxed as possible in order that the <u>catharsis</u> or cleansing flow of negative material could be released.

One other Freudian concept is central to our discussion. He believed very strongly in determinism. Very early infant and childhood experiences, once repressed, could continue an iron clad grip on a person for life, shaping and determining future behavior, decisions, life style, etc. One might think he/she was making independent choices in adulthood, but these were only <u>reactions</u> to earlier, now repressed, factors. This led to the notion that the die was pretty well cast long before adolescence had even begun. This determinism posed a problem for many of Freud's critics. They claimed there was a simplistic reductionism at work. It appeared that religion was <u>nothing but</u> a projection of a cosmic father figure upon the screen of the heavens; the artist's choice of colors was <u>nothing but</u> a reaction to early toilet training; that trouble with one's boss is <u>nothing but</u> an unresolved oedipal complex; etc. But every doctrine comes to be doctrinaire, and disciples are often more extreme than the original master. Lest we focus only on polarization, let us indicate some similarities between the psychoanalytical approach and the religious.

If one were willing to interpret the Old Adam as a basic self-centeredness in contrast to social concern for others, then Freud's libidinal urges would refer to pretty much the same thing since these are related to the needs of the self without all that much reference to the larger society. A basic aggressiveness and even a self-destructive "death wish," the "pleasure principle" and the "defense mechanisms" to avoid dealing constructively with objective reality all represent the problem side of personality. Freud would not have agreed that mankind is by nature good. In fact it takes considerable socialization to tame the descendants of the beasts of the jungle; and what is left of the beast in all of us sounds very much like Original Sin.

Confession is replicated in the long series of sharing deep, dark secrets that Freud advocated. The confidentiality and security of the analytical hour is not unlike the seal of the confessional. The non-judgmental acceptance of this monologue of the patient resembles the grace with which a priest hears the recounting of a list of sins. The analytical process is even more thorough-going since it aims at unburdening the client of unconscious conflicts as well as conscious material. The priest, of course, speaks words of forgiveness and absolution, whereas the analyst aims to remain neutral and objective.

There is some difference of opinion as to whether psycho-analysis tended to loosen the bonds of morality with its un-fettered discussion of sexuality. Some maintain that repression tends to set the stage for explosion and violence; others hold that loosening restraints leads to license. Nowhere is this brought into sharper focus than in the current debate on sex and violence on television. The Legion of Decency and protection of children advocates claim that such exposure is harmful to children, whereas the television producers claim it does them no harm, runs off their backs like water off a duck. Yet we realize that auto manufacturers and brewers are sold millions of dollars worth of advertising using sex and violence to motivate viewers to rush out and purchase product X. You can't very well have it both ways. We leave it as an open question; but one thing is sure, psychoanalysis has had a culture transforming influence of great magnitude. (You may wish to review Chapter 7 and Chapter 8 in the light of this discussion.)

BEHAVIORISM[2]

Behaviorism began in the mouth of Pavlov's dog. By associating a juicy piece of meat with the sound of a ringing bell, it was possible to "condition" the animal to salivate at the sound of the bell even when no meat was present. The conditioned reflex was described as a "stimulus-response" pattern. By presenting rats with certain rewards (food pellet) it was possible to shape certain behavior patterns. J. B. Watson popularized behaviorism as a school of psychology, and B. F. Skinner has been the latest and most prolific interpreter of this way of looking at personality.

B. F. Skinner (1904-   ), a long time Harvard psychology professor, is an enthusiastic campaigner and prophet of be-haviorism. He was so committed to the conditioning principle that he reared his daughter in a specially designed box re-miniscent of the candy factory where the product was guaranteed pure because it was "untouched by human hands." He was in-trigued by the fact that animals could be trained to do fairly

258

complicated sequences of behavior by rewarding the various components of the larger pattern. Extrapolating from laboratory rats to human beings, he conjectured that the reason human behavior seems so mysterious is that we just have not refined our measuring devices which detect all the little conditionings that make us turn and bend and speak and drive automobiles and construct societies. His predecessor, Watson, had boasted that if you gave him a child with full permission to condition him at will, he would be able to condition that child into a beggar, merchant, butcher or thief. It was a matter of programming the correct stimuli to produce the desired combination of behaviors. Granted, humans were more complicated than rats, but the same principles of psychology would hold true.

Skinner claims that the legitimate field of study for psychologists is behavior, not mental states or psychic experiences. Intra-psychic events, so-called, are not subject to scientific investigation, precise measurement, and replication like the behavior of laboratory rats or persons in limited experimental situations. He would not interpret dreams like Freud, but he would check eyelid movements during sleep or other measurable body functions during sleep. He believes that talking about the soul or ego, consciousness and feelings is begging the question. In a paper entitled, "Behaviorism at Fifty," he poked fun at the medieval concept of "homunculus," a kind of little midget inside your head. The Bell Telephone educational film called "Gateways to the Mind" portrayed what happened when a person's finger is pricked. Little flashes of lightning run up the nerve to the brain where a little man is awakened by the alarm, gets up and pulls a lever, sending more flashes of lightning back down another nerve to tell a muscle to contract, thus pulling the finger away from the negative stimulus. Skinner thinks such micro-anthropomorphism is not helpful; and it is not helpful to speak of the "will," "conscience," "feelings," "mind," and "self," all of which are animistic left-overs from primitive times when it was assumed that "something in there" mysteriously activated the person. At least such fuzzy concepts should not be considered legitimate subject matter for behavioral science.

A description of a demonstration experiment epitomizes Skinner's approach.

> "...a hungry pigeon was conditioned to turn
> around in a clockwise direction. A final,
> smoothly executed pattern of behavior was
> shaped by reinforcing successive approximations
> with food. Students who had watched the demon-
> stration were asked to write an account of what
> they had seen. Their responses included the
> following: (1) The organism was conditioned

to expect reinforcement for the right kind of
behavior. (2) The pigeon walked around,
hoping that something would bring the food
back again. (3) The pigeon observed that a
certain behavior seemed to produce a particular result. (4) The pigeon felt that food
would be given it because of its actions; and
(5) The bird came to associate his action with
the click of the food-dispenser. The observed
facts could be stated respectively as follows:
(1) The organism was reinforced when it emitted
a given kind of behavior. (2) The pigeon
walked around until the food container again
appeared. (3) A certain behavior produced a
particular result. (4) Food was given the
pigeon when it acted in a given way; and (5)
The click of the food-dispenser was temporally
related to the bird's action."[3]

The second set of descriptions is objective; the first set betrays the subjectivism which Skinner finds inexact and non-
verifiable. Stick with what you can know, and do not guess at
what you think is going on inside the organism (animal or human).

What are the implications of this theory for therapy? If a
child has a phobic fear of dogs, and you wish to cure him of
this anxiety-laden condition, you may proceed as follows with
behavior modification: Place the child in a location where he
can see a dog at some distance and provide him with a pleasurable
reward. Gradually bring the dog closer, but each time provide
a positive experience for the child so that the child comes to
associate dog with pleasure (like Pavlov's dog associated the
bell with juicy meat). Thus you have desensitized the fear and
avoidance response and replaced it with a pleasure and approach
response. For a time it was popular to use "aversive" stimuli
in association with alcohol so as to make it a repugnant instead
of a desirable commodity. Antabuse would be taken regularly by
the alcoholic, then if he takes a drink of alcohol, he will have
a very unpleasant physiological reaction. The alcoholic had
originally come to associate pleasure with a pleasant sensation.
When he had been troubled, he took a few drinks and his troubles
went away to be replaced by a pleasant euphoria. This pattern
was continually being reinforced. If his sales went down or he
lost a job or a game or someone criticized him, there was always
a ready solution -- all troubles dissolve in alcohol. No wonder
he got drunk; it worked so well. But now, it is a different
story. With Antabuse in his system, every time he takes a drink
of booze, he gets an immediate aversive reaction. Note that in
this type of therapy there is very little time wasted on

"insight," clearing one's "conscience" or "confession." It was altered behavior you wanted, wasn't it? Then get to work on the behavior.

A mental hospital in California initiated a "token therapy" program. Each desirable behavior would bring to the patient the reward of one or more tokens. Such desirable acts were attending group therapy sessions, cleaning one's room, helping with some ward housekeeping duties, etc. No one was scolded for not doing these things, but when it came time for lunch, those with a token got to eat; at bedtime, those with a token got to sleep in a bed -- others might end up on the floor or have to shift for themselves. Sitting around moping in the corner of the day room, "acting out" or "talking crazy" were not ways to earn tokens. There were also ways of using points or tokens to be promoted from the "C Ward" which was very plain and ordinary to the "B Ward" where there was more color, activity, recreation, etc. Some patients who had lain dormant for years finally earned the right to go down town to buy their own shirt instead of getting a denim uniform from the supply room. In certain mental hospitals where behavior modification therapy was being used successfully, it has been halted because of criticism that it was violating the rights of the patients. It has been called "manipulation" and "treating people like objects instead of subjects." What do you think of it?

Behavior modification is being practiced by all of us daily without knowing it. Compliments, "Please" and "Thank you," doing a favor for a friend, a raise in salary, are all positive reinforcers. Criticism, snide remarks, inattention, boredom with another's company, etc., are all aversive stimuli. Skinner says that since we do it anyway we might as well do it intelligently and deliberately. He wrote a novel, Walden Two (1948), in which he created a utopian commune where positive reinforcement would maximize the good life. Work is not odious and constructive social reactions are rewarded. Efforts are made to "extinguish" undesirable responses. Maybe we should take him seriously, after all it is not long until 1984. Perhaps this is the kind of psychology which can usher in Aldous Huxley's Brave New World.

The criticism of loss of responsibility has been somewhat muted by new developments in behavior modification. Rather than assume that the therapist is the conditioner and the client the inert lump of clay to be molded into a more ideal type of person, there is now an emphasis on the client choosing his/her own goals, e.g., weight loss, self-confidence, social skills, overcoming some problem or other. Then the client also participates in designing the kind of rewards or reinforcements to use in the program and also does his/her own record keeping. Such persons

261

say that they are gratified in having taken charge of their own
lives and have grown in responsibility.

*   *   *   *   *   *   *   *   *   *   *   *

Let us pause for an interlude long enough to compare the
previous two schools of thought.

Psychoanalysis relies heavily upon <u>subjective</u> self-report.
The patient describes his/her own inner experiences of anxiety,
loneliness, increasing self-confidence, etc. The same is true
of questionnaires and self-rating scales. When the researcher
asks the subject to describe or rate the relationship with the
spouse, the investigator is dependent upon the respondent to
report accurately. If the persons filling out the questionnaire
all want to lie about the matter, the researcher is just stuck
with a lot of inaccurate data. The psychoanalyst can only work
with the material the patient makes available during the interview. He may respond, inquire, even probe; but the raw data
begin with the patient's self-report.

Behaviorism looks for <u>objective</u> data that are verifiable
and observable. It tends to be more external and tangible. All
the students had the same pigeon available for their observation
and could check each other's observations. As indicated in our
Preface, there are many kinds of information which can be
gathered best by this objective method: census, statistical
information for actuarial insurance tables, divorce by chronological age and decade of marriage, most suitable techniques
for teaching reading or mathematics, and the impact of some
specific feature of our society upon personality (abortion,
handicap, status, retirement, television, etc.). Even closely
related to religious factors we have need for investigation into
child rearing practices which lead to or are associated with
delinquency or social adjustment; rehabilitation of criminals;
medical ethics decision-making; value clarification in the
public school system and/or church and synagogue; what factors
are associated with altruism and which dynamics foster ego-
centricity? Objective research may not provide the ultimate
answer, but could be useful in dealing with some penultimate
issues.

A PERSON-CENTERED APPROACH[4]

Carl Rogers (1902-) agreed with Allport that nothing
short of the whole person should be the concern of psychology

and not just stimuli or behavior or even inner experience; at least Rogers did not want to limit himself to anything short of the whole person. His confidence in the capacity of the client to solve his/her own problems, if given the opportunity, showed an unconditional positive regard for the individual. This is why his early work in a counseling clinic at the University of Chicago was referred to as "non-directive," later "client-centered." The counselor should not lead the client to the solution like a teacher educates a child; nor should the psychotherapist be "in charge" of the patient as though taking a superior and controlling attitude; nor should any judgmental attitude be present to threaten the client who is already battered and vulnerable from whatever failure brought the two together into a therapeutic relationship.

Rogers would agree with Freud that there should be a permissive and non-threatening atmosphere for the counseling session. Rogers parted company with Freud concerning the basic nature of human personality. You recall that Freud posited much destructiveness from libidinous drives.

> "Our mind, that precious instrument by whose
> means we maintain ourselves alive, is no
> peacefully self-contained unity. It is
> rather to be compared with a modern state in
> which a mob, eager for enjoyment and destruc-
> tion, has to be held down forcibly by a pru-
> dent superior class."[5]

In contrast to Freud, Rogers assumes that the individual has positive resources upon which to draw; it is the negative social and experiential factors that have prevented constructive action which need to be removed in counseling. The client needs the opportunity to marshall those resources and draw upon the inner strength and sense which now lie dormant and impotent.

> "A person-centered approach is based on the
> premise that the human being is basically a
> trustworthy organism, capable of evaluating
> the outer and inner situation, understanding
> herself in its context, making constructive
> choices as to the next steps in life, and
> acting on those choices...the choices made,
> the directions pursued, the actions taken are
> increasingly constructive personally and tend
> toward a more realistic social harmony with
> others."[6]

And what facilitates this new and constructive attitude on the part of the client? The client has had the unique opportunity

of "experiencing a nonpossessive caring and love for the other."
This is called "empathy" -- feeling into the situation and
suffering of another person. It is more objective than sympathy,
which gets too emotionally involved and often means drowning in
the same slough of despond as that of the client. It is also not
a condoning of the other's behavior or words just because it is
not punitive. It remains non-judgmental while still being
sincerely concerned. It means attributing to the other the
freedom and capacity to work out her/his own solutions. All of
this implies a basic trust of the other person, the client. It
assumes a basically sound or healthy core inside the person upon
which life can be reconstructed. Clearly Rogers believes that
the Image of God is more characteristic of human personality
than the Old Adam.

Just prior to this section on Rogers, I referred to two
kinds of _knowing_ about personality: subjective and objective.
In the same symposium at Rice University from which Skinner's
pigeon experiment was taken, Rogers proposed a third kind of
knowing about personality: "Interpersonal Knowing or Phenomeno-
logical Knowledge." It is precisely through the interaction
between the empathetic counselor and the accepted counselee that
the person becomes fully known, a knowledge that is free of the
pretense, hypocrisy and defense mechanisms the client had felt
it necessary to use elsewhere in life. This is very much like
the "I - Thou" relationship in Martin Buber. The person is free
to become aware of who she/he really is and does not have to put
forth the "personnage" to which Paul Tournier referred, does not
need to hide behind a mask. It is more than insight; it is a
freeing up of the positive potential within the person.

Finally, Rogers believes there is a place for all three
forms of knowing about the individual in building a "Science of
the Person." There is a place for self-report, certainly a place
for neurological and physiological data as they bear upon
stimulus-and-response; but there is also room for this third
form, which might also be called humanistic psychology. Other
terms applicable to this third school of thought are
"existential," "self-actualization," and "interpersonal."
Allport falls into this category with his concept of
"becoming."

It is easy to see why Rogers' orientation became so popular
with pastoral counselors and chaplains. It preserved the
responsibility and the dignity of human personhood, showed the
importance of grace and fellowship, and held out hope in a
positive yet realistic fashion.

Allport's caveat is still valid. Too many psychological
theories have been built upon work with the disordered, troubled,

and abnormal personalities in clinical practice. More emphasis
needs to be given to those persons who have been self-actualizers
right along, those who have not needed to resort to extreme defense mechanisms, compulsions, and addictions. What of those
persons to whom Allport's mentor, Richard C. Cabot, referred as
using constructively work, play, rest, and worship? Granted,
when you have listed statistically all the deviants in the
nation, there are not many left whose name is not on one list
or another (alcoholics, stutterers, blind, handicapped, mentally
ill, psychosomatically ill, stigmatized for an assortment of
deviations, etc.). But health may be described in more positive
ways than the mere absence of illness.

The reader should be reminded that we have limited our review of the way behavioral scientists analyze personality to
only three schools of thought and a few exponents of each at
that. We could also have included sociologists and anthropologists, educators, and social workers, all of whom have their
notions and theories about the nature of human nature.

NOTES

1. Sigmund Freud wrote voluminously. For starters one might
   consult A General Introduction to Psychoanalysis, trans-
   lated into English by Joan Riviere, Garden City, New York:
   Garden City Publishing Company, 1935. Freud's three books
   especially related to religion are The Future of an
   Illusion, New York: Doubleday, 1961 (translated by James
   Strachey); Totem and Taboo, W. W. Norton Co., 1950; and
   Moses and Monotheism (translated by Katherine Jones),
   New York: Vintage Books, a division of Random House, 1939.

2. The founder of this movement, J. B. Watson, wrote
   Behaviorism, in 1925. It was published by Norton. B. F.
   Skinner's early work was The Behavior of Organisms, New
   York: Appleton-Century-Crofts, 1938. He also wrote Science
   and Human Behavior, New York: The Macmillan Co., 1953. A
   recent statement of his position may be found in About
   Behaviorism, New York: Vintage Books, Division of Random
   House, 1974.

3. Wann, T. W., Behaviorism and Phenomenology: Contrasting
   Bases for Modern Psychology, Published for William Marsh
   Rice University by The University of Chicago Press, 1964,
   pp. 90-91.

4. Rogers, Carl R., Counseling and Psychotherapy, Boston:
   Houghton Mifflin Co., 1942; Client-Centered Therapy, by the
   same publisher, 1951; On Becoming a Person, Boston:

Houghton Mifflin, 1961; and Carl Rogers on Personal Power, New York: Dell Publishing Company, 1977.

5. Freud, Sigmund, Character and Culture, The Collected Papers of Sigmund Freud (translated by J. Starchey), New York: Crowell-Collier, 1963, p. 303.

6. Rogers, Carl, Carl Rogers on Personal Power, New York: Dell Publishing Co. Inc., 1977, p. 15.

7. See Footnote 3 of this chapter (Wann), pp. 115-116.

COMPARE AND CONTRAST AND DISCUSS

1. If you needed help from a professional consultant for the following problems, whom would you engage, Dr. Freud, Dr. Skinner or Dr. Rogers? Place F, S or R in front of each problem.

____ (a)   a morale problem in a football squad

____ (b)   layout of an assembly line in a factory

____ (c)   an aged Sunday School superintendent whom no one likes but whom no one has been able to persuade that retirement is in order

____ (d)   training a retarded person within a sheltered workshop

____ (e)   a formerly handsome and physically fit business man who is going through a mid-life identity crisis

____ (f)   resolving a clash between a vigorous adolescent girl and her establishment-type parents

____ (g)   a boss trying to get across to a worker the idea that her/his performance is not up to par

____ (h)   a university undergraduate student in the midst of a faith crisis (such as the so-called conflict between science and religion)

____ (i)   a "Type A" personality type individual who has already had his first cardiac problem and is not cooperative with the physician's suggestions

_____ (j)   a clergy person involved in an "affair" but will-
            ing to begin marriage counseling and looking for
            a counselor

2. Which of the three schools of psychology discussed in this
    chapter would be helpful for analyzing or studying the
    following religious issues?

    liturgy   group membership   faith and belief
    conversion   ministry to youth   morality
    prayer   religious education   church politics

    If more than one would be useful, how would they approach
    these topics differently?

3. As you studied this chapter, which of these three perspec-
    tives appealed to you most or seemed to fit the human
    condition.as you see it? Why? What was lacking in your
    least favorite school of thought?

4. Compare and contrast these three with the approach of
    Erikson and/or Allport as they have been alluded to in the
    text.

5. I happen to believe that the Sacrament of Penance could be
    studied profitably (in the field of pscyhology of religion)
    from the perspective of each of the three types. May I be
    so bold as to propose the following?

            Repentance - Rogers' increased sensitivity
            Confession - Freud's catharsis
            Amendment - Skinner's positive reinforcement

    Do not hesitate to criticize such an approach and then
    substitute your own analysis.

6. What becomes of the body-mind problem in behaviorism?

7. Is Rogers' optimism about human nature justified? Can you
    give examples or evidence for or against him?

8. Although the "science" aspect of behavioral science pre-
    sumes value-free objectivity, what are the underlying
    presuppositions of Freud, Skinner and Rogers?

9. Do you wish your counselor to be value-free or to have her
    own convictions about morality and the meaning of life?

10. Criticize the statement: "It is possible to be too
    scientific."

CHAPTER 13

SECULAR SUBSTITUTES FOR TRADITIONAL RELIGION

Secular pertains to what is not spiritual, sacred or religious. Often the term "worldy" conveys the same idea only with the connotation of immoral or sinful. For the purposes of this chapter, I do not wish to define it in this negative sense, as though secularism is simply the absence of religion as usually understood. I think of those persons who look out upon the world, and, following the scientific law of parsimony, feel no need to look beyond it.

SECULARISM AS A WORLD VIEW

When did secularism begin? Was it when the divine right of kings was forsaken and the optimists of the French Revolution claimed the power to govern rose up from the masses in democratic fashion and did not descend from above? Replacing faith with reason added momentum to the secular movement. The industrial revolution demonstrated that power could be generated by human inventiveness and effort. Why rely on the faith of a mustard seed to move mountains when you could rely on bulldozers? Is there a problem? Set a task force of scientists at work with engineers to implement their discoveries. Both Karl Marx and Sigmund Freud believed that religion was not helpful, in fact negative, in its impact on social and personal welfare; and it would be more useful to take a secular or this-worldly approach to social and personal problems. A thorough-going secularist simply believes religion is unnecessary and builds his/her world view without the benefit of traditional religion.

The above movement was not one of exchanging one religion for another, such as converting from Roman Catholicism to the Baha'i faith nor converting from Judaism to some so-called "sect." It meant deliberately saying one did not need religion

269

at all with its belief system, practices, and ecclesiastical structures. It may be that a person (or society) does not formally forsake a traditional religion by withdrawing membership, but simultaneously also attributes all the functions of religion to some other entity such as imperialism, democracy, etc. A Pakistani historian claims that British imperialism had all the characteristics of a religion.

> "It is not at all ridiculous to see in imperialism the panoply of an organized church. The works of Lugard and Milner were the Holy Writ. The writings and commentaries of Froude, Seeley and others made up the corpus theologicum. Disraeli, Salisbury and Rosebery were the high priests. Cecil Rhodes and Curzon were the leading missionaries who spread the gospel with the help of a host of devoted workers. Kipling wrote the carols. Henty, Buchan and a score of empire novelists supplied the Books of Prophets. ...little remains behind in imperialism if you take out the religious intensity, the devoted fanaticism, the unbelievable loyalty which the faithful gave to their faith."[1]

Aziz's description of imperialism seems to be self-sufficient, but Englishmen inter-mingled these secular pursuits with the theology of the Anglican faith. Perhaps one could go so far as to say that the Queen of England's title "Defender of the Faith" could have applied both to the religion of the Church of England and to the religion of Imperialism.

There is the more thorough-going secularist, however, who proudly wears the label, "atheist" or "free thinker." Such a person would not resort to any of the religious resources we said applied to the various stages of life (sacraments and ceremonies from birth to death). Even where there might be significant celebrations such as weddings, no hint of a divine dimension or worshipful attitude would be present. Everything is accounted for on the human, this-worldly level.

Secularism places responsibility for management of the world strictly upon the shoulders of its inhabitants. Its adherents rely upon reason, logic, and the laws of nature and do not find worship, myth and mystery, tradition, and the spiritual congenial to their nature. It is not a philosophy of life for weaklings because it takes a certain stoical strength to stand so independently in the world.

THE VACUUM PRINCIPLE

It was fairly transparent that the assumption of Part I of this book was that a variety of religious beliefs, traditions, practices, sacraments and ceremonies, etc., were functionally useful to assist in the process of personality development and adjustment throughout life. If these personality needs are not ministered to via the factors described therein, then one could assume that a deficiency or lack would exist. Such deprivation could be described as a psychic vacuum.

The principle of vacuum comes from physics and describes a condition in which material substance is withdrawn from an enclosed space. It is difficult if not impossible to create a total vacuum. A negative pressure is created within the container (e.g., a vacuum bottle), with the result that pressure is built up to fill that space -- to equalize the pressure. If a person does not have ego needs met through constructive means such as worthy vocation, social support, affiliative relations, etc., the individual will seek out other means to fill the void. If a secularist does not find "meaning of life" or what Allport called a "unifying philosophy of life" through religious resources, he/she will seek out or create such meaning from the world about, from self-contemplation or from some a-religious system. The easiest way to describe what I am talking about is to cite several such systems.

EXAMPLES OF RELIGION-LIKE FUNCTIONS RE-CREATED BY SECULAR COMMUNITIES

Harvey Cox makes a delightful tongue-in-cheek analysis of the Miss America Pageant as an animistic fertility cult operative in the midst of twentieth century scientific America. There is the ideal woman, a virgin, who is selected on the basis of carefully prescribed virtues, attributes, skills, etc. The faithful worshippers of beauty and sex gather in a large cathedral for the final ceremony and millions are tuned in on TV. Meanwhile, of course, the outlying tribes have sent their best delegates for the final test. There is even a set liturgy as the shaman-like master of ceremonies chants his annual song, "There she is, Miss America...your ideal, etc." As in primitive fertility rites, the goddess is showered with flowers and gifts, symbols of reproductive power. The magical powers of THE GIRL are demonstrated in the observable fact that when she blesses something it multiplies rapidly whether it be shampoo, bath oil, automobiles, beer or whatever she deigns to touch with her wand. Some may call it advertising, but those gnostics among us who are enlightened know that she is only one in a long line of all-powerful queens going back to Isis, Siris and Aphrodite.

271

Cox's analysis could be applied to other folk heroes and heroines of stage and screen, boxing ring and baseball diamond, politics and the military. Names like Babe Ruth, Marilyn Monroe, Elvis Presley, Muhammad Ali, General MacArthur, etc., are all names with which to conjure.

I live only two blocks from our university football stadium, which holds about 50,000 screaming believers several Saturdays each fall. When I am swept along in the stream of pilgrims going to or from the place of THE EVENT, I can see in my mind's eye the Crusaders of the Middle Ages heading for their Holy Grail, which was not, as far as we know, made out of leather. I also visualize the great throng of Muslims flowing like a river toward Mecca. Parades and processions have a way of bolstering loyalty to a common goal or object of faith. When we hired our last football coach, he was promised "_total_ commitment."

We are not as concerned with little idolatries, such as worshipping "The Almighty Dollar" or even "Demon Rum," as we are with a community's or society's world view. Several twentieth century societies have deliberately and self-consciously set out to create secular substitutes for that old time religion.

NAZIISM

A dramatic example in recent times to try to create a substitute for traditional religion, or, perhaps more accurately, to leap backward a couple thousand years into pre-civilized Western Europe to find the roots for their religious origin and the meaning of their society, was the Nazi development of new types of ceremonies. For example, the birth festival, the marriage festival, and the festival for the dead were the three official titles for their celebrations of the life-cycle. Under the Führer's direction and by his special commissioner, who was in charge of a cultural revitalization, these celebrations were activated. There was even a substitute initiation rite for adolescents to replace the German Lutheran Confirmation.

In a book called _Secular Salvations_, Ernest B. Koenker describes these ceremonies.[3] Some very interesting attempts were made to say that this would not be religious. These ceremonies were to be rational and logical rather than mystical or magical. Upon closer examination it became obvious that there was a great deal of appeal to awe and faith. Jung's "deep, symbolic representations" were utilized so that the swastika was certainly designed to be an emotionally charged symbol as well as an ensignia. (See "Symbolism" in Chapter 9 above in this book)

Ancient customs capable of transmitting materials viable for peoples' life and work could still gain admittance to festivals. And new forms would come into use which were capable of being handed on. This is the whole point: these forms were to be of such vital nature that they could be passed on. There was the hope that they would become traditional, just as other ceremonies and symbols were traditional for centuries. After all, the Reich was to carry on for a thousand years symbolically, and the folk's symbolic representation should be powerful.

"It is no cultic movement, but exclusively a people's political tenent which had grown out of racial knowledge (this intuitive racial knowledge). In the course of German history, many alien customs arising from alien powers were transformed and transmitted so that they could today become the unadulterated possession of the entire people. It is the task of national socialist folklore to push through here the distinction between what is authentic and what is alien, and to determine what values in the transmitted materials are viable for the peoples' work and their planning and execution of festivals."

The Nazis did try to keep their ceremonies consistent with their theology. The National Socialist celebrations were to be visible images of their world view, living ingredients of the community life of the people, and experiences that work and live on in the celebrators. The celebrations were to call to life a faith in a world order in which the people had their special rank and value. It had this similarity with religion in that it tried to coordinate the systematic unifying philosophy of life with these individual ceremonies, rites, acts and symbols supporting this faith.

COMMUNISM (EAST GERMANY AND RUSSIA)

Koenker refers also to the Communist approach to finding substitutes for religious support for personality. For example, there are several hymns listed. They are party songs in which there is the notion of the people's gratitude to the state, as there would be gratitide to God under the Russian Orthodox doctrine of providence or creation.

One of the songs goes like this:

"She has given us everything,
the sun and the wind;
never is she stingy.

273

Wherever she was there was life.
Whatever we are we owe to her.
Never has she forsaken us.
When the world froze we were warm,
protected by the mother of the masses,
borne up by her mighty arm."

Then the refrain follows:

"The party, the party is always right,
and comrades shall we ever be.
Whoever fights for right is always right
against lies and exploitation;
Whoever outrages life is wicked or dumb;
Whoever defends humanity is always right.
So nourished in the spirit of Lenin
and welded together by Stalin,
the party, the party, the party."

Here is a sweeping hymn of loyalty and gratitude that carries the
people along. It would be a fine way to open a worship service.

Most of these secular approaches have an equivalent also to
sacred scripture, whether it is the Mein Kampf of Hitler, Das
Kapital, The Communist Manifesto, or The Writings of Mao Tse
Tung. In all of these there is always some kind of authorita-
tive declaration which has more than literary value. It almost
has a supernatural significance, a holy aura around it. This
is another characteristic way in which they partake of religion.

In the performance of the ceremonies it is interesting to
see how imitative they are. For example, in connection with the
birth festival (that is, the dedication of children), or the
marriage or death ceremony, the speaker is always the state
appointed representative who officiates or gives the eulogy. And
he is urged to have sessions with the people before the ceremony.
(There is a big stress now on pre-marital counseling.) It is
assumed that if confidence in the relationship is to emerge, the
speaker must learn the people's background, occupations, activities and social and intellectual outlook. If he is to help
guide the people into a strong marriage or family relationship,
he must be acquainted with them personally (pastoral care).

In the Soviet Union there was originally an effort to do
away with the family, or at least to minimize it, under the
assumption that it was a left-over from the burgeois, sentimental
era of the Church. It was assumed that people would really be
loyal to the state if they did not have so much loyalty to
spouse and family. Divorce was made very easy. A person could
be divorced by simply writing a postcard and mailing it to his/

274

her spouse. That was sufficient. (See "Marriage as Religious Support" in Chapter 5 above.)

The Soviets found that the family is essential. They have gone through great efforts to strengthen family life and marriage. The ceremonies are now carried out in an increasingly elaborate form. There is a marriage chamber with special carpet and draperies, there are gifts of flowers to the bride and groom, and there are special speeches and the signing of certificates in a distinctly ceremonial manner.

Both parents participate in the vow. If, however, the mother is not married, there is another form of the vow to use. In general, the vow is to bring up the child in the new system. But it is almost verbatim the same as the baptismal vow made by parents in promising to bring of their child in the kingdom of God and to be faithful to the Church.

> "Before forward striving humanity, we, Emmie and Kurt Eisermann, responsible for ourselves and our child, declare our marriage to be an indissoluble home for our son, Uric Eisermann, born on November 8, 1957, in Stalinstadt." ... "It depends on you, on all of us. We vow to rear our son to be a socialistically perceptive thinking and acting citizen of the German Democratic Republic."

The vow has a place for the signature of the two parties. It may also bear the signature of sponsors ("godparents") attesting to the vow, which is another old religious tradition. The sponsors promise,

> "In order to help fulfill this vow, we vow (as sponsors) to assist in the integration of this child into the Peoples' Republic and to keep him loyal to all these commitments."

In marriage, there is this kind of vow:

> "Before all working people, we, Gerta and Herbert Fischer, responsible for each other and for ourselves, vow to guard our marriage, contracted here this day, in mutual love, as a fellowship for the whole of life. We vow to the worker society to strengthen by our common creative effort the socialist achievements and the Political Power of Workers and Farmers. To one another we vow attentive esteem, thoughtfulness, help in time of need,

mutual encouragement for vocational and cultural development, mutual decisions, and in-
dissoluble faithfulness."

There is also a similar ceremony carried out for burial, in
which the "speaker" has a special role again. In these burial
services there are similarities to primitive burial ceremonies.
Part of the function of the primitive religious ceremony was to
hold the tribe together. When one person left, the tribe was
that much weaker. It was a great loss to have a person drop
from the tribe or from the hunting or food gathering party.

Here is part of the address which the speaker gives at the
funeral or the festival of death:

"The death of a citizen in the German Democratic Republic is a painful loss to all
farmers and workers, for we treasure every
person as a part of our strength in the
building of socialism, of the future, and
of our good tradition. We survey respect-
fully the life which has just come to an end
and stress the energy with which the deceased
has struggled. In so doing, we condemn the
exploiters, the militarists, the fascists,
who misuse human life. We note the good the
deceased has accomplished in the family, among
his co-workers, and for friends in social
organizations. We laud what he has created
in work and social activity in the way of
material and spiritual values, which he be-
queathes as a nameless monument to the
peoples' possession and consciousness. We
mark the breach which has arisen where he
worked in social functions and in the family,
and we voice our grief at the loss of this
person. We invite others to honor the deceased in that we propose, according to the
strength given us, to close the breaches
which have arisen, close the gap, in order
that the good intentions of the deceased may
be realized. The image and example which
the deceased has left in our memory should
incite us to these ends. It is our duty to
commit the deceased to the earth so that,
in keeping with his intentions, we may be
able to foster further the improvement of
life."

There is even the hint of a committal service: "earth to earth, ashes to ashes," which appeared in traditional Russian Orthodox ceremony.

CHINESE COMMUNISM -- DEVOTION TO CHAIRMAN MAO

When I visited the People's Republic of China in the fall of 1976, it was obvious to me that the kindergarteners and elementary school children sang their devotion to their beloved Chairman Mao with the same enthusiasm and warm sincerity as Sunday School children sang of their love for Jesus. Mao's picture hung as prominently in home and school as the Crucifix or picture of The Blessed Virgin Mary would hang on the wall of a devout Catholic home or parochial school. The moving song, "The East is Red," is sung with the combined feelings of "A Mighty Fortress Is Our God" and "God Bless America." This anthem could easily be played on a pipe organ as a postlude to a church service and would not seem out of place. There are many ingredients of worship in the New China even though formally there is no felt need for "religion."

Clearly, Mao is seen as a savior who led his people out of bondage and into the promised land. They speak continually of Before Liberation and After Liberation much as we in the West divide history with B.C. and A.D. The old society before 1949 is always called "The Bitter Years"; now they enjoy life in the "New China" -- much like Christians refer to the Old Dispensation and the New Dispensation. The Long March reminded me of the Israelites' sojourn in the wilderness; struggle, suffering, and faith brought them through their trials. They were also only a remnant; but through them came salvation.

Ideology is not only expressed through "Mao Tse-tung Thought" but through numerous proverbs and categories. Get rid of the "four olds" (old ideas, old culture, old customs, old habits), which are remnants of bourgeois feudalism. They represent sinful forces of an evil world from which one needs to be converted to a new faith or life style. And since sin is always prone to rear its ugly head, there must be constant vigilence (like Saint Paul's daily drowning of the Old Adam). That is why there needs to be a continuous revolutionary activity to keep society pure; since there will always be "Capitalist Right Roaders" who wish to return to "The Bitter Years" of exploitation and greed. Hortatory slogans abound: Serve the people; Rely on your own resources; Follow the mass line; Learn from the peasants and workers; Go down to the countryside; Put politics in command; etc. Mao's social philosophy may be summed up in this quote: "The masses are the real heroes, the masses have boundless creative power, the people, and the people alone, are the motive force in the making of world history."

277

There was a sense of liturgy in the sameness with which each
briefing was begun and concluded whether we were visiting a
school, factory, shipyard, housing complex, or rural commune.
It began with how bad things had been during the bitter years before liberation and went on to cite the progress made by putting
into practice the teachings of Chairman Mao. It always ended
with a kind of benediction ending on an eschatological note: "We
have determined to follow Chairman Mao's behests and continue the
revolution to the end." The "end time" to which they refer is
that day of complete justice and full equality toward which they
have travelled only part way thus far.

We explained earlier that religion provides a person with a
heritage, a destiny, meaning of life, how to fit into the larger
scheme of things. They also have a missionary zeal since they
believe that their way of life is best and would be welcomed by
the downtrodden masses of every country. Hence they were very
eager and willing to help build the large Tanzania-Zambia rail-
way in East Africa (14,000 Chinese workers). They are convinced
that their way can also be the salvation for other third world
countries. It is a missionary faith.

Jerome Frank, in his book Persuasion and Healing, has made
an interesting comparison between psychotherapy, religious revivalism, and thought reform.[4] The impression I received was
that the Chinese operate from a different basic assumption about
social relations and moral values. We think that stealing is a
sin. As our Chinese interpreters explained their handling of
theft, their approach would be quite different from ours. Instead of punishment for sin, they would see a need for thought
reform, "brain washing." Anyone with such dirty thoughts obviously needed his brain cleansed. In other words, they would
think of such anti-social behavior as motivated by strange
thinking, some kind of heresy, rather than a sin. Had the thief
not understood or believed Chairman Mao's teachings, namely, that
stealing is exploitation? We had a whole war to drive out the
exploiters -- Japanese imperialists, rich landlords, etc. -- and
now you turn around and exploit your neighbor by stealing his
bicycle. You had better attend the political thought discussion
meetings more faithfully and learn what the New China is all
about. The culprit needed conversion to the new faith. He was
a backslider or loose liver in Wesleyan terms. He should be
criticized until he was willing to join in self-criticism (repentance) and make his re-commitment "to follow Chairman Mao's
behests and continue the revolution to the end."

Turn to our definition of religion in the Preface of this
book and see if these and other "isms" fulfill the criteria of
religion. Even when a society leaves out God or other traditional marks of religion, the functions seem to remain if one
looks for them.

RELIGION OF THE REPUBLIC

Professor Sidney Mead has used the term "Religion of the Republic." It grew out of the Enlightenment and the necessity for colonial Americans to get along with each other in a religiously pluralistic society.

"This is 'the religion of the Republic,' for I think it provides, or legitimates, the premises of the Declaration of Independence, the Constitution, and a long line of Supreme Court decisions on matters pertaining to religion."[5]

In many ways the American Way of Life has become a kind of religion. Its Sunday School is the public school, which now teaches "value clarification" courses, and generally sets out what is the good, the true, and the beautiful for its citizens. Democracy as the ideal form of government, capitalism as the accepted form of economy, competition as the standard form of motivation, progress and advancement generally, together with the kind of leisure which goes to make up "the good life"; all these are taught by the public school on behalf of the belief system of the Republic. These are not to be seen as imposed arbitrarily upon the citizenry since indeed the values and meaning of life taught in the public schools are the consensus of the vast majority of the populace. The public schools are under the control of local school boards; and if heresy is being taught, there will be excommunication just as in any other religion.

A belief in an overwhelming destiny was sometimes enunciated and at other times taken for granted. The earliest immigrants were extending the Kingdom, were building the New Jerusalem. In an early Wyoming newspaper there is this sense of religious mandate for the westward movement:

"The rich and beautiful valleys of Wyoming
are destined for the occupancy and sustenance
of the Anglo-Saxon race. The wealth that
for untold ages has lain hidden beneath the
snow-capped summits of our mountains has been
placed there by Providence to reward the brave
spirits whose lot it is to compose the advanced-
guard of civilization. The Indians must stand
aside or be overwhelmed by the ever advancing
and ever increasing tide of emigration. The
destiny of the aborigines is written in characters not to be mistaken. The same inscru-
table Arbiter that decreed the downfall of
Rome has pronounced the doom of extinction upon the
red men of America."[6]

279

There is a sense in which any mass social movement needs a theology or ethic to undergird it, even if it needs to be worked out in retrospect as a rationalization. This applies to class, status, property, human relations, and culture. It may well be that when there is an impasse in religion (e.g., Baptists being on both sides of the slavery question yet supposedly having the same Bible and theology), appeal is made to a secular substitute for religion, some culturally based or geographically based reality (like some grew cotton and tobacco while others did not).

It sounds like we have come full circle to our historian from Pakistan who wrote about imperialism as a religion. Yet imperialism may co-exist with another religion in the same society, in the same personality. My grandparents had a disturbing feeling of uneasiness as Indians rode by their Minnesota homestead dragging their belongings behind them on a travois, but they had repressed into their subconscious the fact that they were farming on the Indian's hunting ground. In atonement they fearfully offered them a little food and hoped they would continue on their way west. I doubt if they were even aware there was any religious or ethical conflict in their hearts; their Norwegian Lutheranism was quite untouched by the Indian's plight. And their descendants think it terrible today when one nation drives out another in order that it may fulfill its destiny.

There are many questions we could raise about the impact of our American Way of Life upon mental health and personality adjustment, but we will leave those for the discussion section of this chapter. Have we demonstrated that the functions of religion have been replaced by secular substitutes when the formal aspects of religion have been abandoned? Is it really true that the vacuum principle is at work psychologically as well as in the world of physics?

NOTES

1. Aziz, K. K., The British in India: A Study in Imperialism. Islamabad, Pakistan: National Commission on Historical and Cultural Research, 1976, p. 58.

2. Cox, Harvey, The Secular City, New York: The Macmillan Company, 1965, p. 194.

3. Material on Naziism and Russian Communism is drawn from Secular Salvations by Ernest D. Koenker, Philadelphia: Fortress Press, 1965, pp. 193 ff.

4. Frank, Jerome D., Persuasion and Healing, New York: Schoken Books, 1961, Chapter 5, "Religious Revivalism and Thought Reform."

5. Mead, Sidney E., The Nation with the Soul of a Church, New York: Harper & Row, Publishers, 1975, p. 118. See also his The Lively Experiment, Harper, 1963; and The Old Religion in the Brave New World, Berkeley, California: University of California Press, 1977.

6. This was a statement of the Big Horn Association printed in the Cheyenne Daily Leader, March 3, 1870, and quoted in I Buried My Heart at Wounded Knee.

QUESTIONS FOR MODERNS

1. Can you name some examples of secular art or literature? Be careful because some only appear to be secular but are profoundly religious.

2. Is jazz music a secular form of expression just because it was commonly played in houses of prostitution along Basin Street in New Orleans? Can you think of any jazz pieces which are actually hymns of repentance or confession?

3. How would you distinguish between patriotism and secularism? Does patriotism necessarily mean the worship of the state?

4. Can one be a materialist and a religious person at the same time? Explain.

5. Criticize the "vacuum principle" as applied to this chapter.

6. Is increasing production and consumption of pornography and stress on sexuality a sign of secular attitudes on the part of our citizens in contrast to a religious frame of mind? How about King David? How would you account for the almost total lack of pornography in the People's Republic of China, which aims to be secular; and the proliferation of pornography in the United States of America, which has a very large percentage of religious adherents?

7. Would you suppose that considering theft a heresy instead of a sin would have greater or lesser deterrent effect on an individual's moral behavior? Is classifying exploitation as a heresy compatible with a religious orientation?

8. In this chapter the public school was said to be the current transmitter of moral standards. What other institutional expressions of the Religion of the Republic can you name? How do they function?

9. How has the scientific way of thinking contributed to the secularism of our day?

10. If we assume that there is a psychic and spiritual vacuum because religion has not been meeting the personality needs in the way it had traditionally, what has happened to make this state of affairs come about? Has religion become non-functional for many persons? Comment on such terms as "dead orthodoxy," "formalism," "the institutional church," "depersonalization," "bureaucracy," "professionalism," as these might affect an individual member of a religious group so as to cause him/her to opt for secularism.

11. How would you explain the rapid rise of numerous sects and cults with their intense commitment? Are these attracting persons whose needs are not being met in traditional religious denominations, but who still do not feel drawn toward secularism in the sense of no concern for religious categories?

12. What parallels do you see in America to the secular substitutes described in Nazi Germany or Eastern European Communism?

13. Compare the faith commitment required of a Communist Party member and the standard member of some Protestant group of your choosing.

14. Would a liberal or conservative member of some church be less likely to convert to communism as a faith commitment?

15. How do the level of commitment and stress on high standards for group membership serve personality needs? For example, does a strict group provide the member with a greater sense of personal worth and ego support? On the other hand, is there a personality adjustment price paid for such conformity? What is it?

16. The following are a few quotes from an article in The National Observer, May 26, 1973. React to them from the perspective of this chapter. "The journey from confessional to couch (psychotherapy) may be less a result of psychiatric evangelism than a failure of traditional religion, its authority weakened as science undermines the literal interpretation of one religious myth after another." "Psychiatrists are only falling into a vacuum.... The vacuum used to be filled by priests and ministers."

CHAPTER 14

WHOLISTIC PERSONHOOD -- GETTING IT ALL TOGETHER

"The hand of the Lord was upon me, and he
brought me out by the Spirit of the Lord, and
set me down in the midst of the valley; and
it was full of bones. And he led me round
among them; and behold, there were very many
upon the valley; and lo, they were very dry.
And he said to me, 'Son of man, can these bones
live?' And I answered, 'O Lord God, thou
knowest.' Again he said to me, 'Prophesy to
these bones, and say to them, O dry bones,
hear the word of the Lord. Thus says the Lord
God to these bones: Behold, I will cause breath
to enter you, and you shall live. And I will
lay sinews upon you, and will cause flesh to
come upon you, and cover you with skin, and put
breath in you, and you shall live; and you shall
know that I am the Lord.'" (Ezekiel 37:1-6)

We have all heard the spiritual, which speaks so rhythmic-
ally about "de foot bone connected to de ankle bone.....de leg
bone connected to de hip bone, etc." It takes more than a pile
of bones to make a person; they have to be connected together
with sinew and ligaments. We are reminded that the word
"religion" means literally "to bind again," to tie together.
This is what is meant by a wholistic perspective on personhood.
And finally, breath, spirit is needed for life to come into these
bones.

283

THE WHOLE IS GREATER THAN
THE SUM OF ALL ITS PARTS

Even in the mechanical realm, as any parent knows who has tried to assemble a child's bicycle that came in a box, the whole is quite different from the simple tabulation of all the parts. There is the matter of the relationship of the parts to each other, their organization into a functioning unity. True, every part is needed, but without organizational relationship they are simply a pile of pieces. Somehow, it seems even more like a bicycle when the child gets on it and joyfully pedals away.

When personality is considered as only the sum of its parts, the individual thus evaluated speaks of being de-personalized. "I'm just a number." Or maybe a series of numbers, as in the case of students. It is not uncommon to hear a student described as a 3.56 GPA, A.B., from Ohio State, with a 570 Verbal and a 610 Quantitative on the GRE--should be worth a ¼-time RA." A patient in a hospital may be referred to as "the hypertensive in 206 (followed by statistics about blood pressure, hematocrit value, temperature, and assorted laboratory reports). At the store a wealthy citizen cannot charge an electric razor if he/ she does not have a "credit rating," which is not available since the customer has paid cash for fifty years. When I presented my faculty staff card, signed by the president of our university, for validation of a check signature in our bookstore, I was met with stoney silence and a puzzled look; but when I drew out my Social Security Number, the clerk smiled warmly and said, "Thank You!" Only little pieces of us are recognized here and there, and we crave a more wholistic image, a unified self. No wonder so many persons seem to be having trouble with their identity these days.

The study of personality has become so specialized, and such a vast body of data has been accumulated, that it is understandable that one psychologist is interested in measuring intelligence, another instincts, another stimulus-response, another intra-psychic experiences such as dreams and fantasies, and still others social influences and group dynamics. All of these parts of the person are worthy of study and do add to an understanding of the person, but the picture remains fragmented like looking at oneself in a shattered mirror. There is a pressing need for "getting it all together," as the younger generation has been saying for a decade.

Some religionists must also accept their responsibility for bifurcating the individual. Some have so spiritualized personality as to neglect the physical and material aspects, unwittingly falling back into Platonic dualism. These feel they strengthen the importance of religion by calling spiritual matters "more important" when actually there is no need to choose up sides in such a tug-of-war between body and spirit. They talk as though instincts, endocrine glands, habits, and conditioning were of little consequence. Neither myopia is sufficient for a vision of the whole person.

PERSONAGRAPH--A SYNTHETIC APPROACH[1]

Synthesis means combining various elements into a unified entity in contrast to analysis, which means to loosen up or take apart. In this book we have looked at many parts and separate experiences in the spiral of life; now we will end with an effort to get it all together.

An instrument for summing up the whole person needs to include the tangible and the intangible. So often the tangible is more easily and accurately measured, and thus, in our scientific-technological age gets more attention. We list in the case record the age, sex, address and phone number with ease; and they are also quickly picked up on the computer. It is more difficult to set down the hopes, faith, and ultimate destiny of an individual. Another problem is the different meaning which the same statistic has for two persons. One girl thinks it is perfectly OK to be "pleasingly plump"; another girl of the same age and height is absolutely mortified to weigh the same as her friend. One youth is relieved to have "finished" his/her education at age sixteen, and the family extends congratulations on the new job at the plant. The next family take for granted their child is going to, and through, college and on into some profession; and they would label as "hopeless drop-out" the culprit who failed to live up to these expectations. Ironically, they both have the same I.Q. according to the Stanford-Binet test. It is for this reason that I have chosen to develop a self-rating scale. The person filling it out may use records, reports, diagnoses, etc., which have been accumulated up to this point in the life history; but I want that information to be filtered through the subject's own perceptive screen. If there should be drastic discrepancies, they merely become part of the data which can be dealt with in an interpretive discussion. (Why can't I play basketball at the university even though I am a midget? I have my rights, you know!)

How does the individual interpret the relationship between

the various factors set down on paper? Is the person aware of the significance of past experience (very low grades throughout high school and the first two years of college) for future goals (serving as a medical missionary for the denomination)? How realistic is it to expect to be admitted to medical school with these grades when the admission standard precludes that possibility? Does the person feel pre-destined to failure in everything because of failure in activity A or B? What kind of meaning does the individual ascribe to adversity or success, illness or health, social popularity or prejudice? Toward what goal or goals is the person moving?

Following Allport's lead, I hope the person filling out the Personagraph will be mindful of resources and strengths as well as problems and the negative aspects of personality and lack of status. Statistical precision is not the object of this self-rating scale. Its purpose is to help the individual gain self-understanding, a fuller self-awareness, a sensitivity to life issues and the larger reality in which that life is lived.

Figure 26 shows how the Personagraph is divided into four quadrants. The two more tangible areas are "capacity" and "experience" (the latter is past oriented). The two areas which I feel are often slighted and are surely less easy to measure or document are "meaning" and "goal" (the latter being future oriented).

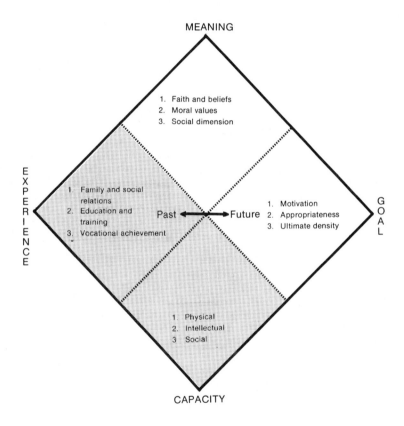

MEANING

1. Faith and beliefs
2. Moral values
3. Social dimension

EXPERIENCE

1. Family and social relations
2. Education and training
3. Vocational achievement

Past ← → Future

1. Motivation
2. Appropriateness
3. Ultimate density

GOAL

1. Physical
2. Intellectual
3. Social

CAPACITY

Fig. 26   Design of Personagraph

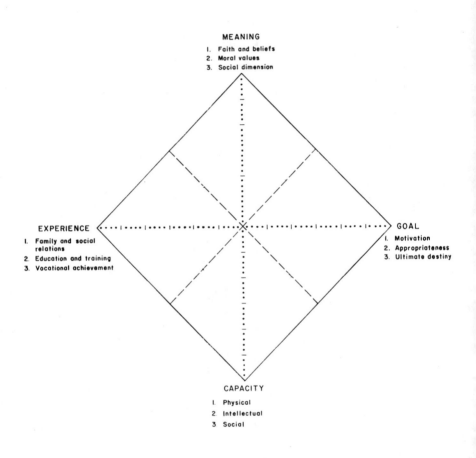

MEANING
1. Faith and beliefs
2. Moral values
3. Social dimension

EXPERIENCE
1. Family and social relations
2. Education and training
3. Vocational achievement

GOAL
1. Motivation
2. Appropriateness
3. Ultimate destiny

CAPACITY
1. Physical
2. Intellectual
3. Social

Fig. 27   Personagraph Rating Form

* * * * * * * * * * * *

Before we go any further, we should explain the scoring method, which is quite simple and requires no statistical skills. It was designed by a simple person for the masses although sophisticates are also welcome to use it.

Begin at the center in each case and proceed outward in this fashion, each dot counting 1 point out of a possible total of 10 points, thus:

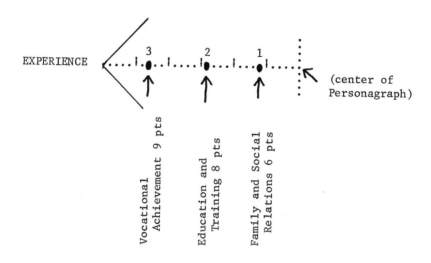

Fig. 28   Scoring the Personagraph

Since the person gave himself 6 points on #1, Family and Social Relations, he puts a mark at #1, six dots out from the center. Then he begins counting from that point outward another 8 dots for his second rating, which is #2, Education and Training. Next, he counts outward from that point another 9 marks for his final rating, #3, Vocational Achievement. The interesting pattern exhibited here is the person's perception that, whereas he began with a modest familial and friendship base, he progressed to a more positive rating on the latter. If these were courses, we might say his grades went from a low C to a B to an A; but the important question is what the subject sees in this pattern.

289

CAPACITY

Capacity includes the basic equipment a person has to work with: to function as an organism, to meet basic needs, and to relate to the environment.

1. Physical capacity is the foundation upon which personality is built. It includes the senses and other body structures such as organs and glands. Unless the heart has the capacity to pump enough blood through the system, that owner of that heart will neither work nor worship, think nor feel. How does the subject perceive of such capacities as physical strength and vitality, physique and body shape? Is there a health problem or handicap, hearing aid or glasses, amputation or limitation? Is the person on medication to make up for some organic deficiency or to stabilize a physiological abnormality? Now here is the important point. If the individual is to rate himself/ herself on a continuum from 1 to 10 (or 1% to 100%--supposedly if one were at 0% death would have already taken place), how is this score to be arrived at? Not according to a national norm or the ideal height and weight chart in the YMCA physical fitness gymnasium. I want the person to put down a score that represents what his/her own physical capacity means to him/her, not to anyone else. The person with epilepsy may very well be so adjusted to the problem and so well medicated for control that. it is not seen as a capacity deficit; well and good, so be it. This is self-report; later we can discuss it.

2. Intellectual capacity means the capacity to think, re- member, grasp relationships, reason, etc. We should distinguish this from learned skills. I.Q. tests have not always been suc- cessful in eliminating cultural factors and educational factors as it had been hoped they would. Self-objectification at this point is very important because the person who has come to grips with this factor in a realistic way is much more likely to find the proper niche in society than the one who uses rationaliza- tion, idealization, or repression to avoid self-understanding and reality. Again, the unique intention of this self-rating scale is not to see where one falls on the normal curve (above or below the 100 I.Q. average), but whether one looks upon his/her intellectual capacity as a positive or negative factor. Is it enough for the goals sought? A 100 I.Q. is quite in- adequate for the Dean of the College of Law, but very "satis- factory" for an unskilled worker. Make sure it is the subject's own evaluation, anywhere from 1 to 10, with 1 being at the ex- treme low end and 10 at the high end of the scale.

3. Social capacity is much broader and involves the capacity to establish and maintain relationships. It is what

Allport called "social intelligence." Some persons just do not seem to be sensitive to the needs or in-put of other persons about them. They miss cues that could alert them to the feeling state of another person. Other individuals without training in social work or counseling are right on target when it comes to sensing where other people are coming from and what is going on in a group dynamics sense. It often leads to fruitful discussion after the form has been filled out.

EXPERIENCE

It is impossible to imagine the millions of sense perceptions, feelings, words and discrete behaviors which a person has experienced by even early adulthood or late adolescence. We therefore, need to group past experiences between birth and the present moment under a few headings for practical purposes. The individual may wish to consult records, documents, and the memory of family members to bring these things into consciousness. Social workers, lawyers, and detectives are skilled at re-creating the case history of the client's past experiences.

1. Family and social relations are primary because they represent the earliest evidences of our developing personalities. The concentric circles expand rapidly but begin with parent-child, sibling, and other immediate family contacts. Were these positive or negative? If these early memories evoke a sense of trust and rewarding experiences, the subject will be inclined to rate this item high. If earliest experiences were of a mis-trust nature, child abuse, and rejection, the score may be low indeed. But the circle expands to include playmates, schoolmates, and social relations in general. Taken all together, what would the composite score be? Let the subject put it down.

2. Education and training goes all the way from kindergarten through formal schooling, but also includes on-the-job training, and self-training such as independent reading and study. Has all of this vast enterprise fitted our subject for today's needs or not? Is education and even continuing education (of CEU fame) perceived as functional or a boring, marking-time kind of experience? School experience may have been so traumatic and painful that the person has made a lifetime commitment never to learn anything whatsoever. He gives education and training zilch. Obviously there is overlapping here because life does not come in nice, neat boxes. A person may have despised the "education" aspect of school but enjoyed the "social relations" side of extra-curricular activities. Now the person wonders why "college ain't as much fun as I thought it was gonna be." Keep the person's nose to the grindstone till

291

he/she has put down a score for education and training experience.

3. Vocational achievement is where the rubber hits the road. This is reality testing and need not begin with the official working papers at age 16. Has the person had little jobs along the way--newspaper route, lawn mowing, baby sitting, etc.? Were these successes or failures? Has work provided ego satisfaction or enhanced one's inferiority complex? Has this individual ever experienced inner rewards of job satisfaction, or did he/she always rely on external reinforcement (usually authority figures)? Was the individual self-motivated in work-related tasks, or were most assignments carried out to avoid punishment and disgrace? As the subject reflects on these aspects, a score will emerge, high or low.

MEANING

Now we turn to the so-called spiritual side, the side of personality explored by some chaplains in mental hospitals who take a "religious history." What provides meaning for all the factors we have discussed so far? What is the guiding principle or governing motif behind all this person is and does? Since many persons have never asked themselves this kind of question, it will have to be broken down into sub-parts and patiently teased out with questions that get behind the obvious. We do not settle for the quick "I subscribe to the Apostles' Creed" type of response, a standard though spiritual testimony, nor any other secondary statement. We are not asking for content as much as we are searching for the function or meaning of this meaning in the life of the subject in his/her own words. Just as previously, concerning education, we were not concerned about the number of grades fulfilled nor the courses taken but with the positive or negative impact of that factor on the individual's personality development; concerning "meaning," we wish to have the subject rate whether this factor has been positive or a negative factor for him/her. (Remember the Danish tailor?)

1. Faith and belief system have been a blessing for some, a guide and comfort; but for others beliefs are the battle ground of the family reunion where relatives choose up sides and doctrines with which to do each other in. Some trace their divorce to disagreements and contentious fighting over "the truth." Some have agonized over their doubts for years and finally have dropped the whole enterprise because it was too destructive and painful. They chose agnosticism as a matter of survival. Others have found what Allport called "intrinsic" religious faith commitments a steadying influence and found therein the resource to handle life's trials and unfathomable

mysteries. Although the subject may be reluctant to set down a number for something as holy as faith, being urged to symbolize this part of life concretely may help to force him/her to think more specifically about it rather than verbalize on in generalities.

2. Moral values may be seen as negativistic restrictions and rigid codes that mostly prohibit self-expression; and the subject has exerted heroic struggle to be freed from this bad side of life. Obviously this would push the score to the lower end of the scale. The score would be elevated in proportion as the individual perceived ethical considerations as ennobling of life and moral values, as making interpersonal relationships more precious. For such a person values striven after enhance self-regard and human dignity. Then values are not bondage but enable a person to live a more worthwhile life. Responsible and ethical decision making is a privilege. How high will the subject rate the moral dimension of personal existence?

3. Social dimension of the meaning of life may be seen in contrast to the individualized or ego-centered way of looking at capacity and experience. Is this person an island unto himself, or is he a "man for others"? She may see herself narcissistically as the center of attention in order for life to have any meaning; or she may be another Florence Nightingale willing to lose herself in the larger needs of humanity. Does the person prefer to share experiences or live a predominantly private existence? While encouraging the respondent to fill out these rating categories, one would do well to refrain from leading the subject with pejorative remarks and leadings toward the "right answer." After all, the object is not to please you, the administrator of this simple form. The purpose is that he/she project onto the paper the real "self" insofar as that is possible. Therefore, this score should also be freely and honestly placed upon the paper.

GOAL

Purposeful striving, goal-directed behavior, moving into the future meaningfully is what life is all about. Having acknowledged my capacities and reviewed my experiences in the light of what I consider important in the universe, I need to ask myself "What am I going to do with all this; whither am I tending and why?" Some persons never do set goals deliberately; they follow the path of least resistance. One of the most helpful questions directed to me as an undergraduate at the University of Minnesota was the one my professor of Biographical Psychology, Dr. Richard Elliott, posed: "What do you want to be doing five years from now? Can you give me the name and address of the person whose kind of work you would like to be doing ten years

from now?" I came up with some answers, and it helped me clarify some matters that had lain dormant beneath the surface in a
nebulous and unhelpful way. If "experience" is what has happened in my life from birth to this present moment, "goal"
stretches on into the future beckoning me hopefully on or scar-
ing the daylights out of me.

1. Motivation refers to what moves a person to action.
Seemingly, some are pushed from behind by what psychologists
call "drives"; others are attracted toward goals in the future.
Personally, I am struggling feverishly to accomplish my goal
for this, which is to have it in on time at the publisher's
office, which means getting into the mailbox on May 15th.
Granted that is not an earth-shaking goal, but it demonstrates
the power of future goals to motivate us forward. Some live on
the goals which others set for them; their motivation is "other
oriented" and not "inner directed." This is a nice way of
avoiding responsibility, because if anything goes wrong it is
the fault of the "other" person who chose a wrong goal for my
vocation, marriage, etc. It is not difficult to see the inter-
connections between motivation toward goals and the several sub-
factors under "meaning." Let the subject set a mark on the
scale indicating what motivation means to her/him and whether it
is an asset or a liability.

2. Appropriateness of goal relates to "capacity" because it
is very frustrating to aim too high and constantly fail or aim
too low and be bored to death. Ideally an appropriate goal takes
both capacity and proven "experience" into consideration. The
student who has consistently done very poorly at mathematics
is ill-advised to pursue mechanical engineering; and the tone-
deaf person might as well discard choir directing as a career
goal. Occasionally, we encounter a dedicated and single-minded
person who stubbornly pursues an inappropriate goal for fear of
being labelled a "quitter." He bravely paddles his canoe over
the waterfall on the strength of a misplaced conviction. He may
mis-apply the aphorism about not turning back once you have set
your hand to the plow. You may wish to re-read parts of Chapter 4 on Vocation. Let the subject wrestle with the appropriateness of the goals chosen and record a judgment.

3. Ultimate destiny seems so far away that many folks
ignore it or ridicule it as "pie in the sky by and by." Polaris
may be a long way off from the explorer, but the "polestar"
turns out to be a better guide than nearby trees or mountains.
Does this individual have an ultimate concern in the Tillichian
sense or are his goals all penultimate or even antepenultimate,
perhaps even more short-ranged than he/she had realized? Members of the TGIF Club simply Thank God It's Friday again; they

294

made it through another week. The Maoist interpreter set her goal "to follow Chairman Mao's behests and pursue the revolution to the end." Another believer speaks of destiny going beyond this present life pressing on to "Eternal Life with God, now and forever." A person may reveal at this point that he is hung up on a mid-life crisis because he has attained all his goals, marriage and family life, business success, financial security, etc.--there's nothing left to live for. This raises again some interesting questions about what he had said about "meaning" and why he responded as he had in that quadrant.

A CASE OF SELF-UNDERSTANDING: A MODERN PRODIGAL SON GETS BACK ON THE ROAD BUT NOT TO FATHER'S HOUSE

A pastor once approached me about a problem which had him stumped. A high school senior had left home, taken a room in the downtown YMCA, and had determined to be independent. Dan supported himself with a night janitor's job in the large department store nearby and continued to attend classes. What puzzled the pastor was that the boy seemed OK as an individual, and the father and step-mother also seemed like average, hard-working people who should be able to get along together; but put the three of them together and you had dynamite. What further distressed the minister was that the son was an acolyte at the 9:00 a.m. service, and his parents attended the 11:00 a.m. service of worship. Yet he could never get them to kneel at the altar rail for communion together, the very sacrament designed to work reconciliation and strengthen the bonds of fellowship. Would I talk to the boy?

In a few sessions it seemed apparent that the triangular impasse of defensive step-mother, authoritarian father, and rebellious adolescent was a clearly defined battleground. After also visiting with the parents, I found even less likelihood of any of the three of them "giving in," since that was how they perceived any form of reconciliation. I decided to concentrate on the son as the primary client, assuming him to be the most receptive of the three. I wondered what kind of pattern he would draw for himself on a Personagraph. The result is Fig. 29.

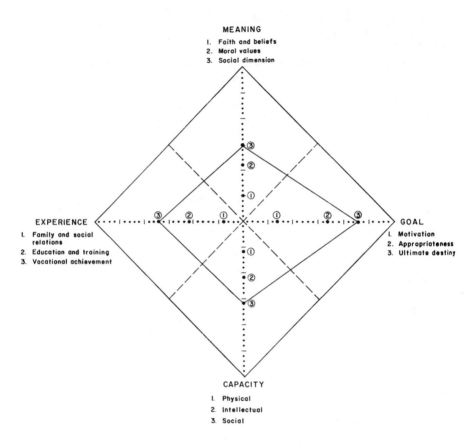

MEANING
I. Faith and beliefs
2. Moral values
3. Social dimension

EXPERIENCE
I. Family and social
   relations
2. Education and training
3. Vocational achievement

GOAL
I. Motivation
2. Appropriateness
3. Ultimate destiny

CAPACITY
I. Physical
2. Intellectual
3. Social

Fig. 29   The Prodigal's Personagraph

Dan spoke of his capacity with a mood of inferiority. The reason he graded himself 6 from a physical standpoint, though he looked handsome and healthy, was a reflection on his lack of attainments in sports. He had also not received any support or approval to amount to anything from his parents. His intellectual rating of 5 corresponded with his school grades, namely, middle of his class. Although he had a girl friend, he felt ill at ease in a social group and hung around the edges of the church youth group. His role of acolyte was a formalized and special role not requiring interpersonal relations, and he liked that Sunday task very much.

In the experience quadrant he quickly jotted down his lowest rating, the same 4 which he gave himself for the social

296

dimension of meaning. He felt he got nothing from his family
other than board and room, and he would rather not pay the
emotional price for those benefits, hence elected to support himself and thus avoid the family tensions and hassles. No one
put him down at the YMCA. Education was positive because in the
large city high school he was also on his own, felt independent.
Although he liked his night janitorial job and was considered a
good worker, he knew his parents (especially his father) looked
down upon this as menial labor. His father was a machinist and
gave Dan two messages: "I surely hope you can do better than I
have; but I doubt if you'll amount to anything because you are
so irresponsible."

One would have expected a higher rating on the role faith
played in his life, since he was so dedicated to the role of the
acolyte in the liturgy. In discussing faith it came out that
he felt very guilty about his alienation from his parents, and
coming to the Lord's Supper accentuated the lack of fellowship.
He recalled from his catechetical instruction the passage from
Saint Paul that those who eat and drink unworthily "eat and drink
judgment" upon themselves. At least that is how he interpreted
I Corinthians 11:27-30. He wanted to be right with God but hated
his parents. This also explains his ambivalence about his moral
values. We have already referred to his feelings of isolation,
which accounts for the 4 on the social dimension. On one occasion the police had found him wandering aimlessly around the
loop of the city at two in the morning on his night off. He was
in a kind of self-contained daze. It was this incident that
prompted both the father and the pastor to seek extra help for
this boy. Although he suffered anxiety, the mental health
clinic had determined he was not mentally ill by any means. He
did lack sufficient sleep and a well balanced diet, as he snacked
on junk food.

It was in the area of goals that the key to vocational
guidance was discovered. He was strongly motivated to go to the
state university, located in the same city. His conviction that
this was appropriate for him is dramatically exhibited in his
rating of 10 points--100% certainty. Concerning his "ultimate
destiny," he spoke the denomination's phrases about eternal life
and salvation but felt little "assurance." His religion was
not intrinsic, but an external formality he hung onto for support, and he was sensitive enough to know that that was not
enough. How could he get it all together?

Upon further reflection, Dan was able to admit that the
reason he wanted so intensely to attend the university was to
show that old so-and-so, his father, that he could make something
of himself. Yet that goal did not correspond with his high

school record nor indeed with the judgment a person might make from conversing with him. It just did not seem that his aptitudes were very strong in the theoretical and intellectual sphere. It also became apparent that there was nothing to be gained by dealing with the educational and vocational goals apart from their motivation--proving something to his father.

The religious meaning upon which we focused was the distinction between liking and loving. Nowhere in the Bible nor in his denomination's teachings does it say that one must like one's father or mother. What is ruled out is hating them. Would it be conceivable that these three could repent of their hatred and confess it to one another? Would they be willing to forgive each other? At the same time, there would be no stipulations about what they must do together including living at home or even coming home for Sunday dinners. I spoke with the parents in their home, and they also saw this as a freeing attitude even as Dan had. They were able to grasp quite easily the distinction between the love of grace (agape - unmerited love of the Gospel) and the love which the Greeks called philia as in philosophy (love of wisdom) and the Romans called socius as in society or social companion.

One Sunday morning we all agreed to meet in the sacristy before the second service and have a ceremony of reconciliation. Each of the three expressed heartfelt sorrow for their individual hatreds and spites, and the right hand of fellowship and forgiveness was shared. I pronounced the liturgical form of absolution. It was as though a burden of guilt and excess baggage had been lifted from their shoulders. There was a feeling of relief in their new freedom. They were no longer to be bound together by negative and restricting and destructive thongs, but free to go their way in peace. Even I, a stoical Norwegian Lutheran, found my heart "strangely warmed" like the Methodist John Wesley at Aldersgate.

In our next session, Dan and I were now free to speak about future educational and vocational plans in a new atmosphere of freedom. I had asked the Personnel Manager of the large department store if they would be willing to give Dan some vocational interest and aptitude tests, which was easily arranged. Dan was willing to think about his future afresh. He now accepted the guidance that grew out of these personnel interviews and tests. He accepted an apprenticeship in the department of the store which sold and serviced air conditioners and refrigerators. Upon completion of his last semester in high school, he was enrolled in a technical school for further training in air conditioning and refrigeration.

Dan had finally gotten it all together: capacity, experience, meaning, and goal. He found a sense of legitimate worth in the eyes of God, his neighbor, and himself, and he was also able to love all three.

"You shall love the Lord your God with all your heart, and with all your soul, and with all your mind...You shall love your neighbor as yourself." (Matthew 23:37, 39)

NOTE

1. The author has used the Personagraph in counseling with both college and theological students as well as in marriage counseling and with a variety of ages. It was first described in Chapter 2, "The Axes of Concern in Personality," in a book he edited entitled, Religion and Medicine: Essays on Meaning, Values, and Health, Ames, Iowa: The Iowa State University Press, 1967.

SELF-APPLICATION AND DISCUSSION

1. Does the case of Dan demonstrate how "the whole is greater than the sum of the parts?" Discuss some of the interrelationships between scores and categories that added to Dan's self-understanding.

2. Does it bother you that the Personagraph is not "scientific" and does not lend itself to statistical exactitude?

3. What are the advantages and liabilities of the Personagraph as an instrument for exploring personality? How could it be combined with other instruments?

4. Don't be intimidated by the Jungian pattern of four (quaternity); you may think that there should have been five or more categories. What would some other dimensions be able to pick up on such a rating scale? Don't believe something just because it is in print!

5. How can you compensate for the deficiency in self-rating scales that the subject may be repressing into his/her subconscious precisely those things that are most important

to be aware of? In other words, the sickest people would yield the most inaccurate ratings and yet need to follow the maxim that is so difficult even for healthy people: "Know thyself."

6. What inner feelings do you have as you even contemplate my invitation that you fill out a Personagraph on yourself? Are you squeamish about doing a biopsy on your own personality? What about it is most uncomfortable?

7. What do you think of the gimmick or method of forcing you to put down a concrete number for some of these nebulous factors? Obviously giving it an arbitrary number does nothing to make it more accurate. My purpose was to help you come to a decision. It is especially necessary for the kind of person whom a friend described in this way: "as hard to pin down as nailing a custard pie to a wall."

8. One purpose of the design of the Personagraph is to overcome the dualistic split between body and mind, "material" and "spiritual" aspects of personality. Was this purpose accomplished? Criticize.

9. Can you improve on the scoring method? If so, please do so, and use this device in any way you wish. I'd be glad to hear from you. Just write to:

Professor David Belgum
School of Religion
The University of Iowa
Iowa City, Iowa 52242

SUMMING UP

It seems like a long time ago that we began to follow the personality on the ever widening and ascending spiral of life. We have thought about the influence of many religious factors upon that growing self, which, in turn, was not above shaping religion for its own purposes. Religion can be either bane or blessing as the individual grapples with the issues and tasks of the "life cycle," sometimes both in the same life, leaving the person ambivalent about religion. There is the subjective and the objective, the intra-psychic and the social, the cognitive and the behavioral to be found in the complex we call religion.

If I have been biased, I hope you have not thought me to be dishonest to boot. If you will recall, I periodically gave you the settings both of my microscope and my telescope. You are free to adjust your own scope to suit your own needs. It is for this reason that one textbook is hardly ever sufficient. This brief psychology of religion has borrowed freely from many sources, but they were all filtered through the sieve of one narrow mind. Nevertheless, I feel about this book much like my father felt about his sermons: "I have milked many cows, but the butter is all my own."

I hope you have found opportunity to apply these various points of view and interpretations to yourself, and that, here and there, you have come to understand someone else better for having read these pages. Perhaps you have seen a facet of religion or a dimension of personality in a new light. This has not been an ambitious project. Any one of the chapters on the spiral of life could be a book in itself, as many of the end notes indicate.

Part II required quite a mental adjustment as you tried to

shift from the individual adjusting to the world view of a specific culture. You were asked to imagine how personality was viewed from that theoretical and cultural construct. It was amazing how frequently the same issues came up. Each culture is confronted with the same basic realities and has to account one way or another for human potential and human experiences. Did you see a progression from primitive to present day perspectives? Are the plot and scenario basically the same, only with different players going through the same classic lines and actions with varying accents? Could you see yourself in primitive animism and in biblical characters? If you consider yourself a secularist, you no doubt have a definite opinion of whether or not I presented that world view fairly.

Some day I would like to do a psychohistory case study on Mao Tse-tung. I would be interested to know if you have been stimulated to study some significant figure in depth. There are many other schools of thought and psychologists worthy of inclusion in this type of study. There are numerous rating scales and other psychological instruments, techniques and therapies. At the end of this book we can say we have come to the beginning of the subject.

APPENDIX

ALLPORT'S PSYCHOGRAPH[1]

In order to show the complex variety of factors that impinge upon personality formation, Allport drew up a list of traits, which could be judged to exist to a greater or lesser degree in each individual. On the left side of the graph were psycho-biological factors such as physique, intelligence and tempera-ment. These are the givens, the equipment of our bodies and endocrine system. Next he considered traits of expression, whether one were ascendant or submissive, persistent or vacil-lating in relating to the outside world. At the right side of the graph were the attitudinal traits, attitudes toward self as well as others. Finally, he borrowed five traits directed to-ward values from Spranger's list of "directions of striving." They include theoretical, economic, aesthetic, political, and religious values. These suggest that an individual considers his/her highest value as a striving for truth, utility, harmony, power, and unity, respectively. He and P.E. Vernon constructed a simple test for determining how a person related to these values (plus the social). Yet Allport's concern for a wholistic perspective of the person is indicated by the following caveat in regard to his own instrument.

> "Use immediately shows up the limitations of this psychograph (or of any other). However carefully the investigator plots the scores, he will find that no personality is accurately represented in a profile. In spite of its con-necting lines, a psychograph fails to express the qualitative balance between two or more traits. A person whose profile dips in "ascen-dance" and rises in "expansion" has not merely low standing in one trait and high in another.

There is a resultant blend in his behavior, colored also by all other co-existing traits, that eludes the psychograph completely. Discouraging as this discovery is, it follows inevitably from the false assumption that personality is the sum-total of plottings of scores on common variables."2

The most direct way to explain what Allport was getting at is to demonstrate his psychograph with a specific case; and what better case can we use than Martin Luther, about whom Erikson was also interested enough to use in a case book, _Young Man Luther_. Figure 30 presents Luther's profile, which will be followed by brief commentary as to how the ratings were arrived at. Rather than clutter the text with complete quotes, Footnote #3 indicates a few sources for the ratings.

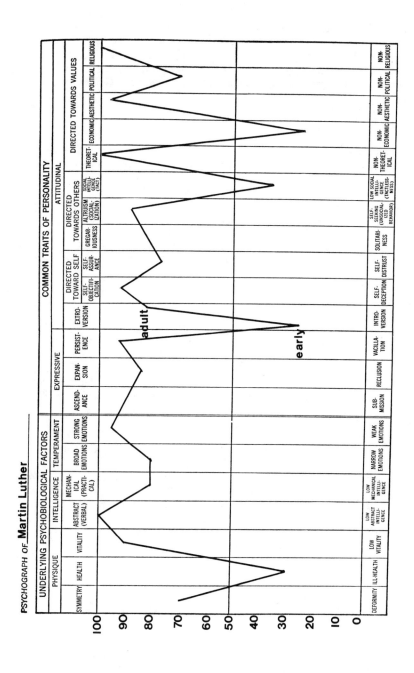

PSYCHOGRAPH OF **Martin Luther**

Fig. 30   Construction of the Psychograph

305

Symmetry--Deformity

Luther's bodily build was normal, and he seemingly had no deformities. His appearance was robust, and pictures of Luther reveal a healthy-looking, well formed physique (a bit over weight). Rating - 70.

Health--Ill-health

External appearance was deceiving because his diseases were mostly internal. It is evident that his health was poor during his monastic days because paintings of him at that time show protruding cheek bones and sunken eyes. After his marriage, he overcame some of the physical ailments which accompanied his self-imposed starvation of monastic days. Luther is reported to have suffered with at least the following diseases: renal colic, rheumatic fever, sciatica, hemmorhoids, dysentery, disease of the middle ear, stone, catarrh, vertigo, and weak heart. Rating - 30.

Vitality--Low Vitality

The fact that Luther accomplished as much as he did is evidence that he had a high degree of vitality. As soon as his splitting headaches would cease he would begin anew on his work. He was continually translating, preaching, and corresponding in spite of his poor physical condition. He studied in the monasteries while the usual thing was not to study. Rating - 90.

Abstract Intelligence

Luther was born with an exceptionally brilliant mind. Luther, at age six, could read and write. In school, ".....Luther made marked progress in the higher Latin grammar, in composition, versification, and discourse, and easily out-distanced his fellow-pupils."[5] Throughout his education, he moved swiftly taking degrees in his stride. "Luther (according to Cattell's list one of the ten most eminent men who ever lived) took the M.A. degree at 22 and became a university professor of philosophy at 25. He had won wide recognition as a religious teacher at 29. At 34 he published his 95 theses."[6] It is said that he translated the entire New Testament from Greek into German in three months; and this was also an important linguistic unifier and standard for the High German language through its use over the years.

A psychologist, Catherine Cox, has undertaken to analyze the geniuses of the past in The Early Mental Traits of Three Hundred Geniuses. Luther ranks as the fifth most eminent of these three hundred geniuses. The minimum amount of intelligence necessary for the accomplishments of each genius was estimated. Luther's IQ for the A I period (up to age 17) was estimated to be 145; for the A II period (age 17 to 26) it was 170. Luther had an extraordinarily high degree of innate, abstract intelligence. This is evident because of his voluminous writings on deep, abstract, theological matters. Rating - 100.

Mechanical Intelligence

Luther had a fairly high degree of mechanical intelligence and manual dexterity. He evidently had an insight into practical affairs and business because he was elected District Vicar to administer ten monasteries. Since Luther was poverty-stricken about the time of his marriage, he did manual labor to support himself; he took up gardening. He laid out a garden and constructed a fountain. He said, "I have made considerable progress in clockmaking, and I am very much delighted at it." Rating - 80.

Broad Emotions--Narrow Emotions

Spells of melancholy came over him intermittently throughout his life even after his great spiritual conflict was over. Yet, he was not always depressed and sad. Once while performing his priestly duties near Erfurt, he nearly burst out laughing at the fumbling, rustic organist. Nor was his entire life wrapped up in spiritual thoughts and aesthetic emotions; he had a very happy home and married life. His table was a jovial and friendly center for his many friends. He was not happy nor satisfied when he was restricted to narrow emotions while in the monastery, but enjoyed himself among many people and in varied situations and experiences. Rating - 80.

Strong Emotions--Weak Emotions

Luther was very impetuous and often used violent language whenever he became angry with someone. He felt strongly about everything that came his way--the Catholic Church, the devil, his sin, his work, and his family. "Temperamentally, he seems to have been high-strung, emotional, sensitive, quick-tempered, impetuous, imaginative, impressionable."[8] His fits of temper of which the devil was usually the victim, and also his fits of fear, in which the devil was the chief offender, may be related to his severe childhood. This may be discussed under the heading of Luther's Neuroticism. Even Luther's closest friends were victims of abuse and temper. He called his enemies dirty pigs and devils without much apparent concern. His violence of language and fits of terror indicate very strong emotional temperament."[9]   Rating - 95.

Ascendance--Submission

One of the things he was famous for was the fact that he did not submit to authority alone, great as it might be. He did not retract unless he was shown wrong by arguments. He did not recant when asked to do so at Augsburg. "Here I stand; I can do no other." Rating - 90.

Expansion--Reclusion

He became despondent and ill bodily when he had to remain cooped up such as in the Wartburg Castle, in the monastery, and in the Coburg Castle. He felt a need for expressing himself among the people, and he felt hemmed in when he had to stay in hiding in the above mentioned castles. In his monastic period, he was moody. In fact, monkery was a vicious circle for a man like Luther, who was by nature expansive. The more depressed he was the harder he practised the ascetic works and the poorer his physical and mental condition became, resulting in more depression. Rating - 85.

Persistence--Vacillation

While in the monastery he was persistent and determined to follow the rules fully. Rituals may have occupied as much as six hours a day to say nothing about private prayers and meditation. He spent almost half of a year fasting. "His intense asceticism threatened, in fact, to seriously undermine his health, and he ascribed the bodily infirmity which he suffered later to these years of excessive bodily mortification."[10]   Yet he did not leave the monastery until many years after he had passed the most rigorous phase of monastic life. Although he had frequent feelings that maybe he should be following a different course, he did not follow whims. Rating - 90.

Extroversion--Introversion

The basic reason for Luther's spiritual conflict was the fact that he devoted so much time to hyper-critical self-analysis. One reason for his turning his attention in toward himself so much might be that he put so much emphasis upon concupiscence, the sexual drive. Whenever the sexual urge came upon him, he soon began to feel sinful and a sense of failure came over him. After he was made instructor at Wittenburg and was elected District Vicar of ten monasteries, he had less time for introspection. Yet, in spite of his active, public, seemingly extroverted life and activities, he was basically introverted.

308

His whole philosophy and theology was permeated with the concept that each individual must look into his own conscience and find sin there.

After Luther's break-through into the joy of grace and justification, he seemed to be freed from the morbid kind of introspection and inward-turning, which had plagued him during his heroic efforts to earn his salvation by scrupulosity and self-flagellation. He was an out-going host and had many students and friends at his table from whence his famous "Table Talks" arose. He also enjoyed his marriage and family life, which may have helped him to turn outward instead of inward upon himself. He also frequently reached out to the sick and troubled in correspondence and was sought out in a way that is usually not true of introverts. I have decided to give him two ratings: During the early and monastic period - 25.
After "conversion" and marriage - 75.

Self-objectification--Self-deception

For his generation, Luther was unusually objective about sex. Although he always thought it was sinful to think about sex, he did admit it. "In his lectures on Romans (1515) he speaks of the 'voluntaria et solitaria pollutio' (masturbation) with sufficient detail to indicate personal experience."[11] He also tried to understand his physical condition as well as he could with his inadequate medical knowledge. "I take it that my malady is made up, first of the ordinary weakness of advanced age; secondly, of the results of my long labours, and habitual tension of thought; thirdly, above all, of the blows of Satan; if this be so, there is no medicine in the world will cure me." Here he is honestly trying to understand himself. Satan is not, in this case, self-deception, but only the unknown quantity which we later discovered to be germs, eyestrain and various nervous disorders. It is unknowing deception not willing and determined deception. He is also objective about his writing ability. If he thinks he is lacking in style, he admits it. He writes to Brentias, a colleague, ".....I prefer your writings to my own....., your words flow in a purer, more limpid stream. I, whose style is impracticable, harsh, rough, pours forth a deluge, a chaos of words; my manner is turbulent, impetuous, fierce....." His objective, humble manner is revealed in the fact that he did not become enamored with himself. Rating - 85.

Self-assurance--Self-distrust

He must have had a great amount of self-assurance and confidence when he refused to recant at Augsburg even though great authorities in the church admonished him to do so. While he was

interned at Wartburg, he began to get ideas that maybe he was
wrong and was leading many people to hell. As his influence
began to grow and people began to riot in public demonstrations,
Luther regained his self-assurance and his faith in his role and
mission (Bestimmung). He almost always spoke with conviction
and sometimes violence. He was certain that he was correct in
his reformation criticisms. This was all in regard to his public
life. In his private life he was not so sure of himself. He
feared the temptations of concupiscence and felt safe from the
sexual drive after he had escaped into the monastery. He became
even more insecure when he discovered that sex followed him even
to the monastery. Self-assurance was another trait which became
more pronounced as he found a resolution to his religious search
and peace of soul. Again we could give him an early and later
rating, but for a composite we can estimate. Rating - 70.

Gregariousness--Solitariness

When Luther was about fourteen years of age, he had a fond-
ness for solitary contemplation. When he was at school, especially at the university, he got along well with the other
students but was not overly social. After he was married, he
had guests almost always at his table, which seems to indicate
that he liked company. (See Extraversion--Introversion above.)
Rating - 60.

Altruism--Self-seeking

He was evidently not self-seeking when he gave up law, the
most lucrative profession of his day, for the monastery. He was
continually lending money to poor students who needed it. He
did this although it left him quite broke much of the time.
Rating - 80.

Social Intelligence--Low Social Intelligence

Luther had a low degree of social intelligence. Whenever
he felt like calling some papist or even the Pope himself a pig,
he would not take the trouble to soften the epithet. He just
called him the name without any concern for how it would look
in print or sound from the pulpit. He even got into frequent
argument with his friends by calling them bad names. He did
not have the tact necessary to bridle such an unruly temper.
Rating - 30.

Theoretical--Non-theoretical

At Erfurt University Martin was called "The Philosopher" by
his classmates. He was called to be professor of philosophy at

Wittenberg University. He was a systematic theologian of great renown, and debated with the great scholars of his day with remarkable success. He was an avid reader of the Latin classics and a prolific author. Rating - 100.

Economic--Non-economic

He had very little regard for material goods. In order to be admitted to the monastery he had to take the vow of poverty. He was continually in debt and yet lending money without concern as to where it would come from. Yet he seemed to have had a practical mind for business as shown by the fact that he was elected District Vicar to administer ten monasteries. He was perhaps too other-worldly minded to care about debts and money for his personal needs. His wife was the one who saved money by planting gardens and keeping cattle and chickens. Rating - 25.

Aesthetic--Non-aesthetic

Ursula Cotta, who took Martin in while he went to school, was attracted by Martin's good voice. Hymn singing was his only pleasant memory from early school years. He loved music and played both the guitar and flute. He thought music helped him overcome temptation and the devil. He wrote many hymns that have become famous and are used in most protestant churches. Rating - 95.

Political--Non-political

Luther was continually interested in politics among the nobility. He took sides back and forth with and against the nobility and then with and against the peasants. He was influential in inciting the revolt of the peasants, and then he admonished the nobility to crush the peasants. He could not stand to be cooped up in the Wartburg Castle when his leadership was so badly needed in the split of the church. Rating - 70.

Religious

There was hardly a time in Luther's life when he was not vitally concerned with religion. His greatest conflicts were spiritual conflicts. He was continually trying to gain peace of mind as far as religion was concerned. All his study after the first few years at the university were devoted to theology. He spent many years in a monastery, in translating the Bible, and more years preaching and writing religious works. Very few people have been more concerned about religion, church matters, and theological problems than Dr. Martin Luther. Rating - 100.

311

It has been a long and laborious journey to travel through Martin Luther's Psychograph, but I hope that the exercise has demonstrated the many faceted personality of this man. Allport was interested in a multi-dimensional perspective, yet we must agree with him that such an excursus "shows up the limitations of this psychograph." We have the further problem that such a famous reformer has two kinds of biographers: enemies and friends; not so many objective reporters, although the climate of ecumenicity has mellowed the critics and made followers less defensive. The most we can hope for is to strive for increasing understanding of the subject at hand.

There are numerous problems connected with "psychohistory."[12] Meanings are related to cultural settings. For example, the fact that Luther spoke very personally about the Devil, threw an ink well at him, and made him (in the form of a black dog) depart, should not be written off as hallucinations necessarily since professors of physics of the day also believed that demons lived in various layers between the clouds and went down to earth to do mischief like making women sterile or causing someone to be born a hunchback. Each person has to be understood in his/her socio-historical context. What is violent language to one is routine debating technique for someone else.

Another problem is the hazard of attributing more psychological meaning to a given experience than is warranted. Luther's "fit" in the choir loft is a case in point. While the Gospel for the day (Mark 9:17) was being read, he was reported to have cried out, "Non sum, non sum!" ("I'm not, I'm not!") and swooned to the floor. First, was the incident accurately reported? Second, what meaning did the text have for Martin? It speaks about the youth who was possessed of a demon and brought by his father to Jesus to have the demon expelled. Young Martin, who had disobeyed his father by joining the Augustinian order, may have been wondering if he had truly heard God's call via the thunderstorm experience, or whether he were mistaken and "possessed." It would be nice to have the luxury of several interviews in depth with the client, Martin, but unfortunately that will have to wait until later. Meanwhile, everyone is free to speculate.

What the Psychograph does accomplish is that it forces us to look at many factors ranging from physique and health to temperament and values. It is an example of Allport's eclectic method as he urges us to be constantly aware of the individual uniqueness of one particular person.

NOTES

1. See Chapter 15, "Common Traits: Psychography: in Allport's Personality: A Psychological Interpretation, the early version of his textbook.

2. Ibid., p. 404.

3. Bainton, Roland, Here I Stand: A Life of Martin Luther, New York: Abingdon Press, 1950.

   Cox, Catherine M., The Early Mental Traits of Three Hundred Geniuses, Stanford, California: Stanford University Press, 1926.

   Friedenthal, Richard, Luther: His Life and Times (translated by John Nowell), New York: Harcourt Brace Javonovich, Inc., 1970.

   Mackinnon, James, Luther and the Reformation, London: Longmans, Green and Co., 1930.

   MacLaurin, Charles, Post Mortems of Mere Mortals: Essays Historical and Medical, Garden City, New York: Doubleday, Doran and Company, 1930.

   Maritain, Jacques, Three Reformers: Luther, Descartes, Rousseau, London: Sheed and Ward, 1932.

   Smith, Preserved, "Luther's Early Development in the Light of Psycho-analysis," Am. Jr. of Psych, Vol. 24, 1913.

   Scheweibert, E.G., Luther and His Times, St. Louis: Concordia Publishing House, 1950.

4. Allport, Personality, p. 403.

5. Mackinnon, Op cit., p. 18.

6. Cox, Op. cit., p. 98.

7. Ibid., pp. 97-98.

8. Mackinnon, Op. cit., p. 98.

9. MacLaurin, Op. cit., p. 118.

10. Mackinnon, Op. cit., p. 93.

11. Smith, _Op_. _cit_., p. 370 ff.

12. See _Psychohistory and Religion_, edited by Roger A. Johnson, published by Fortress Press of Philadelphia, 1977. This book included articles by persons from various disciplines including historian Bainton, psychologist Pruyser, and psychotherapist Meissner.

ABOUT THE AUTHOR

David Belgum was born in 1922 in a Norwegian Lutheran par-
sonage near Glenwood, Minnesota. His childhood was characterized by the shame of stuttering, the joys of 4-H Club membership
and playing saxophone in the school band, with the economic
depression of the 1930's as the backdrop for Act I.

The Second Act included graduating from Marshall High
School in Minneapolis, the University of Minnesota, and North-
western Lutheran Theological Seminary, also in Minneapolis.
After about six years of experience as a parish pastor and grad-
uate study in Psychology of Religion, he received the Doctor of
Philosophy degree from Boston University in 1952.

The Third Act began in 1953 when our hero married Kathie
Geigenmueller, and they began family life in Springfield, Ohio,
where he served for two years as Assistant Professor in the
Department of Religion at Wittenberg University. He returned
to Northwestern Lutheran Seminary for almost nine years of pro-
fessorship in Pastoral Theology. From 1964 to the present,
David has served on the Faculty of the School of Religion and
College of Medicine at the University of Iowa. He is also
Director of the Department of Pastoral Services at University
of Iowa Hospitals and Clinics. There are three children in the
family, now all away at school. Current hobbies include farming, gardening, travel, and writing.